# Bobby Murdoch, Different Class

by David Potter

Foreword by Billy McNeill

First published in 2003.



EMPIRE PUBLICATIONS



ISBN 9781909360013

# Contents

Foreword ....................vii
Celtic Daft ....................1
Initiation ....................17
Rangers and a bad Winter .................... 33
The Continuing Complex ....................55
The Messiah ....................79
Annus Mirabilis ....................103
Marginal Decline ....................125
A Man For all Seasons ....................146
The Battle of the Bulge ....................160
A Funny Old Year ....................174
In and Out ....................190
Middlesbrough .................... 211
Big Jack's Pride .................... 225
On The Bench ....................237
The Hotseat .................... 248
Life as a Legend .................... 260

Career Statistics

Glasgow Celtic ....................273
Middlesbrough ....................291
Scotland .................... 296

# Foreword

I vividly remember seeing Bobby for the first time. I was a member of Our Lady's High Motherwell senior team and when our game finished we stayed to watch the junior side and in particular a young lad we had all been hearing about.

Bobby was sensational, taking control of mid-field and displaying a maturity far beyond his tender years. It was evident that he was an exceptional talent and years later we became colleagues in the Celtic side destined to become the Lisbon Lions.

Bobby was an enormous presence with the Lions taking control of mid-field, showing an amazing combination of skill, artistry and aggressive creative play, looking for the ball all the time and weighing in with a fair share of goals. His delight in playing for his beloved Celtic always showed in his happy expression on the field and he certainly did not hold back in celebrating our share of victories. Off the field Bobby was a happy person, content with his position in football and very much a family man delighting in his time with Kathleen and his children, Bobby, Kathleen and Barrie.

He always had time for his admirers, of whom he had hoards and enjoyed meeting Celtic Supporters at their functions of which he was a regular attender. Bobby was a warm, open, friendly person apart from being an absolutely magnificent player who will never be forgotten by his team mates or by the Celtic Supporters.

***Billy McNeill***

# Celtic Daft

World War 2 was slowly coming to an end when Robert White Murdoch was born on August 17th 1944 at 57 Toryglen Road, Rutherglen. Curiously, quite a few books say Bothwell, but Murdoch was definitely a Rutherglen baby (according to his mother who definitely knows!) and, indeed, apart from the time that he played for and was involved in coaching and managing Middlesbrough, he lived in Rutherglen or the surrounding area all his life.

Bobby was the first born of Robert and Barbara Murdoch. In 1944, Robert was in the munitions industry, working for Stewart's and Lloyd making shells for the war effort. He had started life as a cabinet maker and in later years he would work as a boiler cleaner and various other jobs, notably with the Electric Company and the Water Board. The couple, who had met in Stewart's and Lloyd in Rutherglen would go on to have another three boys, Matthew, Billy and James. Billy was also a footballer, playing for Kilsyth at the same time as Kenny Dalglish played for Cumbernauld and even being selected for Scotland Juniors when the future Scotland, Celtic and Liverpool star wasn't! Billy then went on to play professional football for Bristol City, Stenhousemuir and Kilmarnock. James played for Cumbernauld and then Cardiff City.

The war years had been grim for Rutherglen and indeed for all Glasgow and Scotland. But the devastation that had hit other industrial centres of the United Kingdom had avoided to a very large extent Glasgow - apart from Clydebank which had suffered dreadfully in March 1941.

Glasgow, still calling itself "the Second City of the Empire", had played its part and remained comparatively undamaged. Men in the Forces were lost of course, but on nothing like the scale of the First World War. Nor had there been any great internal dissension problems as there had been in the previous conflict with its "Red Clydeside" tradition of dockyard problems, rent strikes and street demonstrations.

On the other hand, what many historians call "the quiet revolution" was taking place in Glasgow and elsewhere. People's minds began to change. The liberal thinkers of Kelvinside and Bearsden began to look at the horrendous slums of the Gorbals and Cowcaddens and say, "This is not right". Similarly, those who had been condemned to live in such hell holes began to say "We are expecting, nay demanding, something better as part of the deal in eliminating Hitler".

By the time that Barbara Murdoch produced her bouncing baby boy, optimism was indeed beginning to appear. There was still however a long way to go. British and American troops had been in France for well over two months, but the expected German surrender did not happen. Indeed the July 20th plot to kill Hitler having failed, some felt that the Fuhrer was in an even stronger position than previously. Lethal bombs still dropped on London, and many people were yet to lose their lives in what became known as the Battle of the Bulge and other theatres of war, notably the Far East. The European War would eventually finish in May 1945 with the Allies steadily advancing on the West and the Russians mopping up the East. Shortly before Bobby celebrated his first birthday, the Americans dropped the H Bomb on two Japanese cities, precipitating the Japanese surrender.

Four years later, when the young Bobby Murdoch started attending St.Columbkilles Primary School in 1949, a start had definitely been made to improve life for all concerned. The country had voted Labour in 1945 with a virtual unanimity which astonished the Establishment. King George VI was visibly shaken, apparently, as he asked Mr. Attlee to replace Mr. Churchill. The National Health Service, pledged to produce fitter and healthier babies, had been up and running for a couple of years when Bobby went to school. The horrendous diseases of pre-War Glasgow like diphtheria, rickets and polio were quite clearly on the run, housing was steadily improving (as could be seen in the steady statistical rise of houses with indoor toilets, for example) and there was at long last a feeling of confidence that young Bobby's generation was going to have a better deal than the previous ones.

To be a baby or a small child in that era meant that you were cosseted as never before. Milk, cod liver oil, orange juice and other goodies were dispensed to this generation that was going to be so different from previous ones in terms of health. Less pleasant to the recipients, but no less beneficial were the countless injections to kill all the horrible diseases that used to decimate Glasgow. These were normally administered by stern-faced, severe-looking middle aged ladies, totally committed to their calling, who appeared to take a grim pride, even enjoyment, in their necessary task.

And there was a permanent change in the ethos of Great Britain. Even when the Labour Government of Clement Atlee and Aneurin Bevan fell in 1951, it was replaced by Conservatives, certainly, but a benign, paternalistic, blander bunch than the ones of the 1920's whom Glasgow M.P. Jimmie Maxton had, not without cause, called "murderers" and whom Nye Bevan would describe as "lower than vermin". Prime Minister Winston Churchill realised that life had changed, recalled his previous Liberal sympathies and said, "there is no finer investment for the future than putting milk into babies".

But these changes, far-reaching and widespread though they were, would take time. The Glasgow of the late 1940's and early 1950's still bore the ravages of 150 years of industrial revolution, of man's inhumanity to man and the reckless pursuit of profit and warmongering at the appalling cost of human misery. Poverty would not be eradicated quite so easily and the slums would stay for a few years.

In addition there was the sheer filth of industrial Glasgow. Buildings were black with industrial soot and sheer neglect. Fog tended to settle over the Clyde, become smog and devastate the health of those with pre-existing lung or chest problems. Most of the population still smoked, the message of the damages of tobacco not yet getting through. Indeed, the rise of Glasgow owed a lot to the tobacco trade with the Americas in the 18th and 19th centuries, and the lovely large houses still seen in the beautiful villages to the west of Glasgow can often trace their history to a tobacco baron.

And if the population of Glasgow smoked, it also drank. One permits oneself a sardonic smile on occasion when one hears the (admittedly alarming) statistics of alcohol abuse in the early part of the 21st century. This was mild compared to what it had been before. Wife beating, child neglect and other problems are nothing new. They existed in the 1950's as they will in any society where people are not taught to treat each other with respect - in any society where profit comes first.

Allied to this was crime. The novel "No Mean City", describing Glasgow in the 1930's is a classic of its genre. Such conditions had hardly changed over the war years in some parts of the city. Stabbings, razor gangs, murders and armed robberies were common, and it would be some time before Glasgow could rid itself of this image. Some might argue, indeed, that 50 years down the line, it has still not done so.

One thing that was not changing however was football. It remained (and remains) the abiding passion of the Scottish working class. Unlike cricket, for example, which is more sophisticated and expensive, football was reasonably easy to organise as long as somebody had a ball, and Glasgow boys in particular did little other than play football. Crowds flocked back to see the game. The first big game after the end of World War 2 was the Scotland v. England Victory International at Hampden Park on April 13th 1946 in which Jimmy Delaney formerly of Celtic, but now of Manchester United, scored the late winner for Scotland to put the nation into a frenzy.

There is a story about this goal. The author cannot guarantee its authenticity, but it is a family folk tale, firmly believed - and indicative of how much football meant to the Scottish nation in 1946. Imagine if you will, the scene in a respectable Scottish working class household.The mother of the family has saved up her coupons and managed to get sausages for the tea. She is cooking them, humming happily to herself, rejoicing in the recent return of her son from far away fields of glory like Mersa Matruh and Monte Casino. The hero of this hour is sitting in the living room along with the father of the house, a hero of an earlier war and now sadly crippled. Father and son are listening to a commentary of the football.

The old radio, now somewhat worn but with its batteries recently recharged, has done yeomen service over the past few years assuring the population that "we shall go on to the end" and "a bright gleam has lit the helmets of our soldiers" and "we will fight them on the beaches". It is now used for more peaceful purposes with Raymond Glendinning talking about men like Frank Swift and this man who seems to mean so much to her husband and son - Jimmy Delaney, of Celtic and Manchester United fame.

Suddenly, a great cry is heard. Fearing for her husband's

health, she rushes through to find father and son in a "danse macabre" of joy, for Jimmy Delaney has scored. Raymond Glendinning is shouting "Yes it's Delaney - Jimmy Delaney!" Mother, delighted that that is all that has happened returns to her sausages, benignly shaking her head about the passion with football. She sees something magical, however, for the sausages are standing up and cheering, nodding to each other and saying "Delaney! Delaney!" before settling down for the rest of their sizzle.

Even apparently meaningless fixtures like Great Britain v. Rest of Europe had no problem whatsoever in attracting a six figure crowd to Hampden Park, and every club found interest and attendances soaring. One simply could not live in Scotland in those immediate post-war years without being heavily involved in football. Bobby was of a Roman Catholic family, and this inevitably in Glasgow meant a lifelong and passionate love affair with Celtic Football Club.

It is of course an unforgiving love as well, from which there is no escape. Being in love with Celtic is not unlike being in love with a capricious and demanding mistress who is quite happy to cause you misery, knowing that you will dance to her tune and that any consorting with anyone else will be a transitory flirtation. The real love will be Celtic. One does get cynical and incredulous about statements like "I am no longer a Celtic supporter" or "I used to support Celtic but now follow..." Such statements are inevitably rubbish. Once you are a Celt, you are always a Celt.

In the case of the Murdoch family, there was a connection as well. Bobby's father Robert senior had a cousin who played left back for them. He was Alec Rollo, a rugged and determined left back who won a Scottish Cup medal in 1951 and a Coronation Cup medal in 1953. Robert Murdoch senior however had his own hero in Malcolm McDonald - he of the devastating Delaney,

McDonald, Crum, Divers and Murphy forward line of 1938 which swept all before it in Britain to win the Scottish League and then the one-off Empire Exhibition Trophy.

Sadly Bobby's childhood did not coincide with a great time in Celtic's history. Bobby was nevertheless taken to see them by his dedicated father and was frequently lifted over the turnstile to get in for nothing. Honours were spectacular, but isolated. Bobby was not yet 7 when Celtic won the Scottish Cup in 1951, the club's first major honour since 1938. He did remember with a little more clarity the winning of the Coronation Cup in 1953 and the League and Cup double of 1954. And there was a certain League Cup Final in October 1957 when Celtic beat Rangers 7-1! All of these triumphs would trigger off tremendous celebrations with dancing in the streets of the Gorbals and other Celtic enclaves, but it would be wrong to imagine that they were in any way a regular occurrence.

Apart from those triumphs and great players like Charlie Tully and Bobby Evans, there was not very much to cheer about at Parkhead, a mile or so from Bobby's Rutherglen home. His home life was peaceful and uneventful. Cynics often refer to the early years of a footballer as the "poor but honest bit", as if every football writer says this of every player. In the case of Bobby Murdoch, this was no cliche. In his early years, he had the greatest piece of luck of them all - namely being born of good and loving parents in a house where decency and Christian values were uppermost.

His mother confirms that he got his strength from eating porridge, and he needed this from an early age because he was always out playing football. At the age of 5, he was given the unusual compliment by the big boys of being allowed to play with them - a clear sign of burgeoning talent! He and brother Matt once had a fight which destroyed the family's companion set - the brush, poker and other accessories required for stoking the coal fire, but apart from that, his childhood consisted of little other than football.

His own career was taking off. In 1952, at the age of seven and a bit, young Robert Murdoch, a stocky well built lad by now, played for the Under 12's School team at outside left, and the following year, the same team won the Rutherglen Burgh Cup in a game played at the ground of the local junior team, the beautifully named Rutherglen Glencairn. For his progress at the early stage of his life, Bobby was grateful to his teacher Mr.Terry Heaney and the janitor Mr.Frank Daly whose tolerance of boys playing football in his playground at illicit times allowed the skills of Murdoch and others to develop.

School was from 9.00 to 4.00 p.m.- at least those were the times for the girls and the few boys who did not like football. For footballing boys, the day started a good hour earlier - even in the December mornings before it was properly daylight! - and went on until well after 5.00 p.m, or until irrelevant considerations like hunger took over the body and compelled a return home for tea.

Bobby's Secondary School was Our Lady's High School, Motherwell. When he started there in 1956, the captain of the senior school football team, much admired by the girls and much envied by the boys, was a tall fair haired chap by the name of William McNeill. Not only was he a great sportsman, he also seemed to have leadership qualities which marked him out as something special. He was bright as well, and it was predicted that he would go far. Rumour had it that he was already attracting the attention of the mighty Celtic.

As far as football supporting was concerned, Catholic schools in the West of Scotland are fairly monolithic establishments. Everyone supports Celtic. A few will have a preference for a local team like Motherwell or Clyde, but Celtic own the hearts of most from the Headmaster downwards. The result is that although no-one will get a ribbing on a Monday from heartless school mates about how his team did, if Celtic performed badly, it also means that the defeats are even harder to take because there is a sort of communal melancholy which is hard to shake off. Conversely, a victory will cause euphoria. Sadly in the late 1950's, there was far more melancholy than euphoria.

But Murdoch's playing career flourished. This was in spite of the fact that Our Lady's High School played few competitive games because of a legal dispute. Before Bobby's arrival, their team had played at Hampden Park in a Cup Final. It had ended in a draw and when the replay was scheduled not for Hampden, but for the ground of Blantyre Vics, the school and their opponents, Holyrood, deemed it unsuitable and refused to play! This seemed to indicate that childishness was not confined to the young and the school's subsequent suspension for such obduracy meant that Bobby's school career was not the best vehicle for revealing his talents in competitive games.

Yet under the guidance of Mr.Naughton, Bobby played friendly games. He also, of course, played for his Boys' Guild team.There was no hiding the talent of the youngster who could play on the left wing, at inside left and at left half. He played with lads like Benny Rooney (son of Celtic's trainer Bob Rooney) who would go to play for Dundee United, St.Johnstone and Morton, and John Cushley who would play alongside him at Parkhead. Murdoch would also recall playing one game for Lanarkshire Schools against East Lothian and in the team were Willie Henderson and George Graham who made their names with Rangers and Arsenal respectively.

Billy McNeill, several years Murdoch's senior, was impressed by what he had seen and heard about the young Murdoch. Murdoch, in McNeill's opinion, played particularly well at wing half and reminded him of Duncan Edwards, the Manchester United left half who was killed at Munich in 1958. The resemblances lay in the powerful physique and the exciting "flair" for bursting through in attack at just the right moment. McNeill also pays tribute to Murdoch's "reading" of a game i.e.being in the right position at the right time, his inexhaustible energy and his sense of adventure in that he was always prepared to switch defence into attack or to move suddenly to the other side of the field. All this was to come later however. At the moment, Bobby was merely a "promising youngster".

Local team Motherwell showed an interest in Bobby. Motherwell always enjoyed a reputation of being a good football team. Their manager was Bobby Ancell who had played for Dundee in their fine post war team and fine players absolutely abounded at Fir Park - Willie McSeveney, Pat Quinn, Bert McCann, Ian St.John and Andy Weir. Yet even in the boom years of the late 1950's the seeds of future decline had been sown in the shape of disappointing attendances and not enough investment of the money that they did have. It would lead to their short-sighted and ruinous policy of selling their star men.

In summer 1959 the 14 year old Bobby Murdoch was invited to train with them and indeed was offered a full time contract at the enormous sum (for 1959) of £8 per week. Possibly he should have accepted, but two things counted against it. One was the solid advice from parents and teachers that he should have a trade as well as playing football and indeed, he was already learning his trade as a sheet metal worker. The other consideration was the more potent one that Celtic were also interested in having him train with them on a part-time basis.

Possibly basing his decision on emotion rather than anything else, the young Murdoch accepted what Jock Stein (then youth coach at Parkhead) was offering. His mother was happy that he was still doing his apprenticeship as a sheet metal worker, his father was delighted that he was learning about football with the team the family loved, and Bobby had enough sense to keep his eyes open and his mouth shut as he embarked on the learning experience of Celtic Park.

In the first place there was Jock Stein who would be at Parkhead until March 1960 when he left to became Manager of Dunfermline Athletic. Under Stein's tutelage, there were other youngsters like Billy McNeill, John Clark and Pat Crerand now beginning to break into the first team. Another encouraging force was the sheer magic of the name "Celtic", and the very fact of being able to see and talk to legends like the great Charlie Tully (with whom he had the briefest of historical overlaps). Even the thrill of mundane jobs like scraping mud off players' boots, sitting on the first team bus, carrying the hamper out of the boot of the bus and listening in on team talks must have been a great experience for Bobby - albeit that the results on the field that season of 1959-60 remained disappointingly and depressingly poor.

It was however Sean Fallon who did the persuading and the hiring. Sean was a charming Irishman who allayed any fears that the boy's parents might have had, guaranteed that he would be looked after and allowed his own deep love for the club to become infectious. Sean had played well for the club in the 1950's as a full back (and occasionally centre forward), and immediately on finishing his playing career, began to work for the club as part of the scouting, training and managerial set up.

It was also in 1960 that Bobby's social life began to develop. He met and began to go out with a girl called Kathleen Barrie. She was pretty, charming and very soon a romance would develop and blossom. There was a religious difference - something that might have made been important in some West of Scotland households in the early 1960's, but it said a great deal for both of them (and their families) that it was not allowed to stand in their way. There was to be no "Romeo and Juliet" or "West Side Story" theme to this romance! Indeed, Rutherglen being such a small place, it transpired that their parents knew each other!

Sadly, in Glasgow at this time, there could still be quite a problem with religious bigotry (on both sides, it must be said) and quite a few young people found it to be an insuperable obstacle to incipient love affairs. Stories abound of young Catholic boys and girls who would actually give false names to prospective suitors lest they were immediately deterred by the thought of someone with an Irish name!

Yet the circumstances of them meeting each other were somewhat unusual and contain a humorous comment on the sectarian nature of Glasgow in 1960. Kathleen had been invited to a party on 7th August 1960. Bobby wasn't, but he crashed in anyway demanding the return of some of his Buddy Holly or Elvis Presley records that he had loaned. Presumably, this matter was amicably resolved, but Kathleen noticed this boy (apparently he had been playing in one of the Celtic trials that day) - dark haired, handsome, athletic looking and wearing a brown suit and brown winklepickers.

The term "winklepickers" might need some explanation. It refers to shoes worn by young men at the time - uncomfortable but stylish and called "winklepickers" because of their very sharp toe. Kathleen immediately noticed them and correctly deduced that he was a Roman Catholic. She noticed that the toes were curled up - a consequence of the amount of genuflection that is necessary in the Roman Catholic faith! Glasgow is notorious for ways in which one's religion is spotted. Your name and school are the obvious ones, more subtle and sinister methods involve funny hand shakes, nods, winks and (apparently) the rolling up of a trouser leg. All that the bright Kathleen needed to see was Bobby's shoes!

But the winds of change were beginning to blow in

other spheres as well. Music had undergone a total revolution in the past decade when "Rock'n Roll" began to take over the Glasgow dance halls. Bobby was a great fan of Elvis Presley and Buddy Holly, as well as that old crooner Dean Martin. There was a new atmosphere in the city of Glasgow as prosperity and affluence began to replace the austerity of the immediate post-war era. Television was now a feature in most households, and the social tyranny of the cinema, the theatre and the music hall over the Glasgow population began to lessen.

*'Bliss it was in that dawn to be alive*
*But to be young was very heaven!'*

So says William Wordsworth of the French Revolution. Murdoch, living in the early 1960's was also living through the bliss of a revolution - a social revolution, one nurtured by the Labour Government of 1945-51 and tacitly accepted by subsequent Conservative Governments. From the fruits of these changes was emerging a new Glasgow, a self-confident, prosperous Glasgow totally different from the barbarism of the 1930's. It was hardly true to say that crime was being eliminated, but it was at least being tackled with the gradual disappearance of the "razor gangs" who had desecrated Glasgow's image. The slums were being cleared, new towns like East Kilbride, Cumbernauld, Irvine and Glenrothes were being planned in various parts of Scotland to deal with the "Glasgow overspill" problem and optimism for the future was being expressed.

On the football field things were far more democratic as well. The Scottish honours were being shared around as never before. Teams like Clyde, Falkirk and St.Mirren won the Scottish Cup. Hearts did too and following the lead of Aberdeen who won the League in 1955 actually won the Championship twice. Indeed they were the Champions in 1960. Hibs' day had passed but it was they who had opened up for Scotland the vista of Europe - a theatre which seemed to offer unimaginable promises.

It was still Rangers however who were the benchmark for Celtic. They were still the Champions more often than not. It was Rangers with their wealth, their distasteful but financially successful religious policy of refusing to employ Roman Catholics (something which amazes the historian 50 years later and even at the time raised an eyebrow or two in England and Europe, although it was largely ignored by a cowardly Scottish Press) their large and raucous support with their offensive songs and chants about the Pope - it was they who were the team that Celtic really had to get the better of. And Celtic were showing few signs of rising to this challenge.

It has to be conceded as well that Rangers had fine players. They had defenders like George Young and Willie Woodburn (the latter nicknamed "Big Ben" and having the dubious distinction of being the last Scottish player to be suspended sine die), and fine attackers like Willie Waddell. In the later 1950's and early 1960's Rangers recruited from Airdrie a very talented inside player called Ian McMillan, dubbed "the wee Prime Minister" because he had the same name as Harold McMillan, Prime Minister of Great Britain from 1957 to 1963.

But on the wider stage, it was becoming obvious that both Rangers and Scotland were being left far behind. As early as 1958, television had horrified the country by making them watch Scotland going down 0-4 to England at Hampden on a wet dreich April day, then go on to make singularly little impact on the 1958 World Cup in Sweden. In fact, Scotland actually managed a draw with Yugoslavia in 1958, something which represented an improvement from 1954 which had included a 0-7 tanking from a country that few people had heard of called Uruguay.

The way football should be played however was brought

home to Glasgow in 1960 when the mighty Real Madrid came to Hampden to beat Eintracht Frankfurt 7-3 in the European Cup Final, arguably the most famous European Cup Final of them all. It was really superb stuff and thoroughly enjoyed by the Glasgow public. And the team beaten in the final, Eintracht Frankfurt, had thrashed Rangers in the Semi 6-1 and 6-3!

And then came 1961. Scotland, on one of its blackest days, went to Wembley and lost 9-3. Celtic's goalkeeper Frank Haffey must take some of the blame - indeed one got the impression that he made capital out of this dreadful Flodden type disaster - but not all of it. Billy McNeill was making his International debut that day and it says a great deal for him that his career recovered from this early fiasco. The two full backs were Bobby Shearer and Eric Caldow of Rangers.

It says a lot for Scotland's ability to laugh at itself that a joke soon circulated about the real reason why Scotland were so comprehensively humped that day. It was in fact because the ball was orange! The two Celtic players McNeill and Haffey were afraid of it for the contamination that it might cause them if they touched it, whereas the two Rangers players considered it sacrosanct and were afraid to kick it lest the ghost of King William III might be upset at seeing his favourite colour defiled.

Be that as it may, there was further grief for both Celtic and Rangers in that awful year of 1961. Celtic lost a Scottish Cup Final in a way that caused particular grief to their supporters and Rangers were called upon by the Press to restore some of Scotland's lost pride by winning the first ever European Cup Winners' Cup, as they had reached the Final. Over two legs, Rangers lost 1-4 to Fiorentina - in anybody's language, a thrashing.

It was clear then that Scotland's role in European football was not a leading one in those days, however arrogant and patronising the Press might be. Scotland had one of the largest stadiums in Europe at Hampden and there was certainly no lack of enthusiasm for the game, but Scotland had been traditionally slow and complacent about adapting itself to the demands of the European and indeed the world game. "Wake up" calls had not been heeded, and Scotland's role had been diminished as a result.

But young Bobby Murdoch was learning his trade. He was playing for the Celtic third team and he was technically "farmed out" to the junior side Cambuslang Rangers for experience supposedly in the hard school of Glasgow junior football and so that he could play for them if things at Celtic did not work out. He never actually played a game for them however, working hard in the various Celtic youth teams, playing all over the forward line and impressing everyone by his strength and goal scoring capability. His ability to pass a ball accurately was also commented upon. Eventually he made his reserve team debut for Celtic in 1961 against Third Lanark reserves in a game which Celtic won 5-1.

1961 passed, a dreadful one for Celtic with that painful Scottish Cup final defeat at the hands of Jock Stein's Dunfermline and serious problems of hooliganism in a large but frustrated support. Murdoch, however, kept working hard: learning and absorbing the culture of a professional footballer and the enormous onus that the label Celtic put upon anyone. Then 1962 came along. Murdoch was not yet 18 and still only a part-time professional, when one pleasant Thursday evening in August just after his training session, and only two days after he had played in the Public Trial, the invitation to play in the first team came. The season would start against Hearts on Saturday at Parkhead and Murdoch was inside left!

# Initiation

August 11th 1962 was a fine sunny day. 41,000 supporters gathered at Celtic Park, optimistic as always, for the start of the season. There were attractive visitors too in Hearts, and the season as always, in those days, started with the League Cup. Along with Hearts and Celtic, the two Dundee teams would be in contention for the Section. Only one team would qualify, and it was hard to imagine a more competitive Section.

Summer 1962 had seen Brazil retain the World Cup in Chile (although television coverage had been patchy and unsatisfactory) and the emergence of a Liverpool pop group called The Beatles to challenge Elvis Presley and Cliff Richard. All Celtic fans hoped that at long last their team might rise to challenge Rangers and the other fine teams that there were in Scotland at the time. The omens however were none too encouraging other than the permanently optimistic utterings from the Chairman Mr.Bob Kelly who kept on telling us that his young team had "arrived" and that the fruits of his youth policy were about to be plucked.

But we had heard that before. 1961 had seen a painful defeat by Dunfermline in the Scottish Cup Final, and season 1961-1962 had been perpetually encouraging, but never delivering. The team had played some fine football, apparently encouraged by the release in October 1961 of "The Celtic Song" sung by Glen Daly with the immortal lyrics "Sure It's A Grand Old Team to Play For". In particular a run in the month of December 1961 had led to real hope for a Championship challenge, but the weather turned nasty around the New Year and when it did relent a little, confidence had gone and games were drawn instead of won. Crucially the New Year fixture against Rangers at Parkhead was postponed until April because of fears of playing such a game with hooligans on darkened terraces. By that time the League race was more or less over as far as Celtic were concerned. In addition to the plethora of home draws, there were some really shocking performances against small teams with defeats by Falkirk, Stirling Albion, Airdrie and Raith Rovers a feature of that League season.

Such things are of course likely to happen when the team is young and inexperienced. Perhaps a classic example of what happens with a young team occurred on January 13th 1962 at Tannadice Park. Shortly after half time, Celtic having played inspirational football were 5-1 up. Final score? Dundee United 4 Celtic 5 - and the victory only achieved by some desperate defending to the frenzied cries of "Kick it up the park" or "Clear it, you ... ." from those who had half an hour earlier sung the praises of their team.

The League Championship had gone not to Rangers, however, but to Dundee. Celtic, at a late stage of the season, had beaten Dundee and drawn with Rangers - something that made the previous lapses all the more galling. But the major disappointment of that season was the 1-3 reverse in the Scottish Cup Semi Final against St.Mirren at a windy Ibrox.

There were several interesting points about this game, all perhaps highlighting yet again the fact that Celtic were a young side. One was that they had actually beaten St. Mirren 7-1 in November and then 5-0 at Love Street, only 5 days before the Semi Final! The 5-0 game looks like an "ambush", lulling the young Celts into a sense of false security, and masterminded by old Celt Willie Fernie, whom Celtic had now twice allowed to depart, once with crass stupidity (and apparently to pay for the new floodlights!) to Middlesbrough and now, thinking that his career was finished, to St.Mirren.

But the crucial factor of the Ibrox game was when captain Dunky McKay won the toss, and then opted to play against the wind. There was nothing necessarily wrong about this as a tactic, but it was clearly not part of the plan, if indeed there had been anything worthy of the name "plan". The crowd were treated to the amazing spectacle of several players, notably the brilliant Pat Crerand, shouting and arguing with their captain before the kick-off! The team then played with no heart, arguing and bitching with each other and, totally outplayed against the wind, were 3-0 down at half time.

The second half saw a slight improvement, but there was still a lack of commitment or logical thought in the play with several players giving the clear impression that they would rather be somewhere else than trying to rescue Celtic. Celtic supporters will forgive basic lack of skill. They find it more difficult to reconcile themselves to lack of attitude in a game which is crucial to any chance of success or silverware. Ten minutes remained when the crowd turned nasty.

Celtic supporters had a deservedly bad reputuation for thuggery and hooliganism in 1961-62, but this was the worst. Bottle throwing and in-fighting among Celtic supporters led to a pitch invasion. Possibly this was a misguided attempt to get a fresh game, more likely it was simply some idiots, incapable of such rational thought, trying to brighten up a depressing afternoon. The players were taken off with 10 minutes remaining, the Celtic Directors secretly conceded the tie to St.Mirren, but then the players came back for a meaningless 10 minutes during which time Alec Byrne pulled one back - showing what might have happened and that it did not need to be like this.

"It did not need to be like this" - how well that phrase sums up Celtic in those days! The Ibrox Semi Final was one of the saddest days in Celtic's desolate history in the early 1960's, and it showed the depth of the problem. On the day that Rangers won the 1962 Scottish Cup at Hampden against St.Mirren, half a mile away Celtic were playing out a dreadful game at Parkhead in front of 11,000 frustrated but still admirably loyal spectators in which Raith Rovers, by dint of scoring one goal in the first half and packing their goal in the second, saved themselves from relegation. Celtic were going nowhere.

The formula for keeping Celtic fans happy seems to be that management will get off with a lot of money-grubbing and foolish decisions as long as there is an earnest and hard-working team on the park - and, if possible, one of the three Scottish trophies won every season. This had now not happened since October 1957 which granted had been the 7-1 win over Rangers, on the strength of which Celtic's management and fans had dined for far too long. Four barren seasons 1958-59, 1969-70, 1960-61 and now 1961-62 had passed. The support were beginning to get even more restless.

But even in the opinion of more than a few Rangers fans, Celtic did have one jewel in their crown - and that was right half Pat Crerand. The argument that he was the best player in Scotland at that time (and there were many, many good ones among the war babies who were now growing up) had gained a lot of ground by his performance in the 1962 International against England at Hampden Park on April 14th 1962. Scotland won 2-0 and Pat was the man of the match, nullifying the influence of his direct opponent Johnnie Haynes and creating some superb moves for Scotland. There was a down side to him as well in the shape of a disciplinary record and a difficulty sometimes in adapting to the rest of the team but as long as Crerand was in the team, there was still some sort of hope.

This was the background into which the young Bobby

Murdoch entered stage left. He was still a few days short of his 18th birthday. He was young, strapping and athletic - but a total unknown to the Celtic support, apart from the diligent among them who had attended reserve and youth games. But he had impressed in the Public Trial on the previous Tuesday night. Celtic's trials in these days were Greens v. Whites. The Greens were the "probables" and wore the traditional Celtic jerseys whereas the Whites, wearing the white with green sleeves and green shamrock, were the "possibles". Murdoch lined up for the Whites alongside Fallon; Young and O'Neill; Clark, Cushley and Price; Johnstone, Carroll, Rooney, Murdoch and Byrne.

That "Whites" team thus contained 3 of the 11 who would play in Lisbon in 1967, but a great deal of water had yet to pass under a few bridges before that could happen. Talk of European trophies would have sounded absolutely bizarre to anyone around Parkhead in those days - a win over Hearts in the first day of the 1962-3 season would do for the meantime for the support ... then we might begin to talk about capturing a Scottish trophy.

Bobby's debut must have been a great day for his family, especially his father Robert Murdoch senior, who had supported Celtic all his life. There was also Bobby's girlfriend Kathleen Barrie paying a rare visit to a football match watching him that day from the terracing. She had been quite interested in the game, but never actually been to Parkhead. This time she went with two friends and stood on the terracing. A certain amount of naivety however was displayed by one of her friends who went to the game wearing blue trousers! She found herself thus subjected to a certain amount of mild, vulgar, but good-natured ribbaldry from the punters!

Parkhead, for all its glaring inadequacies as a stadium - cinders rather than concrete steps on the terracing in places, the "Jungle" resembling a cow shed with its holes in the roof, the cover at the Celtic End which only reached half way down the terracing, toilet accommodation limited for men and barely existent for women - was still "that dear old Paradise" for the faithful, who for all their agonies, never deserted them. The ground did look good that day with the green and white scarves and rosettes of an optimistic support very obvious in the summer sunshine. TV cameras were there as well, for highlights would be on both channels, BBC and STV, that night.

It is remarkable how little has essentially changed about match day at Parkhead in these past 40 years since Murdoch's debut. Fashions are obviously different, and prices astronomical in comparison to 1962 when the programme cost 6 old pence and a Macaroon Bar about the same. Spearmint chewing gum, bars of chocolate and potato crisps were also on sale inside and outside the ground and there was the ubiquitously raucous cry of "Cellic Soovenir Speshul" - an early edition of the Evening Citizen with a team picture on the front. There was also the trams and buses stopping outside the ground, disgorging passengers all filled with the almost tangible thrill and excitement of a new season.

There is a false impression, which the Press at the time encouraged, that Murdoch's debut was an accident. What happened was that John Divers did not have his boots with him. He had been playing for a Glasgow Select at Hampden on Wednesday night and had taken his boots home. They would normally, of course, have stayed at Parkhead. He forgot them on Saturday morning, had to go back for them, was caught up in traffic jams, arrived late and was dropped. A debutant Bobby Murdoch ran out with the team. The Press put these two events together and assumed that Murdoch got the nod when Divers was late.(In any case it made a fine story!) This was not so. Murdoch had been selected all along at inside left. It was in fact Charlie

Gallagher who was drafted in as inside right to replace Divers.

The experience of a debut is one that presumably stays with you all your career. Murdoch recalled the words of encouragement from Billy McNeill and in particular Pat Crerand who told him not to exhaust himself but to keep something in reserve for the second half. This is none too easy for a 17 year old debutant, and by the second half Bobby realised that the sheer pace of the first eleven was something that took a great deal of adjusting too.

What highlighted Murdoch's arrival on the scene was a goal scored by the debutant in the first 7 minutes. It was a simple enough opportunity following a Hughes cross which the Hearts defence failed to clear, but it was crisply taken by the apparently calm youngster, and the team went on to win 3-1. Paton had equalized for Hearts half way through the second half, but Celtic had then upped a gear after the interval and Charlie Gallagher and John Hughes added two more. It was a convincing debut for Bobby and he had the satisfaction of seeing his name in the headlines of the Evening Citizen that night for scoring the opening goal. A Motherwell fan was less impressed. His team had put 9 past Falkirk, but this performance by a provincial team was eschewed by Celtic scoring 3. Twas ever thus.

Parkhead emptied that fine sunny afternoon to the tramp of happy feet and everyone believing that a new era was indeed beginning. The capacity for self-delusion is of course infinite, particularly when all round you are also doing likewise. Crerand was praised, as was McNeill. Hughes "Yogi Bear" had had a fine game ... and yes, that young lad Murdoch had done well. He looked as if he had what was required, as far as Celtic fans were concerned. The team which had done so well that day were Haffey; McKay and Kennedy; Crerand, McNeill and Price; Lennox, Gallagher, Hughes, Murdoch, Byrne.

Murdoch himself spent a happy weekend, not least during the dinner that the club treated the team to on the Saturday night, during which men like McNeill and Crerand (as well as McGrory and Kelly) talked to him as if he were an equal. His career was well begun, but a more difficult task awaited him. Wednesday night saw a very much more meaty encounter at Dens Park, Dundee. Dundee were of course the League Champions, and although they had lost their opening fixture to Dundee United, this was their first big home game of the season. For Bobby Murdoch it was another great occasion - and he was still two days short of his 18th birthday!

With crass insensitivity, Dundee had decided to unfurl last season's League flag before the game. If it was meant to be an attempt to say "Up you Celtic", it was a colossal public relations disaster.The Lord Provost had a microphone and he did try hard, but not a word was heard over "Sure, It's A Grand Old Team To Play For" belted out by the massive Parkhead support.This particular song had been out for almost a year now and was now accepted as Celtic's song, even though the quaintly banal lyrics of Glen Daly "we don't care if they win, lose or draw, darn the hair we care" had been substituted. The memory remains of the poor Lord Provost going red in the face, trying to make himself heard, and Celtic's Chairman Robert Kelly on the platform party trying to look gracious, but having to hold his head in embarrassment at the churlish behaviour of his fans.

As befitted the occasion between two of the country's best sides, it was a fine game of football. It had rained all day, but the rain had now eased and the pitch was in immaculate condition. Celtic edged it in the first half and almost totally dominated the second, but the ball simply would not run for them in front of goal. As it happened, it was Dundee who scored the only goal of the game through veteran

Gordon Smith who had now won three League medals with three separate teams viz Hibs, Hearts and Dundee.

Celtic pounded the Dundee goal but could not score, being denied a penalty late on as well. Murdoch tried hard, but as in the Hearts game was found wanting in the latter stages as the pace did not slacken as much as it would have in a reserve game. More crucially it was Ian Ure of Dundee who won the battle of the Yogis. Both he and John Hughes were called "Yogi Bear", and it was Ure who came out on top on this occasion, beating Hughes, particularly in the air. The game finished 1-0 for Dundee, but a moral victory for Celtic, something that would be an all too familiar occurrence in the early years of Bobby's career.

Saturday revealed another bizarre facet of Celtic Park in the early sixties. Celtic actually beat Dundee United 4-0 - but the crowd booed and slow-handclapped them! It was indeed a shocking game of football, played on a hot day on a pitch which, having been inadequately watered, was surprisingly fiery for this time of year. Passes went astray, constructive play was nowhere to be seen, and although Celtic went in one goal up at half time thanks to a very early John Hughes goal, the 35,000 crowd were restive and unimpressed. Only when Pat Crerand scored a penalty on the hour mark did Celtic settle and go on and add another two goals.

Part of this unhappiness on the part of the fans was caused by the continued absence of John Divers, still kept out of the side by the vindictive management of Mr.Kelly who clearly felt that Divers had let Celtic down. Chants of "We Want Divers" were heard towards the end of the first half, and it would hardly have been surprising if the young inside forwards Charlie Gallagher and Bobby Murdoch had taken this personally. In truth, Bobby had a bad day - something that is liable to happen to a youngster struggling to come to terms with the pace and demands of the first team - but one wonders what Dundee United thought of all this? Celtic were hammering them 4-0, but were being catcalled by their own support! It didn't really say very much for the men from Tannadice!

A League game was now played at Falkirk on the Wednesday night. Divers and Mike Jackson did indeed return as the inside forwards at the expense of Gallagher and Murdoch - and Celtic won 3-1 on a ground, Brockville, which was one of the many bogey grounds of the early 1960's. Then incomprehensibly Murdoch and Gallagher returned for the trip to Tynecastle to play Hearts in the League Cup! It was as if Divers was serving a League Cup suspension.

The folly of all this was seen to its full effect when the strong going Hearts beat the young Celtic 3-2. Yet credit deserves to be paid to Murdoch for his part in a fine fightback which actually deserved more than it got. Hearts were 2-0 up at half time, then got a dodgy penalty to make it 3-0 when Willie Wallace (who would join Celtic in 1966) converted. Then, gallingly, Celtic too got a penalty kick which seemed to give them a window of opportunity. Pat Crerand however saw his kick saved by Gordon Marshall senior (father of the Gordon Marshall who played for Celtic in the 1990's). Ironically, now with the game lost, Celtic started to play the way the supporters had expected. With nothing to lose they threw everything forward and, after Murdoch pulled one back, other chances were missed and Celtic might well have drawn or even won. Hughes did add another very late on, but by then it was too late.

In 1962 it was 2 points for a win and 1 for a draw. This game then left Hearts with 6 points and Celtic 4, but then things took a turn for the better on the following Wednesday night when Dundee came to Parkhead. This time Hughes won the battle of the Yogis, and Celtic totally dominated. Charlie Gallagher scored in the first minute from a Hughes flick, then Murdoch, staying a little further back than normal, took possession of the midfield, spraying passes like a veteran. The wonder was that Dundee kept it at 1-0 until John Hughes added two late goals. The fans were delighted at all this, and their pleasure was increased by the knowledge that Dundee United (having kicked off earlier as there were as yet no floodlights at Tannadice) had, contrary to all expectation, beaten Hearts.

All this meant that Celtic and Hearts each had 6 points and both Dundee teams 4. Celtic had a better goal average, and knew that any sort of win in their last game at Tannadice Park would qualify them. It was a fascinating end to the Section with even the two Dundee teams in with a theoretical chance as long as each did the business for the other! Celtic travelled to Dundee United that first day of September 1962 full of hope that their young side (still admittedly showing more than the occasional piece of inexperience) could win the Section. The Celtic players and supporters would notice something quite different about Glasgow when they returned - no tramlines! This was the last day of the Glasgow trams. Times indeed were changing.

Dundee United were coy about saying what the crowd was that day, but it certainly looked as if safety limits had been exceded. It was not an all-ticket game, for the match had only become vital after the Wednesday night results, and there was no time to print the tickets. The all-ticket limit in these days was 20,000. There were at least 25,000 packed that hot day into the tight provincial ground with its quaint, recently built stand that actually, like that of Raith Rovers, turned a corner!

In fact that stand was the subject of a song over the tannoy system which had the Celtic fans convulsed with laughter. This was the era in which every football club were following the lead of Celtic and issuing their own 45 rpm record. "The Celtic Song" of Glen Daly had been a great success, Rangers issued their "Follow Follow" and Hearts and Hibs issued one between them. The Dundee clubs were now doing likewise. Dundee of course had the tune of the Jacobite anthem of "Bonny Dundee" and added some lyrics

*"Oh there's Penman and Cousin and Alan Gilzean*
*The best centre forward the world has seen"*

Dundee United (who had only been in the First Division for two years) had less to be proud about in playing terms but they had their stand. The lyrics ran along the lines of

*"There's a grand stand, the finest in the land*
*At Tannadice."*

The Celtic fans found this one somewhat funny and retaliated with their own Celtic Song and (less respectably, perhaps) the hauntingly lovely rebel song "Sean South of Garryowen" - a song commemorating an I.R.A. raid on the Brookeborough Barracks, County Fermanagh on 31st December 1957. This song reached its peak in the eyes of the Celtic fans in the early 1960's and is sadly therefore associated with failure on the field;

*"Twas on a dreary New Year's Eve*
*As the shades of night came down*
*A lorry load of volunteers*
*Approached the border town.*
*There were men from Dublin and from Cork*
*Fermanagh and Tyrone*
*But their leader was a Limerick man*
*Sean South of Garryowen!"*

The atmosphere was tense, and the young Murdoch would have been forgiven a few butterflies in his stomach for such an important occasion. It was not as if there were a great wealth of experienced players in the team to calm him down. Captain MacKay was only 25, left back Jim Kennedy being the only man in his late 20's. Lennox was a year older than Bobby Murdoch, and similarly nervous. Crerand and McNeill were a little older, but had yet to be part of a winning Celtic team. In such circumstances a good manager is required to pep them up and keep them confident, but the gentlemanly Jimmy McGrory, for all his fine qualities, lacked that ability, and all that could have been expected from Bob Kelly, a politician rather than a football tactician or motivator, was a pious homily on the need for good behaviour. McGrory would take someone aside and make a few suggestions, then wish everyone all the best - but there would be little in the way of inspirational oratory.

The huge Celtic following, dwarfing the home support, roared them on from the start to the finish - but it was the one game that typified Celtic in the early sixties. A dreadful refereeing decision, inept finishing, sheer bad luck and cruel misinformation all combined to make this game a collector's item in the catalogue of Celtic heartbreaks. Celtic started off playing towards the Dens Park end of the ground and looked as if they would overpower Dundee United. A few half chances were missed, and then came the moment that haunts and enfuriates the writer some forty years later.

The ball was many inches over the line in an undignified goalmouth scramble in front of the Celtic fans when left half Fraser fished it out, fully expecting to see the referee point upfield. But both the referee and linesman were unsighted, apparently, and no goal was given. The photographer for the Sunday Express situated in front of the terracing agreed with the Celtic fans that the ball was over the line ... but unfortunately didn't get a picture of it! Press reports the following day conceded that "the ball appeared to have crossed the line", but this was of no consolation to the outraged green and white hordes.

Half time came with still no reward for the efforts. Dundee United, it appeared, had been over the half way line very seldom, but Celtic for all their pressure had been unable to score. After half time, the pressure intensified, but still a goal would not come. Several times, it looked as if Celtic must score, (including once when Murdoch put the ball past the post from about 8 yards) but United usually managed to get bits of bodies in front of the ball, and clear it. A desperate final effort which saw Frank Haffey on the half way line to release more defenders into the front line came to nothing, and the game finished 0-0. Celtic could not be faulted for lack of effort, but it was the same old story of hysterical pressure, sheer bad luck and no result.

Even at that, the cause was still not yet lost, for Hearts still had to beat Dundee at Tynecastle. Half time had seen the score at 0-0 there as well, apparently, and a final score like that would have been good news for Celtic. Half time scores were given in a quaint and amateurish way with a board with letters down the side. Shortly after half time a man would appear with a piece of paper and put numbers opposite these letters, using a pulley rope. Thus A might read 0-0, B 0-1 and so on. It was absolute gibberish unless you had bought the programme which gave you the code that A, for example was Aberdeen v. Kilmarnock, B was Dunfermline v. Airdrie or whatever.

This was all one had to go on for, in 1962, radio commentary was by no means as comprehensive or efficient as it is now, and although one game was the "commentary" game, the rest of the results were not imparted until 5.00 p.m on the radio. Recently David Coleman's Grandstand programme on TV had introduced the teleprinter (having acquired it apparently from the Admiralty) which gave results sooner, but the fan at the game had no real idea of how other games were going.

In the absence of hard fact, rumours could easily start. Mischievously people did just that. Although rumours that Rangers had lost 0-5 to Raith Rovers were not likely to be believed, a story that they had lost 1-2 might be. The full time whistle had just gone when the Celtic end erupted with the "news" that it had stayed 0-0 at Tynecastle, and that Celtic therefore had qualified for the Quarter Finals of the League Cup.

Scenes of hugging, kissing and dancing were suddenly cut cruelly and abruptly short when the Dundee United tannoy sparked into life and sadistically told the exultant masses that Hearts had in fact won 2-0. The public address man could not resist adding also that Rangers had beaten St.Mirren ... and the deflation of the Celtic support was complete.

What the young Murdoch made of all this, we can but imagine. A year previously as a supporter or a reserve, he would have been part of the grief. This year, it was all the worse, for Bobby was now seen as partly responsible. The fact that he was only just 18 years old and was himself Celtic daft cut little ice with the upset and frustrated Celtic fans who turned on everyone in sight to blame for their failure and unhappiness. "That young Murdock (sic) is nae use" "He'll never mak it" were comments made by the desolate supporters on the way out of Tannadice that afternoon. The buses home were silent vehicles that night - or at least some of them were. Others sadly stayed on to commit a few acts of drunken hooliganism, living up to this sad aspect of the Celtic support in those unhappy days.

In retrospect, of course, the fault lay with the management. Divers should indeed have been brought back - at least for the Tannadice game where a calm head might have made all the difference. In those days Celtic seldom dabbled in the transfer market. The question might reasonably have been asked why no effort was being made to buy an established player to bring out the best in the youngsters. Later events would prove that Lennox and Murdoch were indeed world class players. But at outside right and inside left respectively as they were in late summer 1962, they were hideously out of position. Hughes' inconsistency would drive supporters to dementia. His apparent desire to run through a player was a constant source of puzzlement to his own supporters and amusement to the opposition.

Yet it was only the start of the season. Murdoch's first six games had been a real microcosm of Celtic in the early 1960's. He had seen triumph and disaster. He had been adulated and reviled. He must have experienced bewilderment, anguish and euphoria. His Celtic career had been well begun in the tradition of many other young hopefuls at that time. As yet there was no indication whether he was going to "make it" like Crerand and McNeill or disappear like Conway and Colrain - the ones who started off promising and remained ... promising (as the excellent book "The Glory And The Dream" put it). There was a long way to go yet.

# Rangers and a Bad Winter

Season 1962-63, Murdoch's first, was thus ill begun. The fact that Murdoch had only turned 18 and was really just a young lad (and still only a part-timer, at least at the start of the season) was something that seemed to escape the notice of those who were running the club - and also those who supported the team! Like many other youngsters, he had talent, but talent takes time to develop. It must be nurtured, fed and watered before it can ripen. Yett those in charge of Celtic Park's green shoots of recovery were not good gardeners.

Murdoch was simply thrown into the fray, almost in the manner of a callous World War One general like Douglas Haig at the Somme, without any consideration being given to his development. This was of course the era of the Celtic Youth policy. A wise Youth Policy can provide great benefits, and indeed this particular one could with justice claim to be the foundation for the 1967 European Cup, but at this stage the thinking was haphazard, erratic, ill thought-out and on occasion gave the distinct impression of being a way to build a team on the cheap. Occasionally, there was a good public relations coup - the great Real Madrid, for example, were coming to play at Parkhead on September 10th - but supporters would have preferred a more systematic approach to team building... or the purchase of some established stars.

Murdoch played 34 games in season 1962-63 (including the Glasgow Cup) sometimes at inside right, sometimes at inside left, occasionally at outside right, and seldom had the same partners in the forward line. This was a shocking indictment of those in charge of the club that a youngster (and certainly a talented one) should be mucked about in this desultory and disorganized fashion.

But even if team organization was a shambles, as it undeniably was, there can be no excuse for the attitude of some so-called supporters to what was going on. Understandably frustrated at the lack of obvious success or even obvious team direction in these dreadful years, the support was nasty. Several times the nastiness took the form of hooliganism, bottle throwing, vandalism and sheer naked violence at innocent citizens of towns like Falkirk, Dundee and Perth. More often, it took the form of venting their spleen at the men (or boys) wearing the green and white jerseys. Sociologists would of course have a field day on this adducing factors like "boring jobs", "ghetto housing", "cultural under-achievement", "deprivation" and of course in the case of Celtic "ethnic minority" and "slave mentality". Whatever it was, the young Celtic players were often on the receiving end of vitriol from those with massive personality disorders.

Murdoch was no exception to this. A bad day would often end with dog's abuse hurled at the unfortunate young man. Endlessly compared unfavourably with recent heroes like Willie Fernie or Bobby Collins, or even more distant ones like Patsy Gallacher or Tommy McInally, Murdoch was frequently told that he was not Celtic class, that he would never make it and that we weren't coming back next week to see any more of this.

It wouldn't have been so bad if they had carried out this threat (or promise), but they did in fact come back to deliver their constant verbal diatribes at young men who were trying their best. Supporting Celtic is of course a drug, a dangerous and addictive one sometimes. To be fair to the fans, the results were poor sometimes, and even the hardest hearts ocasionally wilted, but supporting Celtic in those days was not always a pleasant experience when it was done in the company of some people whose attitude towards the team often made one question whether they deserved the name "supporters" at all. There was almost a perverted crowing and a gloating when the team did lose, for they had been accustomed to little else. As happens with victims of abuse, the real horror is when they come to first accept it and then even to enjoy it!

In contrast, Rangers were efficent, organized and had great players like Jim Baxter, Willie Henderson and Davie Wilson. They also possessed what we would have called luck, but which their own supporters would have described as professionalism. It was the ability, quite simply, to win games, even on occasions when they did not deserve to.

For example, let us examine Murdoch's first Old Firm game at Parkhead on September 8th 1962. It was a fine day with a large, singing, chanting crowd. It was the first day of the "Celtic Cha Cha Cha" chant at a full Parkhead - and awe inspiring it was. The standard of play however was unimpressive. Celtic had most of the play, but threw away a golden opportunity when Pat Crerand allowed himself to be psyched out by streetwise Rangers opponents.

It was in the first half and Celtic had deservedly been awarded a penalty when Crerand was tripped up by Brand in the box. Crerand himself took the penalty, but not before several Rangers players, notably Jim Baxter, upset him by arguing that the ball was not placed on the spot. Crerand made it obvious that he was upset by such gamesmanship, then indicated by his run up where the ball was going and Ritchie saved well.

Even at that, Celtic remained marginally on top well into the second half and both Hughes and Murdoch had half chances to score. Both were spurned, and then with time running out, Celtic were even denied a deserved draw. Henderson of Rangers shot from the left, the ball was deflected when Haffey had it covered and Jim Kennedy was just unable to clear it off the line. By any standards it was a lucky goal, and even the Rangers apologists owned it to be so, but it seemed to be the way that life was for Celtic in 1962. There almost seemed to be a belief that Celtic were not allowed to beat Rangers.

Murdoch was one of those dropped in the aftermath, at least temporarily, and he missed the opportunity to play in the prestige friendly against Real Madrid on the Monday night after the Rangers game. Gloom was quite clearly the order of the day at Parkhead, but Bobby was young and realised that he had no divine right to be in the team. He was sufficiently confident in his own ability to know that if he worked hard, he would be restored ... and he was.

And in November, there was a slight glimmer of light, if that is appropriate for a misty murky quintessentially Glasgow November day. It was a Glasgow Cup First Round Replay at Celtic Park, played on the afternoon of Wednesday 21st November. The policy in those days was to play Old Firm games in daylight if at all possible rather than risk the two sets of supporters meeting each other in the dark.

Celtic's form had been haywire that autumn, and Murdoch oftener out of the team than in. His place had been further threatened by the arrival of a much travelled player called Bobby Craig, who had seemed, for a spell, to be the answer to a few problems. Craig had joined the club from Blackburn Rovers, and although his debut game (a matter of hours after his signing) saw Celtic exit from Europe at the hands of Valencia, the club then had a couple of good games beating Airdrie and St.Mirren by big margins. Then, incredibly, at Parkhead, they managed on November 10th to lose 0-1 to Queen of the South!

Murdoch was not involved in any of this, for he had been out of favour since early October. He thus missed Celtic's first ever European adventure against Valencia. He would have worried perhaps about the imminence of nuclear war from the reserve team. October 1962 was the time of the Cuban missile crisis, when the world came as close as it had ever done before or since to self termination. The posturing ended in an honourable draw, however much Western propaganda tried to state otherwise, and all of this tended to overshadow what was going on on the football field. The facts were that Hearts (whom Celtic had defeated on the first day of the season) won the League Cup beating Kilmarnock in a contentious Final, Dundee were progressing in the European Cup at the expense of Sporting Lisbon and Rangers were exiting from the European theatre at the hands of Tottenham Hotspur ... and Celtic were nowhere.

The defeat from lowly Queen of the South saw the usual panicky changes for the next game, and Murdoch found himself restored (but on the right wing!) at Dens Park against Dundee on November 17th. The game was played in wintry conditions, but ended in a fair 0-0 draw. Murdoch did well enough to earn his place for the Rangers game on Wednesday afternoon, but came in at inside right (for the injured Bobby Craig) in a forward line whose only recognisable centre forward, Steve Chalmers, played on the right wing, and the no.9 berth was taken by inside forward John Divers.

This was no way to approach an Old Firm game, but this time it actually worked! Glasgow was shrouded in freezing fog, dreadfully unhealthy conditions which combined with industrial pollution to produce the hated "smog" for which Glasgow was in those days notorious. 24,000 attended this game, not a bad attendance for a working afternoon, and they saw (whenever the mist allowed them to) a great game of football in which Celtic triumphed by 3 goals to 2. There was a school of thought, even at the ground itself, of those who believed that the referee should have called the game off because of the weather, but was afraid to do so because of possible crowd reaction.

Murdoch scored 2, and may even have scored 3. Celtic's first goal came after a Crerand free kick cannoned off the Rangers wall and beat the goalkeeper. Murdoch would claim that it was he rather than a Rangers defender who touched the ball, but newspaper reports generally tend to give the goal to Crerand (neither Murdoch, nor an own goal). Celtic's second goal came when Murdoch picked up a Divers cross from the right wing and hammered home. The other was in extra time when Murdoch made space for himself and was on the right spot for a good through ball from Divers. Celtic were worthy winners, (having hit the woodwork on two other occasions) and although Rangers would claim that the Glasgow Cup didn't really matter, their demeanour at the end showed how disappointed they were. It hurt Jim Baxter to shake hands with the young Murdoch, but to his credit he did so.

Celtic fans left Parkhead that afternoon convinced that the corner had been turned and that Celtic after their indifferent and inconsistent start to the League, could now rally, and with Murdoch and Divers as inside forwards, make a strong challenge. It was a feature incidentally of the Celtic support in these days that, in the same way as defeats produced excessive introverted melancholic depression, a good result, however isolated and insignificant, could induce unwarranted traces of well being and optimism. Sadly this optimism lasted only as far as the following Saturday.

A dismal defeat by the strong going Partick Thistle, who scored two goals in the first half hour, left the team and its supporters demoralised with the second half being played out in an eerie silence. There followed a depressing stagger to the New Year in which once again the forward line was experimented with repeatedly in an effort to find a credible blend.

Murdoch scored a goal against Hibs at Easter Road in the 75th minute. A good goal it was as well, and it looked enough to win a hitherto dour game. The press men picked up their phones and announced it to their offices for the evening's editions of Glasgow's Evening Citizen, Evening Times, Edinburgh's Evening News and Dundee's Sporting Post. While they were actually on the phone extolling the virtues of young Murdoch's strike, a roar drowned them out, for Hibs had equalized. The young Celtic defence had fatally relaxed and at their most vulnerable of moments, been caught off guard.

The following week saw Hearts at Parkhead. A good game ensued but once again another late equalizer for an Edinburgh side deprived Celtic of the points; Johnny Hamilton doing the needful. Murdoch then missed the next two games (one of them a dreadful defeat by Third Lanark, the other a lucky odd goal win over Dunfermline) but Bobby had other things on his mind.

At Christmas, he announced his engagement to Kathleen Barrie whom he had been dating now for some time. As if in celebration, he was restored to the Celtic team (at inside right) for a game against Falkirk at home on December 29th. This game was won, albeit unconvincingly, 2-1, and thus Murdoch retained the inside right position for the Old Firm game against Rangers at Ibrox on New Year's Day 1963.

He must have wished that he hadn't, for this one was another collector's item in Celtic horror stories, bad even in the context of the dreadful days of the early 1960's. The Ibrox pitch was hard and barely playable, but that does not excuse the appallingly inept team performance. Undeniably, certain players thought that the game should have been off and quite openly spread disaffection. With an attitude like that, however justified, one may be about the actual point in question, the team is heading for disaster. The young Murdoch was thus exposed to yet more of this negative, destructive atmosphere.

Yet until half time, things were not going too badly. Admittedly Rangers, apparently wearing more suitable footgear, were a goal ahead, but it was a flukish one which had been deflected off Pat Crerand. Celtic were at least playing respectably, and on the tricky pitch might well have fought their way back into the game. In the second half, given the conditions which militated against Rangers' ball players as well, a concentrated, determined effort might have obtained a draw. The going was tough, the Celtic End, loyal as always, now expected the tough to get going.

Unfortunately, it was the said Pat Crerand on whom controversy centred. Pat, for all his faults, loved Celtic and had been a great help and role model to Bobby Murdoch to whom he gave all the tips about pacing himself and keeping something in reserve for the last ten minutes. A brilliant player, and understandably frustrated at the way in which things were going both in this game and in others, Pat allegedly had an argument with Assistant Manager Sean Fallon in the dressing room at half time. The force of Pat's venom seemed to be directed at John Hughes who, admittedly, was having a shocker of a game.

Now a little anger may be no bad thing on occasion, but this was not one of these occasions. The spat, given the lack of strong leadership, was not resolved the way that it should have been with handshakes, jokes and "Let's fight back - against Rangers, not Celtic!". Had substitutes been available in 1963, Pat would have spent the rest of the game in the stand, but as it was, he had to be persuaded to go out and play in the second half - having apparently at one point thrown his hooped jersey to the floor.

One has to draw a more recent parallel with all this - and one that was even more disastrous for the team. One shudders to recall the Inverness Caley Thistle catastrophe of 2000. The team were behind at half time, but not necessarily totally beyond redemption. A concerted second half effort might yet have saved the day, but a strong figure decides to pick a fight with management - and there is no way back after that.

Back in 1963 "The Glasgow Herald" puts it rather well when it says euphemistically that "more than one player did not seem to have much liking for the task". Basically, Celtic crumbled and Rangers must have wondered what was going on as they romped to a 4-0 victory. Frank Brogan on the left wing looked as if he might have done something for Celtic, but was starved of the ball. Murdoch and others barely got a kick and the collapse of Celtic was a talking point for the rest of the New Year period.

It was a traumatic experience for Bobby Murdoch. In fairness, it must be stressed that his recent recovery from an ankle injury possibly made the playing conditions seem that little bit worse, and he was also still very young, emotionally unfit for the demands of playing in that game against that opposition and in those circumstances. The game finished in a vindictive, triumphalist atmosphere of vitriol and racist hatred against the Irish, the Pope, the Virgin Mary and anyone else whose existence might somehow irritate the consciousness of sub-human intelligence. The Celtic end had evaporated with only a few pockets of defiant resistance, as the snow flurried around them - sadly not in enough quantity to get the game abandoned. One of these pockets solidified round a lone accordian player who tried to rally spirits with his plaintive "We will ch-a-a-nt the Soldiers' Song" before he too, in circumstances reminiscent of the sinking of the Titanic, decided with two minutes left that the cause was lost, and packed up and went.

The game was indeed seen as a gross betrayal of Celtic traditions by the management, and the axe fell on quite a few players, notably Pat Crerand who never played again for the club and departed to Manchester United in February. Murdoch was caught up in the maelstrom of droppings, and it was widely believed by the support at this point that Murdoch was a youngster who had started deceptively brightly, but was destined to join the incredibly large pile of those who were not up to it. It cannot have helped Murdoch's confidence that on January 5th Celtic went up to Pittodrie without him and thumped Aberdeen 5-1. John Hughes, who had played against Rangers as if his boots had been laced together (as one unkind punter put it), had one of his great days and scored a hat-trick!

The game at Aberdeen was remarkable. Celtic were seemingly at rock-bottom (in fact they weren't, for that had still to come!) yet their supporters travelled north en masse, green and white scarves hanging out of train and bus windows in a tremendous display of loyalty and love for the team. They were rewarded by the sight of a new full back pairing of Young and Gemmell - tall youngsters with their hair brushed back who quite simply played the game as if they were enjoying it, refusing to give either of their Aberdeen opponents, Cumming and Thom, a kick of the ball.

Such enthusiasm infected the rest of the team and it was one of Celtic's best performances in this dismal decade. The contrast between Ibrox and Pittodrie could not have been more marked. One supporter summed it all up as he sank into his seat on the 5.15 train to Glasgow that night when he said "Tuesday (New Year's Day) didnae need to be like yon". But where did it leave Bobby Murdoch, part of the Ibrox disgrace, but uninvolved in the Pittodrie fight-back?

The bad weather which descended over most of Great Britain in January and February was probably no bad thing for Murdoch. Between New Year's Day and March 2nd, Celtic played two games - beating Aberdeen 5-1 at Pittodrie on January 5th and Falkirk in the Scottish Cup at the end of that month, but on neither occasion did Murdoch feature. Yet he did not get discouraged, kept training hard and crucially kept faith in himself. It also gave him breathing space to regain confidence. And his life was hardly at an end - he was after all only 18!

The cause of the bad weather was the big freeze which caused more postponements of football matches in Scotland than in any other winter. There had been more snow in 1947, but this time the problem was frost and as heated pitches had not even been thought of, the effect was catastrophic. Celtic took their players to Ireland, where the frost was not so severe, to play a few friendlies, simply to give them some match practice and Murdoch was still sufficiently in favour to be brought along.

But the major casualty of the bad winter as far as Celtic were concerned was the loss of Pat Crerand, transferred to Manchester United in early February for £56,000. After what had happened at Ibrox at the New Year, a departure was probably inevitable, but it was distressing for supporters nevertheless. History has yet to make its mind up about Pat's departure. The stories are confused about whether he wanted to go or was made to go or whether Celtic were just wanting the money, but as far as the support was concerned, it was a major body blow at a vulnerable time when body blows had already been dished out in large quantities.

Pictures of Pat Crerand which had adorned bedroom walls were torn down by youngsters with the same sort of ferocity that is normally kept for jilted lovers. Indeed the parallel is quite striking, for we now had to face the future and the Rangers without our one undeniable world class player (as he had proved in that friendly against Real Madrid at the start of the season). What made matters worse was that the club showed no interest in immediately going out to buy a replacement wing half.

We did not of course know at the time (nor did anyone at the club) that Celtic already had someone on their books who would be a better wing half than Crerand. It would take a few more heavy dunts and a total change in direction before this became apparent. Two long painful years would pass before Scottish football would see someone who could fill the right half position with distinction. He was of course that young forward over whom there currently hung a huge question mark - Bobby Murdoch.

When the frost eased on March 2nd 1963 (to be replaced by an equally severe and predictable thaw which caused floods and landslides galore) and football was restored, Murdoch appeared on the right wing. Loads of games remained to be played, but Celtic, now without Pat Crerand, had no hope of winning the League, such had been their desperately awful form before Christmas. Team selection continued to be bizarre, as indeed was the resultant form. A very fine 4-1 win over European Cup Semi Finalists Dundee at Celtic Park, for example, was followed by a severe 0-6 thumping from Kilmarnock at Rugby Park - an occasion which Murdoch had done well to avoid.

Yet the Scottish Cup provided some hope. On the Wednesday (March 6th) after the snow disappeared, Murdoch scored Celtic's first goal in their emphatic 3-1 victory over Hearts in their much postponed tie. It was a good win against a strong Hearts team (although Roy Barry and Willie Hamilton were absent from the Edinburgh side, serving a club suspension). The consequences of losing that game would have been too fearful to contemplate, and young Murdoch had every reason to be proud of himself for his part in the victory.

But this was the game in which Murdoch sustained his ankle injury. It was a totally accidental clash with Hearts goalkeeper Gordon Marshall senior, but Bobby was taken off. Funnily enough, there were no apparent immediate effects, for Bobby was able to train the next day and indeed to play on the following Saturday in a League game against

St.Mirren, scoring Celtic's only goal. In fact he missed very few games between the injury and the end of the season. This may have been unwise. Perhaps a few games off at this stage might have prevented a great deal of trouble in the future. But at the age of 18, after an enforced lay-off because of bad weather, who would want to drop out of the team and risk losing his place permanently?

This fine win over Hearts was followed by wins over Gala Fairydean, St.Mirren and Raith Rovers to reach the Final. The St.Mirren game brought back memories of previous disasters, for it had been the Buddies who showed Celtic the Scottish Cup exit door in 1959 and 1962. The support were by no means optimistic as they travelled to Love Street on March 30th to see the Quarter Final but this time they saw a business like Celtic team who scored early through Frank Brogan and were professional enough to maintain their lead. Murdoch had a good game that day, playing significantly better in the second half when the Buddies upped a gear and put on more pressure for the equalizer. This compelled Murdoch to move back a little into the midfield, leaving John Hughes and Steve Chalmers up front. It was from this and similar games that the more intelligent of the support began to question whether Bobby was in his best position as a forward. Was he not a better midfielder?

That same day at Dens Park, Dundee probably saw Celtic's best chance of the Scottish Cup go out the window. Rangers went there and in an ennervating but ultimately indecisive contest, peppered with funny refereeing and a penalty for each side, the game ended goalless. The following Wednesday night in the Ibrox Replay, Dundee were 2-1 ahead at one point before succumbing 2-3. This was a shame as far as Celtic were concerned, for Dundee in 1963 seemed to be about the only team capable of beating Rangers. Certainly Celtic looked anything but capable of that, but Dundee were hampered by being involved in Europe (they had now reached the Semi Final) and the incipient hints of player unrest which were to lead to their downfall and long term collapse.

The Semi Final draw threw up Celtic v.Raith Rovers and Rangers v. Dundee United two weeks later. As they travelled to the Semi Final at Ibrox against Raith Rovers, the support tried their best not to think of a year previously when Celtic had collapsed at this stage and at the same venue. Their confidence cannot have been helped by the loss of the Glasgow Cup to Third Lanark the previous Monday. Murdoch scored Celtic's only goal in a lacklustre Final, but generally speaking it had been a shocker of a game.

The Raith Rovers game was well summed up by the Glasgow Herald as being "devoid of excitement and finesse", yet Celtic still managed, with the aid of two penalties, to beat the Kirkcaldy men 5-2. In fairness, it was a windy day and the game was played on a hard pitch, but it was still a poor performance. By an odd coincidence the score in the other Semi Final was the same, 5-2 for Rangers over Dundee United.

By this time Murdoch seems to have flitted between inside right and inside left in a haphazard, whimsical sort of way, yet occasionally the support were beginning to see glimpses of a potentially great player at work. Although he sometimes appeared hampered and cramped in the forward line, Murdoch could certainly take a goal (he had scored a hat trick against admittedly weak opposition in Gala Fairydean) and showed increasing signs of being able to prompt John Hughes to do likewise.

Another modest cause for optimism lay in the fact that two wingers had emerged in Frank Brogan on the left, by some distance the best forward at Parkhead in those times, (yet ludicrously underplayed) and a tiny red haired lad called

Jimmy Johnstone whom the support had instantly taken to their hearts. If everybody played to their potential, there was just the chance that the Scottish Cup might be landed.

The problem was that the opponents were Rangers. Already by some distance League Champions, Rangers exuded confidence, arrogance and more than a little professionism. Yet they were not invincible. Their repeated failures in Europe as well as the Glasgow Cup result the previous November showed that they were susceptible. Most recently, there had been a struggle against Dundee in the Quarter Final. A Celtic performance worthy of the traditions of the club might just win the day, it was felt by the ever optimistic support. The problem was the Celtic "death wish" "inferiority complex" or "freezing on the day" - call it what you will. The problem lay in the mind.

Saturday 4th May was the date set for the Scottish Cup Final, much delayed by the backlog of fixtures. It was the first Old Firm Scottish Cup Final since 1928, and excitement ran high in Glasgow. The 134,000 tickets were all sold with reports of black market prices and counterfeit tickets on sale. In fact only 129,527 appeared on the day, such was the appalling weather. Curiously, in view of Rangers success and status as favourites, the counterfeit tickets were for the Celtic End, indicating a massive degree of affection, love and confidence, the latter perhaps misplaced, for the men in the green and white.

It was a very unpleasant day with wind and rain, and Murdoch found himself lining up at inside right along with wee Jimmy Johnstone. It was a grossly inexperienced right wing, and Murdoch's position of inside right meant that his direct opponent was none other than Rangers' left half, 'Slim' Jim Baxter. Murdoch would cheerfully admit that nerves got the better of him in the build-up to the Final, and that he was possibly, at the age of 18, still a little on the young side to be plunged into that particular cauldron.

As it turned out, both Murdoch and Celtic had a good day. Rangers, the better team on paper at least, had more shots at goal but could not get past Frank Haffey who had one of his better games in the Celtic goal. Frank had of course been the Scotland goalkeeper who had conceded 9 goals at Wembley two years previously, a game much enjoyed, it would appear, by some Rangers supporters who constantly referred to the fact - the first indication that large sections of the Ibrox support favoured England over Scotland. On this occasion however Frank quietened them.

Yet the newspaper headlines of "Fantastic Frank" and "Franktastic" tended to obscure the fact that there were other good Celtic players on view and that with a bit of luck, victory might just have been gained. Rangers were, for example, lucky when Johnstone's lob late in the game went just wide of the goal with Ritchie spreadeagled on the ground.

Murdoch in fact scored Celtic's equalizer just before half time when he was on hand to take advantage of a John Hughes inspired cavalry charge. Rangers had just scored, but as teams do, dropped their guard. Murdoch pushed through a fine ball for Yogi, whose shot beat Ritchie but Shearer was on the line to stop it. Murdoch followed up and scored to release bedlam in the Celtic End behind that goal.

Half time was thus spent with the Celtic supporters outshouting their counterparts. The second half saw the crowd in a state of permanent agitation with the Celtic End hoping against hope that their day was at hand, but dreading a late, lucky Rangers winner. Murdoch played well in midfield, getting the better of Baxter on several occasions and feeding wingers Johnstone and Brogan who might just have, with a little luck, won the day.

But full time came with the teams locked at 1-1. Celtic had caused more than a few flutters down Ibrox way and had earned the respect both of their opponents, and more importantly, the Scottish media who had had to drop their patronising talk about "youngsters", "Kelly Kids" and "colts"and minimise their adulation of Rangers and Jim Baxter - at least for a spell. That night some Celtic players, including Bobby and girlfriend Kathleen, met by chance Jim Baxter at the Buchanan Hotel. In circumstances which would have baffled and humiliated the bigots of both sides, a good relationship (which would lead to lifelong friendship) sprung up and Baxter at one point told Murdoch that he would be a good player ... as long as he stayed off the booze! The irony, in view of later events, was telling.

The Replay of the Scottish Cup Final would not take place until the following Wednesday, 15th May. This was because Wednesday May 8th saw an International game against Austria at Hampden. This game became in itself infamous and possibly unique because it was abandoned with ten minutes to go when a sent off Austrian refused to go! English referee Jim Finney quite rightly picked up the ball and walked off! It remains one of the very few International fixtures ever to have been abandoned. The Austrians retained their hatred of both Scotland and England for a long time after this, and Celtic the following year may have indirectly suffered because of this in the Cup Winners' Cup.

All this had little immediate effect on Murdoch or indeed Celtic who had no representative in the Scotland side that night, Ian Ure of Dundee favoured at centre half ahead of Billy McNeill. But Celtic played off three meaningless League fixtures in the meantime, wiping out the backlog of the bad winter. The form was as inconsistent as the selection of the forward line. They beat Clyde 2-0 at home on Monday May 6th, collapsed abysmally to Dundee United 0-3 on Saturday May 11th at Tannadice and then on Monday May 13th, two days before the Cup Final Replay, delighted supporters by whipping Motherwell 6-0 at

Parkhead.

The forward line permutations ran Johnstone, Murdoch, Hughes, Divers and Chalmers against Clyde, a similar set up against Dundee United, and then what everyone presumed to be an experimental line-up of Brogan, Craig, Divers, Chalmers and Hughes against Motherwell. The problem was that against a Motherwell side that had given up for the season, the team did deceptively well with Chalmers scoring a hat trick from the inside left position.

Murdoch might well have expected not to feature in the Cup Final Replay. In the shocker against Dundee United at Tannadice, he had had a dreadful game (although, in truth, no worse than anyone else) even on occasion lacking pace and strength and looking dreadfully jaded and unfit. This was hardly surprising for a youngster at the end of his first season (and a lop-sided, topsy-turvy, emotional season at that) but his cause was hardly helped by the chorus of boos from the supporters every time he touched the ball after his ineffectual first half hour. Yet this bile and venom was directed against the boy who had scored the equalizing goal the previous Saturday in the Cup Final!

In spite of being absent from Monday's 6-0 win, Murdoch was hopeful about a place in the team for the Cup Final Replay, yet apparently the team bus travelled to Hampden with no-one aware of what the team would actually be! Murdoch was delighted to find himself in the team, but the forward line read an incongruous; Craig, Murdoch, Divers, Chalmers and Hughes. Both wingers from the first game Johnstone and Brogan dropped, Divers, a slow although talented forager, was at centre forward, and Chalmers either a speedy winger or a goalscorer now finding himself at inside left! Hughes could play on the left wing but was dreadfully inconsistent, and on the right wing appeared Bobby Craig, the inside forward who had joined the club the previous autumn but who had now flopped after a promising start to his Celtic career. We thus had a failed inside forward on the right wing, and Bobby Murdoch was the only man in his recognised position! In a Cup Final!

This was crazy, irrational, illogical stuff and more than one punter at the Celtic End straining to hear Hampden's inadequate tannoy system could not believe what he was hearing. "We're f---ed" was the general opinion as that team took the field. Indeed we were. The defence played tolerably well for a spell, but Rangers quickly realised that the Celtic forward line hardly knew each other in this formation, and took full advantage.

2-0 down at half time, the Celtic End seethed with discontent and depression. Allegations of having bets on with the bookies, vitriolic diatribes about weak and foolish management and foul-mouthed hatred about the desertion of Pat Crerand to Manchester United (he would win an F.A. Cup medal a few days later) cascaded like a torrent down the terracing that fine spring evening. Twenty minutes into the second half, another goal went in and, in a scene which baffled the many visiting English and foreign journalists, the hitherto packed Celtic End terracing emptied itself of supporters. They felt themselves betrayed by people unfit to run the club and who had reduced the green half of Glasgow to a laughing stock. 50,000, more or less unanimously, turned their back on Celtic.

Murdoch barely kicked a ball that night, numbed by the enormity of it all. The game passed him by, even though Rangers, to their credit and apparently acting on orders of Scot Symon, the Manager, stopped at 3-0 and did not, other than by a little clowning by Baxter, humiliate their opponents. Almost forty years later, the memory stays of the Celtic End that night - the tears, the dejection, the old men who thought that the team of Patsy Gallacher and Jimmy Quinn was gone, the young men whose entire lives had been spent in ignominy and humiliation, reviled in many cases for their religion and the nationality of their grandfathers... and unable to say anything to those who tormented and taunted them, except silently agree with them. It was indeed the slave mentality!

It so happened that on that very night Tottenham Hotspur, by beating Atletico Madrid in Rotterdam, became the first British team to win any European trophy, in this case the Cup Winners' Cup, having beaten Rangers in a previous round. If anyone had said that night that Celtic would be the first team to bring the European Cup back to Britain in four years time, it would have been a joke in the worst of bad taste. That Celtic performance that night was a sham, a masquerade, a parody, a burlesque of all that Celtic had done over the previous 75 years of their history. It so happened that 1963 was 75 years on from the first game in 1888. It was a mercy that if there had ever been any plans for some vainglorious celebration of these 75 years, they were quickly shelved.

The atmosphere in the dressing room that night can only be guessed at. There would have been all the feelings of the supporters - depression, dejection, shame - but in addition the professional side of it all, that they had been humiliated and degraded by their oldest and most bitter rivals. This had to raise questions about their future involvement with Celtic. Murdoch's youth may have to a certain extent protected him - but even so, his future in the game must have been brought into question.

Murdoch's first season thus ended in the nadir of Celtic's fortunes. He had indeed joined them in an evil hour. There was no sign yet of the wheel turning. Yet there were positives for young Bobby. He was gaining experience. He could take a goal and a certain ability to pass a ball was becoming evident. He had learnt some basic tenets of Scottish professional footbal - such as it was not a good idea to dwell on the ball. Tackles in the Scottish First Division in 1962-63 were crunching, with some brutal defenders around. You either got rid of the ball quickly or made sure that you found space on your own. And you watched your back!

Bobby was still on a learning curve, young enough to benefit from bad times. He still retained the support of his family who, while just as distressed about the fortunes of the team, were as helpful as ever to him. "We'll come again" his father said to him, and even though there were few grounds for such confidence, it was good to know that Celtic were not entirely broken. In addition, the engagement to Kathleen was a great source of strength ... and marriage was being planned.

★

The "Midnight Mail", as it was then called, was gradually picking up a little speed on Wednesday 15th May 1963 as it left Glasgow's Buchanan Street Station on its way to Aberdeen. Three desolate youngsters, dejected and dismayed, sat in a carriage of the train. The last of the money had been spent on a bag of chips and a copy of next morning's Daily Express, which gloated exorbitantly over Rangers' 3-0 triumph. Songs of triumph were heard from down the corridor as Rangers fans shouted their anthems about guarding walls and what their fathers used to wear, as well as offensive remarks about other people's religion.

The train had travelled about quarter of an hour with the boys in gloomy, morbid introspection. A man entered the carriage, politely asking the boys if they minded if he joined them. Seeing the drooping green colours, he sympathised and started to talk about Delaney and McGrory. The boys were in no mood for any sort of cheery conversation and allowed him to drool on. Occasionally he said things like "we will rise again" "all Europe will rise to the name of Celtic" "McNeill will be pummelled as he goes to get that big Cup" "Murdoch will be considered the best of them all".

In spite of themselves, the boys had to laugh at this idiocy. Drink must be a terrible thing if it made you say things like that, but they let him haver on about Leeds United, Inter Milan, Wee Jimmy, "nine in a row" - and someone he called "Murdie". In truth, the boys were nearly asleep, trying to blot out the horrible reality. They did not notice whether it was at Bridge of Allan or Stirling or Larbert or whatever station that the "Ghost of Celtic Yet To Come" disembarked.

# The Continuing Complex

The summer of 1963 was glorious. The Beatles continued to charm the young and appall the old with their music - raucous yet melodic, the West Indians played some lovely cricket against England, Ronald Biggs was part of a gang which held up a Royal Mail train and the Conservative Government of Harold McMillan tried in vain to hush up a security scandal brought about by the revelation that the Minister of War (now it would be called Defence) John Profumo had frequented and patronised the same prostitute as a Russian Naval Attaché.

The same summer should have been spent at Parkhead with a wholesale clear out of coaching staff, the resignation of a few Directors and a frantic search for new talent by a new Manager. Nothing like this happened. Chairman Bob Kelly continued as serenely and complacently as ever, pleased that for all his team's problems, they did at least acquit themselves well in a behavioural sense. This was very important for Bob in his perpetual quest for high office within the corridors of power. The semblance was more important than the substance.

There was also something very quintessentially Celtic about this Kelly obsession with fair play. Kelly's father, James Kelly, had of course been signed from Renton (some would say poached or even stolen) in 1888 to play in the first ever Celtic team alongside the likes of Willie Maley. This began a long and honourable association with the club until his death in 1932. He was not technically a "founding father" of the club, but it was on men like Kelly and Maley that the initial success of Celtic very much depended. More exactly, perhaps, in those days it was the acceptance and integration of the Irish into Scottish society that was at stake.

It was with this in mind that men like Kelly and Maley laid down the strictest guidelines for fair play. The Celtic team must not be seen to be cheating or fouling or reacting badly to provocation. Good behaviour was paramount if the bigots of the Orange Order and the Church of Scotland were to be silenced.

These noble sentiments, although not always lived up to, remained within the ideals of the Kelly family. Robert Kelly (whose damaged arm and other health problems prevented him playing for the club) was always punctilious about the club's image. This was why "bad boys" like Crerand and Auld were often allowed, even encouraged, to leave, no matter how talented they were nor how much the team would suffer in their absence. It also explains stories that Sean Fallon, for example, would tell about how sometimes bonuses were even paid for a defeat - as long as the defeat had been accepted in the "Celtic manner", whatever that might mean!

Jimmy McGrory, the nominal and token Manager, was presumably shattered at what had happened on May 15th 1963, but kept smiling at the Press and the public, puffing away at his pipe and looking like everybody's favourite uncle. Such had been his legendary playing career that he was comparatively immune to the vitriol and hate of the frustrated masses of the broken green and white brigade. What he really thought in private as he sipped his sherry is not recorded. Certainly he never seemed to entertain the thought of resignation at this time, although he did say that he would have had to in 1948, if Celtic had been relegated!

Murdoch, of course, was very much in favour in the eyes of the Establishment at Celtic Park. He had basically made a good start to his footballing career, although there had been a few rough edges which needed to be smoothed. But in the eyes of Mr.Kelly he was a fine upstanding athletic lad, a perfect example of what a young Celt should be. He was polite, personable, affable - a good specimen product of the "Kelly Kids" youth policy.

Kathleen and he were very much in love, and he had no real problem in that side of his life, but what about his football? A bright start and several indications that he was a player of quality, but also the sickening feeling that his Celtic career was to be extinguished almost as soon as it was starting, such was the effect of May 15th 1963.The Book of Revelation, in its description of the end of the World, talks about "the abomination of desolation". Celtic supporters in 1963 felt like that was what they were suffering - and it was a feeling that lasted all summer.

Yet Pandora's Box, which in Greek mythology unleashed all the evils on the world, also released Hope. "They'll come again" said a few wiser souls, and a small piece of encouragement came the way of the supporters a couple of weeks after the Cup Final when Celtic signed a player called Paddy Turner of Morton. Murdoch was hardly likely to be uplifted by this, however, because Turner, an Eire International, was an inside right, and Murdoch may well have now felt that his future in the game lay somewhere other than Celtic Park.

Yet, Bobby was a Celtic supporter. He was hurting inside just as deeply as any supporter and his pre-season training saw him working hard. If Turner was to be inside right, this did not necessarily mean that Murdoch would not play, for none of the other forwards was guaranteed a place either. Indeed, there was always the chance that Turner might produce something special for the chronically dysfunctional forward line and bring out the best in Murdoch, albeit in a different position.

But no-one could have predicted where Bobby would find himself on that rainy afternoon of the opening fixture.

Cruel Fate had decreed that Celtic would find themselves in the same League Cup section as Rangers, and that Rangers would be the first visitors to Parkhead on Saturday August 10th. Jimmy Johnstone was on the right wing, partnered by Paddy Turner, and John Hughes was in the centre. But the left wing comprised (to the horror and bewilderment of the Celtic faithful) Chalmers and Murdoch.

It was Murdoch's first appearance for Celtic on the left wing, where he used to play as a schoolboy and presumably had impressed someone in pre-season training. Against Rangers on a slippy, wet pitch, against a brutally determined Rangers right back in Bobby Shearer, Murdoch had no hope. He was indeed cynically fouled early on - in circumstances which, thirty or forty years later, would almost certainly have produced an instant red card - and was visibly afraid of Shearer for the rest of the game. Elsewhere, Hughes showed a certain amount of bustle, but persisted in his bizarre attempts to run through Ron McKinnon, Chalmers had one chance early on which he muffed, Turner was no place in sight and Jimmy Johnstone was well policed by the elegant Eric Caldow.

In spite of all this, Celtic, playing with loads of energy and enthusiasm, were well on top for the first 30 minutes until Billy McNeill made a mistake with a pass back and Jim Forrest nipped in to score, thus beginning a complex about Forrest that McNeill took a long time to shake off. Confidence now oozed out of Rangers, and Celtic collapsed, predictably, like a pack of cards in the second half. Like the Scottish Cup Final, they were lucky to get off with a 0-3 defeat, and the steady streams of departing fans throughout the second half bore grim testimony to that.

The same forward line then played a feckless goalless draw at Kilmarnock in midweek in front of a still large but obviously traumatized travelling support. Murdoch is barely mentioned in reports of this game - perhaps the most eloquent testimony of all to a player having a bad game - but at least for the next game against Queen of the South at Parkhead, Murdoch was restored to inside right with Turner at inside left. It was another draw, this time 1-1, but the ugly atmosphere and the wholesale barracking of everyone (Murdoch included) made constructive football virtually impossible. Readers may recall the atmosphere at Parkhead on New Year's Day 1994 when another generation of Celtic fans turned on another generation of the Kelly family. August 17th 1963 was like that.

After the game London Road was the scene of a virtually unprecedented demonstration against Mr.Kelly and the Celtic management. The said Mr.Kelly had wisely taken himself off to Dumfries to watch the reserves, and it was just as well, for this demonstration (a forerunner of the massive ones that were soon to hit the streets of Britain to protest at the Vietnam War) was an inch away from turning nasty. Threats were heard from hotheads about burning cars, some people were clearly visible with stones in their hands, but the main emotion was sheer frustration from people who had more or less impoverished themselves in their love of their team, and were being rewarded by this. The Glasgow Police eventually persuaded everyone to go home by dogged determination rather than any kind of heavy-handed overreaction and the peace was kept.

Murdoch was one of those dropped to appease the mob. He missed the rest of the ill fated League Cup campaign and the whole desperate month of September, before he was eventually restored in the first weekend in October. By this time, the League Cup was gone and any idea of winning the League was virtually a non-starter, but a good start had been made to the European Cup Winners Cup against Basle of Switzerland.

September 1963 was in fact a good time for Murdoch to be out of the team. On September 7th, Celtic lost in the

League at Ibrox, (this time an unlucky 2-1 affair after Celtic scored first) making it three defeats to their Old Firm rivals within a month and then on September 14th came the craziest single game of all those crazy years. Third Lanark came to Parkhead. Celtic, minus Murdoch, entralled and amazed everyone by scoring 4 goals in the first 15 minutes - and good goals they were as well, each the reward for some well developed, intelligent attacking play. The "faithful" (at 19,000 more than a little diminished in numbers) had seldom seen anything like this since the 7-1 thrashing of Rangers in 1957. Yet just as people were beginning to speculate about double figures, Thirds pulled one back. Final score? Celtic 4 Third Lanark 4 - and Thirds missed a good chance just at the death, which would have made it 4-5!

The European trip to Basle was the catalyst for some precipitate action by Bobby. He was not even in the squad of 17 to travel. Peeved at being deprived of a trip to the land of William Tell, the Alps, clocks and anonymous bank accounts and also a little concerned about where his long term future lay, Bobby determined to put in a transfer request. Fortunately for Bobby, as everyone was in Switzerland, there was no-one to hand such a request to, and in any case he was talked out of it by his wise father who pointed out, perceptively, that he might get his place back on the harder grounds of winter and that ironically, it would benefit Bobby if the team beat Basle without him - for there would then be more games to be played and more opportunites for him to be recalled. In any case, which other team would take him on when he could not even get a game for the shambles that was Celtic at that moment? Dad was not stupid, and Bobby never actually delivered his transfer request.

Celtic did indeed triumph in Switzerland, and a certain boost would soon be given to the team by Rangers' collapse against Real Madrid in the European Cup. Real Madrid were much loved by Celtic fans in those days. They had twice been in Glasgow in the past few years, once for the famous European Cup Final against Eintracht Frankfurt in 1960 and they had also played a friendly against Celtic at Parkhead in September 1962. Celtic fans had now greater cause to love them. Rangers had lost narrowly at Ibrox and were severely battered at the Bernabeu. Celtic supporters could even make a few jokes about Rangers not doing so well in the "real" world of Europe, as distinct from the artificial one of Scotland. It was however a particularly Glasgwegian example of gallows humour.

Another example of how Celtic fans adopted a love for Real Madrid came in the singing of The Soldiers' Song. Very few Celtic fans knew what the "bhearna bhaoil" was as they sang "To-night we man the bhearna bhaoil". In fact it means something along the lines of "we face the moment of maximum danger", but now one heard things like

*"Tonight we go to the Bernabeu*
*On Erin's cause, come wail or woe*
*We'll sing a song, a soldiers' song*
*We will cha-ant a soldiers' song!"*

But Celtic fans had little to laugh about. Such "Schadenfreude" or gloating at the misfortunes of one's enemies gave a little feel-good factor, but there was still no great sign of improvement at Parkhead. Shocking defeats at Falkirk and St.Mirren led to more talk of crisis, but this time there was a more constructive development of a meeting with Mr.Kelly and the Supporters' Association in which one of the points made was that the recall of Bobby Murdoch might be at least worth considering.

Celtic did this, just as Murdoch pére had predicted and the team suddenly stabilised, then flourished. With Murdoch now settled in the inside right position, the team hit a rich vein of form which lasted right up until the New Year.

There was a good 3-0 win at Tannadice Park, for example, in which Murdoch scored, then Airdrie were thrashed 9-0 at Celtic Park. This was the game in which goalkeeper Haffey (perhaps deliberately) missed a penalty which would have made it double figures, and on several other occasions, five goals were registered. Murdoch himself registered a hat trick against St.Johnstone in early December, and the only "reverses" were draws at Easter Road, Dens Park and Tynecastle. No disgrace in that, and on each of the three occasions, Celtic might well have won the day with a bit of luck.

Thus the assassination of John F.Kennedy and other events in November 1963 were of less concern to Murdoch and the Celtic fans than that their team had apparently recovered from the disastrous start to the season, had a settled team, and were in fact only four points behind Rangers on Hogmanay. A major propaganda coup was registered on November 23rd, the day after the Dallas shooting, when Celtic Park was impressively mute during the minute's silence before the team delivered a spectacular thrashing to the strong going Kilmarnock. In the meantime at East End Park, Dunfermline, some Rangers fans (not all of them, it must be stressed) booed the dead President for having been a Roman Catholic! Even the Scottish press, which tended to turn a blind eye to such things in those days, felt compelled to criticise such bigotry.

Meanwhile at Parkhead, not only were attainment and performances in Scotland good, but progress continued to be made in Europe with the mighty Dinamo Zagreb bending the knee in December. On December 4th, Celtic showed 42,000 and a large TV audience (unusually for these days, the game was shown live - albeit only the last half hour) what they could do with a competent 3-0 win which could have been a lot greater.

The following Wednesday in Zagreb, it might have been

a different story but for a brilliant Murdoch goal which killed the uncompromising Slavs. Celtic were struggling under almost incessant pressure on a difficult pitch all first half, when Murdoch picked up a pass from Chalmers and hammered home from the edge of the penalty box. This was in the 41st minute. It was thus 4-0 on aggregate, and although Zagreb scored once in the 65th minute, they didn't score again until the minutes were ticking away and Celtic were winning well.

Billy McNeill tells the story about this game that Celtic wore rubber boots to cope with the slippy conditions and hard pitch, but they noticed nevertheless that their opponents, apparently wearing conventional studs, were keeping their feet a little better. This was because their studs had been pared back to allow the nails to come through, and that the footwear was not entirely dissimilar to the "spikes" of athletes! This is of course grossly illegal and highly dangerous, but the referee did not seem to notice.

There was thus some justifiable euphoria at Parkhead because of this famous victory, but there was still something missing - and that was a victory over Rangers. New Year's Day 1964 at Parkhead would give us proof whether this could justifiably be called a Celtic revival or not. On form, Celtic were playing the better football, but sadly for the young Celts, there was still the psychological barrier.

It is generally agreed by all those who have played, watched or talked about the game of football, that it is played in the mind as well as on the field. Phrases like "psyched up" and "up for it" are common currency to-day. In 1964, the problem was quite simply the fact that Celtic lacked anyone to tell them how good they were, and conversely how fallible Rangers were. Any unfortunate occurrence in the shape of a bad refereeing decision or a miss in front of goal, was taken as proof that God, Destiny, Fate, Allah or whatever deity one recognises had decreed otherwise. Ancient Romans would throw up their arms in despair and say "Dis aliter visum" - "the Gods willed otherwise". To Celtic, it always seemed that the deities did not like them. Sadly, this attitude was all-pervasive in the Boardroom, dressing room and terracing. There remained the feeling that this was the way that things were and the way that they had to be.

1964 dawned with a fine New Year's Day at Parkhead, and Celtic started off by far the brighter team with the right wing pairing of Johnstone and Murdoch looking particularly menacing. A few half chances were missed, Ritchie in the Rangers goal had a great game, and half way through the first half came a real piece of injustice. Chalmers was through and bearing in on goal when he was brought down by Ron McKinnon. It was as clear a penalty as anyone was likely to see but the referee waved play on.

The Celtic End became quite introspective after that, seething with mutterings about conspiracies and handshakes, but there was nothing anyone could do about that. The team kept plugging away, but half time came and went with the score at 0-0. We could then of course have written a script for the second half. Celtic tried but the steam seemed to have gone out of them, Rangers scored a goal half way through the second half, then were professional enough to cope with the renewed Celtic pressure near the end. It was a bitter occasion, made all the more so in Murdoch's case when he aggravated an injury to his ankle.

Murdoch missed the following day's game against Third Lanark - a good game to miss for it was a miserable 1-1 draw played in an atmosphere of total lethargic depression (another example of the team lacking someone to pick them up and help them bounce back from adversity), but he returned for Saturday's 7-0 whipping of Falkirk, a game which did a certain amount to release frustration.

The season continued with Celtic and Murdoch doing

well and impressing everyone with fine play. Murdoch had a good game and scored a fine goal in the game against Third Lanark which saw them through to the Glasgow Cup Final. The Scottish Cup saw a famous game at Cappielow, Greenock. Morton were runaway leaders of the Second Division, and when they were drawn against Celtic on January 25th, the Scottish media managed to convince Hal Stewart, his men and all the good people of Greenock that they would beat Celtic. In truth, Morton started well and Alan McGraw scored first, but Celtic, inspired by McNeill in defence and Murdoch in the forward line, turned it on.

John Hughes scored a marvellous solo goal after a run from within his own half, another one was scored by Charlie Gallagher direct from a corner kick, and the third was a wonderfully well developed goal. Ian Young the right back found Bobby Murdoch who played a quick one-two with Hughes, then found Johnstone to finish the job. Celtic ran out comfortable winners, although goalkeeper John Fallon received a reprimand from an embittered policeman for raising his arms in triumph to his own supporters!

Although there was an unlucky reverse at Dunfermline on February 1st, the rest of that month was a fine one with progress in all three competitions. A fine victory at Pittodrie in the League was followed by the defeat of Airdrie in the Cup, and in between these wins, the management at long last made a good decision. Neil Mochan was brought back as trainer. In future years, Mochan would make the team the super fit professionals who would take on all Europe.

It was interesting in that Neil Mochan had never been a favourite of Mr.Kelly when he was a player. It was believed that this concerned Mochan's being fined for illegally possessing a radio without a licence - something that reflected badly on Celtic! Consequently, Mochan would be omitted from the team in circumstances where he should have been played. But this was now a welcome straw in the wind. Mr.Kelly was now tacitly admitting that he had been wrong.

A certain amount of enthusiasm among the support was indicated in a new Celtic song current at the the time;

*"There's Fallon, Young and Gemell, they proudly wear the green*
*Clark, McNeill and Kennedy the best you've ever seen*
*Jim Johnstone, Murdoch, Chalmers, John Divers and John Hughes*
*Plus 60,000 Celtic fans who proudly sing the news*
*Oh, it's Celtic, Celtic that's the team for me*
*Celtic, Celtic On To Victory*
*There The Finest Team In Scotland, I Hope You Will Agree*
*They'll Never Give Up Till They've Won The Cup*
*And The Scottish Football League."*

The words were of course doggerel but the song did at least reflect the new upbeat atmosphere permeating Parkhead... if only they could rid themselves of their Rangers complex.

In Europe, Slovan Bratislava came to Parkhead on February 26th and Celtic outplayed them ... but could not score, apart from a Murdoch penalty. The crunch would come in early March. Celtic had to go to Czechoslovakia on Wednesday March 4th, then return to Ibrox for a Scottish Cup Quarter Final game against Rangers on Saturday 7th. It would be a brave man who would predict how these games would go. Most realistic Celtic fans, if given the offer of one victory would have opted for a defeat of Rangers. But you cannot negotiate with God, and certainly not about football matches. The optimistic, of course, prayed for victories in both, while the pessimists feared the worst.

The game in Bratislava was an afternoon kick off, and

thus it was the BBC News programmes of about 6.00 p.m. that gave the good news. Celtic, having put up an excellent defensive and midfield performance, and having John Clark reduced to being a virtual passenger because of an injury (this was before substitutes were allowed), rounded things off with a lovely John Hughes goal. The man of the match, of course, was Jimmy Johnstone who won the hearts of the hitherto partisan Czech crowd (red curly hair and dribbling with the ball being novelties among Central Europeans) but Murdoch was also given a good press for his efforts. Celtic were now in the Semi Finals of the European Cup Winners Cup.

The return to Glasgow was not so much euphoric as hysterical with fans, desperate for success, showing the same sort of adulation that used to be reserved for John McPhail and Charlie Tully in the great days of the past. The Scottish press was similarly out of control, (lauding Celtic for a change!) and even Rangers showed respect by clapping them on to the park at Ibrox in the Scottish Cup tie. It was a move which did them credit, and was clearly designed to quieten the hotheads of both camps, but it may also have unnerved Celtic as well.

The game saw Murdoch at right half rather than inside right. This was of course a harbinger of great things to come, but it was forced in this instance on Celtic by the injury to John Clark, sustained in Czechosolovakia. There had already been a certain amount of debate within the support about whether this would be the best position for Bobby. He had often seemed a little clumsy in the forward line when the ball was coming to him from behind, and arguably lacked just a little pace. On the other hand, his powerful style of play might be put to better use in the midfield, as indeed would his accurate passing of a ball.

There was a fanzine called "The Shamrock" based in Edinburgh, in an age when fanzines were a rarity, and as well as being very representative of the "vox populi" in other respects, it showed a great deal of prescience in respect of the value of Bobby Murdoch, for it told us time and time again that Murdoch would be a finer midfield player than he would a forward. The seller of these fanzines seemed in many ways to symbolise the Celtic support in these days. A shabby raincoat, down at heel shoes, standing in the wet on Janefield Street with his City of Glasgow Trader's badge selling his magazines. We called him "the downtrodden man" from a line in the rebel song about the 1798 rebellion "Kelly, The Boy From Killan"

*"Glory O, Glory O, To the Brave Bhoys Who Died*
*In the cause of long downtrodden man*
*Glory O to Mount Leinster's own darling and pride*
*John Kelly, the boy from Killan."*

"The downtrodden man" was perpetually depressed and never afraid to deliver a broadside of oaths against those in charge of the club, yet he always had a kind word for youngsters and remained indefatigably optimistic as well that things would one day be turned round. Curiously, both he and his magazine seemed to disappear from the scene soon after the arrival of Stein. One hopes that he lived long enough to enjoy Lisbon - and to see his point proved about the best position of Bobby Murdoch.

On this occasion, by serendipity rather than forethought, Murdoch found himself at right half. Indeed Murdoch did have a good game that day, but as often seemed to happen when Celtic played Rangers, the rest of the team selection was erratic and ill thought out. The forward line had to be rejigged by Johnstone being put at inside right, and the forgotten Frank Brogan (that talented and grossly underused left winger) played on the right wing.

Success in Europe the previous midweek or not, this game at Ibrox on March 7th simply and inexorably followed the normal template for Old Firm encounters in season 1963-64. Celtic on top for more or less all the first half, a goalkeeping error allowing Forrest to score just before half time, another goal when the defence ran away from Willie Henderson early in the second half, then a dismal surrender to the apparently pre-ordained order of events. Murdoch fought hard, too hard perhaps, for he was booked by the referee for a wild tackle on Wilson, but long before the full time whistle, Celtic were a beaten team, the now customary trickle of Celtic fans going away home having begun about halfway through the second half.

Celtic had thus lost all three competitions in Scotland to Rangers, for psychological reasons, one felt, rather than footballing ones, but this year there was still Europe. The season was not yet entirely lost. There was still a massive, heartbroken support who deserved more than what they were getting. A minor consolation for the support, and for Murdoch himself, came in the shape of his first ever Cup winner's medal. This was in the Glasgow Cup on March 25th when Celtic beat Clyde 2-0 at Parkhead. It was at least something - and a possibility of greater honours hove into sight.

Wednesday April 15th 1964 saw 51,000 at Parkhead to see M.T.K. Budapest of Hungary in the Semi Final of the European Cup Winners' Cup. Scottish football was deservedly on a high. The previous Saturday, Scotland had beaten England for the third time in a row. Celtic had had two players in the Scotland team - Billy McNeill and Jim Kennedy, and both had deserved their fair share of the plaudits.

This night was a great night for Scotland as Celtic, playing with flair and panache, defeated the Hungarians 3-0. The forward line was much praised, Johnstone and Chalmers (twice) scoring the goals, and indeed their speed and ability to read one another had been a feature of the game. The prompting and feeding by Bobby Murdoch had also been much commented upon. Highlights had been shown all over Europe, and everyone had been mightily impressed. The Final in Brussels (by 1964 just about within the range and the pocket of Celtic fans) beckoned.

There only remained the return leg in Budapest on April 29th. The precedent of Manchester United, who had lost a four goal lead to Sporting Lisbon, was pointed out but there seemed little chance of this happening to such an exuberant, confident bunch of boys as Celtic. Indeed, Mr. Kelly had stated openly that Celtic would go for more goals. It was the duty of Celtic players to entertain the people of Budapest, he stated with breathtaking bombast.

It was just as well that hardly any Celtic fans travelled to the grim Eastern European city of Budapest. Barely eight years previously the country had been savaged by the might of the U.S.S.R. for attempting to assert its independence and the country remained more or less under martial law with very few Western Europeans permitted lest they spread their "decadent" ideas. The game (somewhat pathetically) was not screened on television and thus we were dependent on BBC Radio for that terrible second leg, the pain of which is up there with all the other horrors of that era.

Sometimes the Glasgow quality of being "gallus" is a good thing; but not if it descends into naivety. Celtic would complain about the referee, an Austrian called Dimitri Wlachojanis. Not without cause, and the story is well documented of his sitting at the post match banquet with a couple of blondes on each side of him, but Celtic were foolish to believe that anything approaching fair treatment would be offered them in an Iron Curtain country (i.e within the influence of Soviet Russia) in the 1960's. Celtic would have had to have been particularly good or simply plain cunning to get the better of M.T.K. in those circumstances.

There was even something more subtle perhaps going on here. The Austro-Hungarian Empire had of course been dissolved by the victorious British in 1919, and there remained (in spite of or perhaps because of Adolf Hitler and other horrors) a certain nostalgia in both countries for such a union. A year previously, an English referee had abandoned a Scotland v. Austria International at Hampden Park because an Austrian was sent off and refused to go, no doubt seeing an Anglo-Scottish conspiracy! Now we had an Austrian referee for a game between a Hungarian team and a British team! Revenge was on the cards, even though Celtic were far from being the best example of a "British" team!

Two goals were in fact scored by Celtic, but both were chalked off, and a relentless series of fouls were given to the Hungarian side. Any student of "bent" refereeing will always agree that the awarding of such a series of fouls will have more effect than the blatant awarding of a penalty when somebody falls down. The 4 goals for the Hungarians came because Celtic had their men in the wrong places, still committed to that crazy attacking formation, which had been so brilliant in different circumstances at Parkhead. The return leg was surely a game for Murdoch to be brought back to midfield, but this move would not be countenanced. By the time the fourth goal went in, Celtic were totally demoralised, and although time remained for them to fight back, little constructive play was forthcoming.

Thus ended with a whimper Murdoch's second season. Rangers had won the Scottish domestic treble, but had flopped spectacularly when they came up gainst top European opposition. Celtic encountered lesser European opposition and with a little more knowledge of the ways of the world, might well have won through against them. They might even have beaten Sporting Lisbon in the Final. Certainly if they had played like they did against M.T.K. at Parkhead, they would have needed some stopping.

Would Celtic ever come back, either in Scotland or in Europe? Murdoch himself claims that the return flight was the longest he had ever been on. It was like a funeral, he said, with no-one saying anything, everyone immersed in his own private melancholic thoughts over a season that had at one point promised a great deal and ended up with nothing other than the insignificant Glasgow Cup. It was at least a medal - of sorts.

But something very important happened for Murdoch in the summer. On 6th June 1964 (by sheer coincidence, exactly 20 years after the Allied landings on D-Day in 1944) Bobby married Kathleen Barrie. The two had met in 1960, and the marriage was a happy one until Bobby's death in 2001. Pressure was apparently put on players by the autocratic Bob Kelly not to get married during the football season, lest connubial and conjugal bliss might affect their playing, presumably!

On the footballing front, Hope sprung eternal yet again over the summer, and the start of the 1964-65 season saw Celtic hit a rich streak of form. After an appallingly inept opening 0-0 draw against Partick Thistle in which the punters quite justifiably condemned the authorities who had raised admission charges to 4 shillings i.e. 20 pence, the team suddenly thumped Hearts, Kilmarnock and Thistle to qualify for the Quarter Finals of the League Cup without much trouble. In fact the 20 pence was quite cheap in comparison with other things. 45 r.p.m records, for example, like the current favourite of Manfred Mann "Do Wah Diddy Diddy Dum Diddy Dae" (no kidding!) cost 6 shillings and 8 pennies (33 pence).

Murdoch was instrumental in all this fine start to the season, scoring for example a hat trick against Hearts at Parkhead and generally showing the sort of form that his admirers expected. He had a particularly good relationship with Jimmy Johnstone, fed the ever eager Chalmers and amazed defenders by his sheer power. Bobby Lennox on the left wing was also maturing fast and amazing everyone by his speed. He also teamed up well with the ball playing talents of Charlie Gallagher who was now at inside left. Most important of all, this now looked like a settled Celtic team. And it was a distinctive feature that it was a team performance with Celtic firing on all cylinders and raising all sorts of expectations for the ever optimistic (some would say gullible) support.

It may be that the Celtic forwards were enlivened by a bizarre and high profile attempt to sign the famous Alfredo di Stefano from Real Madrid. It was of course a good thirty years before foreigners would come en masse to Scotland (other than a few Scandinavians who played for Morton and Dundee United) and the whole matter was treated with a certain amount of ridicule in the Scottish press. But Celtic were sufficiently serious to take John Cushley (the reserve centre half and a graduate in French and Spanish) with them. Cushley spoke to di Stefano only by telephone, had problems with his Argentinian accent but he was able to make out that di Stefano would not be too interested in coming to Scotland.

Publicity stunt or not, this curious affair did however send out two signals. It showed that Celtic were prepared to embark on novel adventures and it also told the existing players that there was nothing guaranteed about their place at Parkhead. It certainly seemed to have that effect. The Press, for example, were so impressed by Chalmers at this time that they said things like that the answer to Celtic's problems lay with "Stevie", not "Steffie"!

But all this success in the League Cup came at a price. The last game of the sectional stages was played at Rugby Park, Kilmarnock. Kilmarnock, who had been second in last season's League Championship and who had the reputation of being perpetual bridesmaids rather than blushing brides, had been more than a little put out by Celtic's success, and a certain amount of cynical revenge was taken. Murdoch and McNeill were both carried off, the victims of sinister tackles. McNeill's injury was the more serious. It was a chipped bone and he was out for several months. Murdoch was only out for a couple of games, the victim of strained ligaments, but it was once again an injury to the ankle that would effect him so badly in the long term for the rest of his career and in later life.

Bobby thus missed Celtic's classic 3-1 victory over Rangers in the rain on September 5th, their first for many seasons. He was however given a standing ovation as he took his seat, along with Billy McNeill in the Parkhead stand to watch that game. More tellingly, he also missed the dreadful defeat by lowly East Fife at Methil the following Wednesday in the First Leg of the Quarter Final of the League Cup. This reverse was more than made up for in the return leg (by which time, Murdoch had returned to feed Steve Chalmers for most of his five goals) but the month of September saw Celtic's usual bogey of inconsistency return.

McNeill was adequately replaced as a player by former schoolmate of McNeill and Murdoch, John Cushley, but McNeill's leadership qualities were sadly missed. Murdoch, too, looked less than 100% fit as draws were registered against Clyde and Dundee United and the team went down 2-4 to Hearts at Tynecastle.

But the team progressed in Europe, beating a rough team called Leixoes of Portugal and had also reached the Final of the League Cup thanks to a competent (although no more than that) victory over Morton in the Semi. Their opponents were, as if by fate, Rangers. The Ibrox men were however themselves struggling, being decidedly lucky to get the better of Dundee United in the other Semi Final. In addition before the Final on October 24th, Celtic's League form improved with wins over Aberdeen, Morton and a particularly impressive 4-1 demolition of St.Mirren.

The League Cup Final was surely at last to be Celtic's day. They had already beaten Rangers this season, thus destroying, one hoped, the myth of Ibrox invincibility, and that things can change had been proved by events on the political front. On October 15th 13 years of Conservative rule in Great Britain had come to an end with the return of Labour under a dynamic young leader called Harold Wilson. There was thus nothing sacrosanct about the Conservatives. Was there anything sacrosant about the other blues, Rangers?

In addition for Murdoch, there was another piece of news. Kathleen had told him that she was expecting a baby next May. Coincidentally, goalkeeper John Fallon's wife had told him a similar story - and their baby was expected at about the same time as well. What better way to celebrate a wife's pregnancy than by a League Cup Winner's medal?

91,423 saw that match, with Celtic fans clearly outnumbering Rangers ones. Optimism radiated from the Celtic End before the match... but by half time it was a different story. Once again, Celtic had let their fans down by not taking chances, one in particular by Jimmy Johnstone being an absolute howler and there was also the denial of a stonewall penalty by referee Hugh Phillips of Wishaw. Murdoch had played well, but only in patches, and centre forward Steve Chalmers had been well shadowed by Ron McKinnon.

The 0-0 half time scoreline was a travesty in the context of the amount of pressure that Celtic had applied, but it was already clear from the sounds of the Rangers End that they now fancied their chances. So it proved. Tragically, the Celtic defence creaked and broke twice when Jim Forrest took advantage of slack play, and after only 62 minutes, we once again saw the spectacle of the Celtic End beginning to empty of supporters; dispirited, demoralised and defeated.

Yet their pessimism, although ultimately justified, was premature. Celtic did fight back, swapped wingers and Jimmy Johnstone was on hand to give Celtic a lifeline. The cause could yet have been saved if either Murdoch or Divers had played to his potential. But Divers was slow and ineffectual and Murdoch simply disappeared, the heart having gone out of the youngster (he was still only 20) in the same way as the heart had gone out of those who had chosen an early departure from the terracings. Rangers switched full backs to counteract Celtic's change of wingers, and the middle of the attack had no real answer to Rangers' power.

In spite of all this, hard luck played a part as well, and the Press were unstinting in describing this game as one of the best Old Firm games of all time. Celtic fans were less magnanimous. For some it was the end of the line. There are limits to how much even the most loyal of fans can take, and people despaired of Celtic. The pain was intense and unremitting.

Celtic, as often happened in these days, went into free fall in the wake of a defeat from Rangers. Before the New Year, Celtic went out of Europe to Barcelona (no disgrace in that) but also lost to Kilmarnock, St.Johnstone, Dundee and Dunfermline. Attendances were as miserable as the weather and although the team bought an unknown called Hugh Maxwell from Falkirk, little else was done to arrest the seemingly irreversible decline of the great club who were now openly referred to as "the poor team with the big support", as newspapers gloatingly carried in depth analyses of what was going wrong.

As far as the fans were concerned, the blame was put at the door of no-one other than Chairman Bob Kelly. A letter appeared in a Sunday newspaper with the brilliant and unusual allegory of a ship called H.M.S. Celtic heading for the rocks. Everyone was aware of this, crew, passengers and all, but the Captain kept shouting "It's all right, I'm in charge!" as the rocks approached ever closer.

At this dark hour of Celtic's existence, Murdoch was given a few games at right half. He played in that position in a disgraceful game at Perth in which Celtic were 3-0 down at half time before an incredulous St.Johnstone support, and more laudably in wins over Falkirk and Third Lanark, but this experiment was not persevered with at this stage, and indeed must be seen in the context of the innumerable "games" that seemed to be played with players in an attempt to find that elusive blend.

It was a grim time to be a Celtic supporter and what it must have been like for a young player (Murdoch was only 20, after all) is hard to imagine. He and Kathleen did reportedly consider emigration to Australia ... and worse was to come for Bobby at Ibrox on New Year's Day 1965.

In fact, it came at the end of an unexpectedly spirited second half Celtic performance. Down 0-1 at half time and having seen Jimmy Johnstone sent off after a violent lunge, born of frustration and anger, at an Icelander called Theorolf Beck, the sadly dispirited and underpopulated Celtic End had little cause to expect much. But the team played manfully, Murdoch included, although he did miss a couple of good opportunites. Six minutes remained when Celtic were awarded a penalty which would have given them a deserved draw. Murdoch was the recognised penalty taker.

Ignoring the gamesmanship and comments about the Pope from Rangers defenders, he stepped forward, looking confident. He placed the ball, but crucially did not take a long enough run. He seemed anxious to get it over with. He ran, fatally leaned back and ballooned the ball yards over the crossbar.

Rangers could hardly believe their luck as Murdoch collapsed to the ground, so upset that he had to be rested from the next day's game against Clyde. Life could not really get much worse for Bobby Murdoch. The Rangers complex was still there in full force.

# The Messiah

Christmas 1964 had thus been spent in the deepest melancholy. So were most Christmases in Celtic families in those days. The Beatles did spread some sort of cheer with "I Feel Fine", but for the Celtic faithful, the suffering had gone on too long and was simply too intense. Taking up a new hobby like snooker or golf or even reading a book or watching TV were far more attractive options than football in those dreadful days. Boxing Day, for example, saw a frozen pitch and a crowd of little more than 8,000 to watch Celtic take on Motherwell and John Hughes with sandshoes (trainers, as they are now called) scoring two good goals. It was some sort of cheer, one supposed, in a wilderness of despair.

Yet those who paid attention to their Advent and Christmas Hymns might have gained a little heart. If one could allegorically link captive Israel with suffering Celtic (a curious mixture of faiths, it would have to be said!) then one could hear lines like "Rejoice, Rejoice, Emmanuel Shall Come To You, O Israel", "Late In Time Behold Him Come", "Hail, Redemption's Happy Dawn". The Jews of ancient times needed their saviour; so too did Celtic in those awful weeks of December 1964 and January 1965, when newspapers ran articles saying "Are Celtic finished?" and members of the Celtic backroom staff said that they were. More than one of the players would admit later that they were contemplating careers elsewhere.

The Saviour might have been Bertie Auld who returned from Birmingham in mid January. To continue the religious metaphor, however, Bertie was merely the John the Baptist.

"The one to come after me is greater than I, and I am not fit to tie his boots", Bertie might have said. The Messiah was yet to come, but he was now very close.

The Murdochs spent their first Christmas together in 1964. Both were delighted about Kathleen's pregnancy, but must have wondered about whether playing football for the disorganized shambles that was Celtic in late 1964 was the best option for a young man, however talented and loving of the club. Bobby had already had a few ankle knocks (as well as a few psychological knocks) and both he and Kathleen were aware that, even in the best of circumstances, a footballer's career does not go on for ever. Current wages were adequate, it would have to be said, but hardly excessive and certainly not enough for Bobby to hang up his boots when he reached the age of 35 and retire!

The possibility of emigrating to Australia was mooted. Kathleen had many friends who had done just that, and Australia and Canada were offering "Assisted Passages" for about £10, so keen were they to get young people to their rich and under-populated countries. But did they need professional footballers? They played cricket in Australia and ice hockey in Canada, didn't they?

It would have been interesting to see what would have happened if the Murdochs had gone. Certainly, Celtic and Scottish football would have been infinitely the poorer, but had things not taken a turn for the better at Parkhead in 1965, the Murdochs might well have been forced into that decision. Murdoch might not have quite managed to open the batting for the Australian Test team, but there is a true story of a player who struggled to get a game in Forfar Athletic's forward line, emigrated to Australia and ended up playing in the Socceroos' World Cup and Olympic Games team - as centre half!

Bertie Auld's debut game was against Hearts at Parkhead, the game often referred to as the nadir of Celtic's existence.

To be fair, it wasn't a bad performance against a good Hearts side who would almost win the League that year and Murdoch in particular looked sharper than of late. But the weather was bad, the crowd was poor (Hearts fans clearly outnumbered the Celtic diehards - and at Parkhead!) and the team went down 1-2, the referee even appearing to cut the game short and deny Celtic time for a deserved equalizer.

It was only at the end of January following a month which contained three beatings and two unsatisfactory draws that something began to happen. In the week that the whole of Great Britain was in mourning for the death of Sir Winston Churchill on January 24th 1965, hints began to be dropped that something big was coming at Parkhead. The players, as if aware of it, lashed Aberdeen 8-0 on January 30th, the day of Churchill's funeral, at a sadly underpopulated Parkhead. It was a performance, however welcome, totally out of character with what had gone previously, and Murdoch's own performance was one of his more gratifying, and he scored a good goal. Bertie Auld had taken a penalty. The hero of the hour was however John Hughes, forever unpredictable and quixotic, who had gone nap that day with five goals.

The Sunday papers made good reading on the 31st - the first time the Sunday Post, Mail and Express had been enjoyed by Celtic fans for many months. Not only was yesterday's victory dwelt upon in detail, but the journalists and scribes, without being any too specific, all perpetuated stories that changes afoot on the management front. That very day came the official announcement that Jock Stein was to take over at Celtic Park.

It must have hurt Mr.Kelly to admit that he had been wrong. It must also have hurt (however much anyone denied it) that Stein was a Protestant, although not a practising one. Kelly himself apparently worried that the support might not have accepted him. This was total rubbish. Apart from anything else, any such concerns were an insult to the very many Celtic supporters who were non-Catholic. Most Celtic supporters, in any case, in 1965 were moderate Labour Party supporters. This implied religious acceptance and tolerance.

No-one, other than Celtic's enemies, ever made Stein's religion an issue, and certainly the players had no problems with it. Murdoch, a practising Catholic who went to Mass every Sunday, thought nothing about it, nor did anyone else. The acceptance of Stein by the Celtic support and the Celtic team contrasted starkly with Rangers' undeclared but nevertheless inflexible policy of not signing Roman Catholics.The 1960's were of course an era in which people began not to turn the other cheek about such things. South Africa and Rhodesia's racial policies were now openly questioned, not least by the Harold Wilson Labour Government. In a few years time Northern Ireland would similarly be put under a microscope and found wanting, and as part of this general liberal trend, moderate Scotland, including even the Church of Scotland, began to swing towards Celtic's broader based selection policy as distinct from the sectarian mentality on the other side of the city.

Stein's "Protestant Accession" to the reins of power at Celtic Park was the first shot in the propaganda war which, under Stein, Celtic would win time and time again over Rangers, and which was of crucial importance for the Celtic "feel good" factor. What was of more immediate importance, however, in strict footballing terms, was that Stein would take over on March 8th 1965. It was important to remain in the Scottish Cup, the only trophy left that season, until that time to give Jock a chance to work one of the miracles that he had performed hitherto at Dunfermline and Hibs.

Three Scottish Cup ties had to be played. Even in the

dreadful recent past, Celtic had always made some sort of an effort for the Scottish Cup which was indeed their favourite competition, even though almost eleven long years had passed since green and white ribbons last adorned the trophy. Celtic were usually out of contention for the League well before the New Year, but the Scottish Cup, which only started in January normally, acted as some kind of a spur. This year, it took on even more significance.

Credit must be given to Jimmy McGrory and his Assistant Sean Fallon for getting things right on the left wing. Auld's first game had been as an out and out left winger, but he was now tried as an inside left with Bobby Lennox on the wing. Murdoch continued at inside right. It would need Jock Stein's arrival to point out where Murdoch's best place was, but at least things were better on the left.

Celtic beat St.Mirren quite easily in the end at Love Street (although the goals came late), but then in the middle of February had a terrible job to beat Queen's Park at Hampden, being indebted to Bobby Lennox to score the one and only goal of the game. They played that game in all green for the first time in recent memory, but the most noticeable feature that day was the obvious spring in the step of the support. They were, after all, going to Hampden. They wanted to keep going there. Lennox's goal came in the 61st minute after a somewhat nervy and frustrating wait, but once the goal was scored, the 31,000 crowd relaxed and enjoyed the good play of Auld and Murdoch.

The Quarter Finals on Saturday March 6th (which would be the last game in which McGrory was Manager) brought Kilmarnock and 47,000 spectators to Parkhead. It was a hard fought, typical Scottish Cup tie as one would expect with ex-Rangers Willie Waddell in charge at Kilmarnock. Kilmarnock in fact would win the Scottish League that year in a League race which was strange and refreshingly welcome for those more interested in the wider concept of Scottish football! It featured neither Celtic nor Rangers in the closing stages, and Kilmarnock had to fight off Hearts, Hibs and Dunfermline.

In this torrid Cup tie, on a pleasant spring day in front of a 47,000 crowd, Celtic, playing in their "Hibs reverse" strip of white shirts with green sleeves, were leading 1-0 before Kilmarnock equalized. They then took a 3-1 lead but Kilmarnock pulled one back so that Celtic had to fight to the end to hold on to their 3-2 lead, with Murdoch perforce deployed as an extra defender and showing that he could do it.

Just as that game was finishing, dramatic events were occurring at Easter Road where Hibs (in their last game with Stein as Manager) edged out Rangers with a last minute goal. Thus even before he became Manager of Celtic, Stein had established an Indian sign over Rangers, whose season then spiralled out of control and ended in oblivion.

The playing scenario, then, of Stein's arrival was a host of meaningless League games to play and a Scottish Cup Semi Final line up of Celtic v. Motherwell and Hibs v. Dunfermline. All the players, Murdoch included, were aware of the intense pressure they were under. Stein would certainly have a huge clear out of unwanted players at the end of the season. No-one's place was guaranteed. On the other hand there was a huge air of optimism about the ground that something big was about to happen. No-one however could possibly predict just exactly how big it was going to be.

Stein's reign began at Airdrie on Wednesday 10th March with a 6-0 tanking of the Broomfield men. Those who thought that Nirvanah had arrived instantly were given a shock with several players given a row for showing off, and in any case everyone came down with a very large bump on the following Saturday when St. Johnstone stilled an exultant Parkhead with a 1-0 victory. "At least now I see why I am here" growled Jock in a BBC interview that night.

One of his first thoughts concerned Bobby Murdoch. Stein was of the persuasion (as indeed was a growing body of more perspicacious Celtic supporters) that Murdoch might be a better wing half in the middle of the park than a forward. Murdoch was, in Jock's view, just a little too clumsy when the ball came to him. He was also perhaps a touch on the slow side. He was a far better playmaker, in that he was a powerful, aggressive ball winner who could pass better when kicking up the field rather than across it.

Indeed it was Murdoch's passing of a ball that was his hallmark. In a nutshell, it was the inch perfect pass which finds a man and conserves his energy because he does not have to run for the ball but on the other hand compels the opposition to chase shadows. Stein was convinced that this would be Bobby's contribution to the club. Neither for the first nor the last time, Jock's footballing judgement was as spot on as Bobby's passes would become.

Stein's first playing of Murdoch with the number 4 on his pants came at Dens Park on March 20th. It was less than a totally devastating success for Murdoch had the misfortune to score an own goal! Otherwise he played very well in an entertaining 3-3 draw. The following Monday, Bobby was back in the forward line but the team lost 4-2 to a strong Hibs side... and Murdoch was totally out of touch. This convinced Stein that Bobby should be right half rather than inside right for the Semi Final against Motherwell on the following Saturday.

The result at Hampden that windy March day was 2-2. Celtic had a poor first half and were indebted to Bertie Auld to rescue them with a penalty kick to level the scores in the 60th minute. It was in the last half hour that Murdoch's value as a wing half was seen. He supplied ball after ball to the forward line as Celtic pounded and pounded that Motherwell goal in search of an elusive winner. This seemed to have come when Johnstone scored, but was given offside. Glory was only postponed however until the replay on Wednesday 31st March when a rampant Celtic side, inspired by a midfield of Murdoch and Auld, took Motherwell apart and won 3-0.

It was just as well that the League did not now matter, for form was totally haywire, as Stein experimented with his line-ups to find the winning blend. Hibs were totally outplayed at Easter Road as Celtic won 4-0, but that has to be balanced against a couple of feckless displays against Third Lanark and Partick Thistle and a really baffling and irrational trouncing at the hands of Falkirk to the tune of 6-2. The support did not really know what to make of all this. On the one hand there was the upbeat euphoria of the arrival of Stein and the certainty that in the long term things were going to improve, but the immediate present was disorientating and more than a little alarming.

But all this was of no consequence compared with the Scottish Cup Final against Dunfermline on April 24th. Stein announced at an early stage in the week preceding the game to the Celtic party what his team was to be, and although no offical announcement was made to the Press, a few nods and winks were given to the more perceptive journalists. The team would read Fallon; Young and Gemmell; Murdoch, McNeill and Clark; Chalmers, Gallagher, Hughes, Lennox and Auld. Apparently, Bob Kelly expressed his surprise that Murdoch was at right half, saying that he was a far better forward. Stein replied "You'll see on Saturday how good a right half he is".

It was indeed hard to predict this one. Dunfermline were a good side, Willie Cunningham having built upon Stein's good work. (Stein had been in charge at East End Park from

1960-64). On the other hand, the Pars had the previous week lost their chance of winning the League when they could only draw with lowly St.Johnstone in circumstances where they had to win. Celtic's form was so quirky as to defy analysis, but there was definitely the psychological advantage of Jock Stein, and the perhaps dubious benefit of having a huge, desperate support who had been let down so often in the past. A tremendous weight went on to the shoulders of Celtic's 11 young men that day. Cliches like "date with destiny" and "history looks down upon Celtic today" filled the Saturday morning papers. But they were not cliches. In this case they meant something.

Words can almost fail the historian as he tries to describe the titanic battle between Celtic and Dunfermline Athletic on April 24th 1965. Seldom has so much importance ever been placed on one single game, seldom has a game ever had such a Boy's Own, fairy tale ending. "We'll forgive everything, Cellic, if ye'll win the day" bawled a frantic fan beside me; there was a middle aged, middle class man with a tie and a soft hat collapsed over a hedge in Aitkenhead Road after the game thanking God for deliverance and telling the world that he could not have stood it if they had lost again; and the author himself could not eat his fish and chips after the game for sheer delirium, mingled with the gnawing fear that it had all been a dream and that he was about to waken up. Such was the psychological torment of being a Celtic supporter in 1965.

The Pars scored first, Harry Melrose taking advantage of slack Celtic defending. Then Celtic equalized. It was a weird one too. Charlie Gallagher who had a deceptively powerful shot, hit the bar from about 25 yards. The ball ballooned high up in the air, but such was the Hampden swirl that it was blown ever so slightly back into play. Bertie Auld noticed this and followed up to jump high and head the ball down into the net. Dunfermline scored before half time, (a crazy loudpeaker announcement distracting the Celtic defence as John McLaughlin took a free kick) Celtic replying immediately after the break following a nice move between Lennox and Auld, and it was then that Murdoch began to grow to the awesome task delegated to him by Stein and Celtic's Destiny.

He took command of the midfield, collecting the ball, distributing and spraying passes and proving a dynamic and inspiring presence in the centre of the Hampden sward. Slowly, almost imperceptibly, Celtic began to gain ascendancy over this hard-working and talented Dunfermline side. Nine minutes remained when Celtic forced a corner through the hard working Lennox. Charlie Gallagher took the corner, up rose Billy McNeill "Captain Courageous", "Celtic's King Billy" to head home a glorious and somehow archetypical Celtic goal in the tradition of Jimmy McGrory, Jimmy Quinn or Sandy McMahon.

Nine minutes remained to be played, and it was here once again that young Murdoch proved his value to the team, tackling determinedly and fiercely on the half way line to prevent any Dunfermline counter-attack from developing. The nine minutes were like nine hours on the terracing. What they were like on the field cannot be imagined. Murdoch's reaction at the final whistle mirrored that of every Celtic fan; his tears of joy were every bit as genuine as those of the rest of us.

Back home, little more than a mile away as the crow flies, Kathleen Murdoch was listening to the radio. She was imminently expecting her first baby, and it had been considered not a good idea for her to go to the game. But as any Celtic supporter knows, the hell of listening to a radio commentary can frequently be more nerve wracking than actually being at a game. The last nine minutes after McNeill's goal would not have done any good at all for her blood pressure, something that is important in the later stages of pregnancy.

But Mr.Phillips did blow the final whistle, and Kathleen's husband had a Scottish Cup Winner's medal. Kathleen was able to go to the celebration party at the Central Hotel that night. There she met John Fallon's wife, Essie, a good friend of hers, who was even more imminently about to give birth than she was. In fact, Mrs.Fallon went into labour that very night and had to be taken to hospital from the hotel! Kathleen "survived" for another week before giving birth to young Kathleen on May 2nd, a couple of days after Murdoch had been in the Celtic team which beat Rangers in a Glasgow Cup tie.

In fact Celtic and Murdoch went on to celebrate the Scottish Cup win and the arrival of young Kathleen by winning the Glasgow Cup. Indeed, Celtic had done very well in this tournament in recent years, having won in in 1962 and 1964. The difference this year was that Celtic, with the strain now off them, relaxed and played with flair and panache. On May 3rd, new dad Murdoch starred as Clyde were beaten 3-0 at Parkhead in the Semi Final and on Tuesday May 11th, Celtic beat Queen's Park 5-0 in the Final, Murdoch scoring one of the goals.

History had indeed changed on April 24th. Before the 1965 Cup Final, we seldom had a victory; after that date, we seldom had a defeat. The summer of 1965 was spent in contrast to previous ones in a mood of euphoria and anticipation. "The new season starts seven weeks on Saturday" was the way that supporters greeted one another. Joe McBride was signed from Motherwell to pep up the forward line, and pre-season matches were arranged against Motherwell (on the Isle of Man), Shamrock Rovers and Sunderland.

Indeed it would be hard to over-estimate the effect of that 1965 Scottish Cup victory. The support was born again, the mood mirrored in the 1797 rebel song that was currently on sale in Lewis's Polytechnic in Argyle Street

*"What's the news, what's the news, oh my bold Shelmaleer*
*With your long barrelled gun of the sea?*
*Say what wind from the south blows its messenger here*
*With a hymn for the dawn of the free?*
*Goodly news, goodly news do I bring man of Forth*
*Goodly news shall you hear Bargy man,*
*For the boys march at morn from the south to the north*
*Led by Kelly the Boy From Killan!"*

Supporters walked about with their heads held high and their shoulders back for the first time since the 7-1 win in 1957 and for some younger supporters, for the first time ever. Stein was quick to capitalise on that mood for the following season. He had the wit to ensure that Celtic were never out of the headlines, but it was hardly necessary. Celtic supporters talked about little else.

Murdoch was as upbeat as everyone else. His private life with a beautiful wife and a young baby girl was happy. There was a pop song at this time called "Bobby's Girl", released in 1962 by Marcie Blaine and also by Susan Maughan. Photographs were taken at their nice home in High Burnside of the devoted father with his wife and daughter under the heading "Bobby's Girls".

At Parkhead, he was now confirmed as the right half of this potentially great team. Yet, "right half" was now no longer an appropriate term for the team was slowly developing into a 4-2-4 formation with Murdoch and Auld the formidable pair in midfield. It would be some time before this concept was honed to perfection but Murdoch was told by Stein that this was what to be. This would have been imparted in one of the many informal tactical discussions that were the order of the day. Changed days from previously where the players were not even allowed a ball to train with!

Training indeed was a pleasure. Under the enthusiastic guidance of Neil Mochan but the overall tutelage of Stein himself, the team grew to enjoy training. The emphasis was on ball work and speed. Aware of the propaganda value of such days, Stein invited the Press in on several occasions just to watch how the players trained. This filled the otherwise empty sports pages in July, knocking out Wimbledon, the Open Golf and the Test Match cricket between England and South Africa, and earned the gratitude of scribes and editors, (a potent consideration for the future) but more importantly filled the opponents and the rest of football with dread about what Celtic were about to do. In another propaganda coup, "The Celtic View", the first official newspaper of its kind, was born and had its first edition in August 1965.

Pre-season games were a rip-roaring success. Admittedly, the first was a poor 1-1 draw with Motherwell on the Isle of Man, but it was was followed by crushing victories over Shamrock Rovers in Dublin and then Sunderland at Roker Park. The Sunderland game was a treat, made all the sweeter by the presence of Jim Baxter in the Wearside line-up, which was also managed by ex-Ranger Ian McColl.

Although the team lost its first League Cup game at Dundee United and another game against Dundee at Parkhead a week later, the team recovered brilliantly to qualify for the Quarter Finals. The icing on the cake was a marvellous performance at Dens Park, Dundee in which all the team played wonderfully well, and John Hughes scored a goal which would be hard to parallel for its sheer class.

This was only a step on the way to the winning of the League Cup itself. The team had tasted blood, as it were, by winning the Scottish Cup and were now back for more. Yet they were very nearly defeated in the Semi Final at Ibrox on Monday October 4th. Their opponents were the strong going Hibs (still very obviously of course "The Team That Jock Built", although he had been with them for less than a year!) and their excellent forward Neil Martin had scored twice to put them 2-1 ahead after Joe McBride had scored early for Celtic. The pitch was heavy and quite a few of the 50,000 thought that Celtic were defeated as ex-Celt John McNamee marshalled his defence to keep out wave after wave of attacks.

Indeed the pace seemed to have slowed as quite a few of the more slightly built Celtic players - Johnstone, Gallagher and Lennox - seemed to have peaked as the game entered its final phase. In times like this men like Murdoch are called upon to make an extra effort and it was he who picked up a pass from McNeill, made ground then found Gemmell on the wing. Gemmell's weakish shot lost pace on the wet ground, but goalkeeper Wilson could not hold it and Lennox scored with the rebound.

Celtic were thus given a late reprieve and although extra time saw 22 tired men and no further goals, the replay a fortnight later was a different matter and Murdoch inspired his team to a 4-0 romp, scoring the final goal himself. This was on the Monday night before the Final and the opponents in the Final were again to be... Rangers.

This was to be the acid test of the new Celtic. A good Celtic team must be able to beat Rangers. Too often in the past, a superior Celtic team had collapsed against Rangers when they were required to play well. But this time, although Rangers had narrowly beaten them in a League game at Ibrox in September - something that might have encouraged the Celtic inferiority complex - there were vital differences. One was the sheer presence of Stein and the almost magical belief in his talismanic powers. The other was the fact that Bobby Murdoch was now playing in his correct position and exuding confidence. His presence would be inspirational, although oddly enough (if we ignore Glasgow Cup games) Murdoch had never been in a Celtic side that had beaten Rangers!

Another factor in Celtic's favour was that for some reason or another, penalties were awarded to Celtic that would not have been given previously! One of Celtic's backroom staff put it rather well when he said that "Stein cowed referees into fairness". In 1964's League Cup Final a stonewaller was turned down. In 1965 a soft one was given by the same referee when the contact between Provan and Johnstone was minimal, to put it mildly. This was after a previous penalty had been given after Rangers' centre half Ron McKinnon had had a brainstorm and handled the ball in the box when there was no real danger.

John Hughes converted both penalties, and Celtic thus began the second half two goals ahead. It was to be however a stern test of their new professionalism as Rangers threw everything at them to get back into the game. Murdoch was one of those "booked" (a yellow card in modern parlance) for "impeding the progress" of Davie Wilson by throwing his arms around him! It was a game which showed that Celtic could handle the physical side of the game as well, even if journalistic phrases like "orgy of crudeness" and "roughhouse" were somewhat hyperbolic. Rangers did score an extraordinarily lucky goal in the 84th minute when Rangers' John Greig and Celtic's Ian Young went up for a ball, the ball hit both of them but cannoned into the goal! Celtic however held out and Murdoch now owned two Scottish medals. He had a League Cup one to go with his Scottish Cup one - and had now beaten Rangers! He was not even unduly depressed with his "booking".

Before Stein arrived, Bob Kelly had laid great store on discipline and players not being in trouble with referees. Jock Stein was realistic enough to realise that in order to win trophies, occasionally a little "meat" had to be dished out. This incurred the risks of punitive action from referees.

Stein could accept that occasionally a rough tackle had to be made "just to let him know you're there" - and a booking might ensue. He was less happy about players being booked for retaliation or arguing with the referee - that was unnecessary. On occasion Jock might have done well to heed his own advice and not argue with referees!

The significance of this League Cup victory in October 1965 should not be underestimated. It confirmed that the Scottish Cup win was no fluke, and that winning trophies was one thing that Celtic fans should now expect as a matter of course. Proof of the swinging of the pendulum in Celtic's direction could even be seen in the behaviour of the fans. Some Rangers fans actually invaded the field at the end while Celtic were doing their lap of honour in order to attack the Celtic players. It was just as well that they did not quite make it. What a fit young man like Bobby Murdoch might have done to an undernourished youth from Larkhall does not bear thinking of! The Celtic fans maintained a dignified low profile.

The author recalls himself at Mount Florida railway station that fine autumn evening awaiting for his Blue Train (as they were then called) to take him back to central Glasgow. He soon realised that he was, as it were, cut off from his unit and deep behind enemy lines and that the train was far from the only thing that was blue. He crammed his green scarf into his pocket as he wandered alone among the blue hordes. "Look unhappy! Look unhappy!" he kept saying to himself. He managed it, but it was far from easy!

The Murdochs had a party that night at their new house in Islay Avenue, High Burnside. Ronnie Simpson was one of the invited guests. In some ways, Ronnie had been the hero of the hour in that League Cup final. His goalkeeping had been inspirational and at several points he had been seen to calm the defence, not least captain McNeill, when things were getting flustered. That night Simpson wandered about the house of the Murdochs, glass of lager in hand, singing "It's a Blue, Blue Day" - a significant occurrence in his family, presumably, for his father of course, had been Jimmy Simpson, one of Rangers' greatest ever players in the 1930's! Rumour had it that Jimmy had been seen at the Final - and supporting Celtic!

In the League, progress continued to be made. The defeat at Ibrox was immediately atoned for by a 7-1 beating of Aberdeen at Parkhead, and until New Year, only one League point was dropped, and that was when a lacklustre Celtic team could not quite break down a defensive minded Partick Thistle at Parkhead. The week before Christmas, an important victory was registered at East End Park against the strong going Dunfermline, then Christmas Day saw Morton put unceremoniously to the sword to the tune of 8-1, Murdoch contributing one goal and loads of creative play.

At New Year the good form continued. On 3rd January 1966 at a misty and frosty Parkhead with the pitch heavily sanded, Celtic hammered Rangers 5-1, the highlight being Murdoch's 30 yard drive to bring the 4th goal. It came from a pass by Joe McBride through the ample legs of the massive referee Tom "Tiny" Wharton. Murdoch's subsequent leap and punch of the air showed his adoring masses on the terracing that his joy was no less than theirs. Like the fans, Murdoch was glad to hear the final whistle that day, for the fog was closing in and an abandonment would have given Rangers an undeserved reprieve.

January 1966 also saw an epic two-legged encounter with Dinamo Kiev in the European Cup Winners' Cup Quarter Final. (Celtic had reached that stage by disposing comfortably of the strangely named Go Ahead Deventer of Holland and the more conventionally monikered A.G.F. Aarhus of Denmark.) The first game at Parkhead saw a rampant Celtic performance with Murdoch scoring two great second half goals as Celtic beat the Ukranians 3-0.The second game was played a fortnight later in Georgia and Celtic, with two centre halves McNeill and Cushley in the team, were professional enough to earn a 1-1 draw, in spite of the sending off of Jim Craig.

Few people remember that game however as well as they remember the odyssey of Celtic's return. A combination of bad weather, bureaucratic incompetence, deliberate Soviet obstruction of westerners for sheer spite, red tape and a very convoluted route via Stockholm meant that it was late on Friday night before a weary and stressed Celtic party returned. Hardly surprisingly, they lost to Hearts at Tynecastle the following day!

It was only one of a very few blemishes that season, however, for the play was generally good. (Curiously enough, they also lost to Aberdeen at Pittodrie the Saturday after the first leg of the Dinamo Kiev game). Murdoch, while still retaining his goal scoring ability (normally when used as a surprise weapon as an extra attacker) was now a visionary midfielder with an extraordinary ability to pass a ball that had old timers remembering Peter Wilson of the 1930's or even "Sunny" Jim Young from before the First World War. His play, and his infectious effect on the rest of the team was a joy to watch.

Often he was noticed in a negative sense in that if Murdoch had an off day, so too did Celtic. February 26th saw the return of one of the distressing traits of the bad old days - namely losing to small teams, in this case Stirling Albion. For some reason, on the heavy ground at Annfield that day, Murdoch simply did not click and the team went down to a 0-1 defeat.

It was against Hearts, however, in the Quarter Final of the Scottish Cup in early March that Celtic had reason to be grateful to Murdoch. 46,000 were grossly overcrowded into Tynecastle to see a remarkable game that ended up 3-3.

Crowd problems were acute that day, not from any huge amount of hooliganism from the Celtic support (although the Hearts fans did not help matters by singing "The Sash My Father Wore" - the start of a disagreeable trend of Gorgie supporters aping Rangers) but more because of sheer crowd congestion. There were actually probably more than 46,000 in the ground because someone (in a brilliantly pre-arranged coup) with a ticket, entered the ground through the turnstile and managed to release the bolt on the Exit gate at the Gorgie Road end and allow in his ticketless friends!

Hearts went ahead, Celtic equalized, a crowd invasion took place, Hearts again went ahead, Celtic equalized then themselves took the lead before Hearts grabbed a late equalizer. The game was hot and frantic and a draw was just about the fairest result. Murdoch would admit that this was one of the toughest games all season.

72,000, a record attendance for a midweek match at Parkhead, turned up for the Replay. Once again Hearts tried hard, but this time Murdoch took control of the game in a way that he hadn't on Saturday and following a blistering opening, Johnstone scored an early goal, then Murdoch himself pounced on a slack pass and added a second. Celtic scored again in the second half - and Murdoch looked world class. Significantly, it was only as Murdoch tired late in the game that Hearts scored their consolation goal.

To a Celtic support already upbeat and euphoric about life, further joy was given that night with the news from transistor radios that Falkirk had beaten Rangers 3-2 at Brockville in a League match, thus strengthening Celtic's position in the title race and allowing everyone to think that Celtic would sweep the boards at the end of the season. Certainly, the standard of play (and the word used was "consistent") gave one loads of optimism and confidence.

Yet, everything might well have gone pear shaped at the end of that fine season. In mid-April Celtic were involved in three trophies - the Scottish League, the Scottish Cup and the European Cup Winners' Cup. In the same way that success becomes infectious, so too does failure. The Semi Final of the Cup Winners' Cup saw Celtic playing Liverpool. Hard luck does not do justice to the emotions as Liverpool edged it after a legitimate Lennox goal was chalked off for offside by a linesman who could not believe how fast Lennox was.

The team were reeling from this massive blow when they had to face Rangers in the Scottish Cup Final. Once again, luck deserted the team when Rangers won 1-0 in the replay after a dull 0-0 draw. Rangers' goal was good, but it was Celtic who had had the bulk of the play. Murdoch however had nothing to reproach himself for, because he played soundly in both games, the first one in particular when many fans though he was the best player of the 22.

Celtic were now however in a position where they might lose the League as well. In circumstances like this, the team looked to their midfield to take a grip of the situation and produce the goods. This effectively meant a huge burden of responsibility falling on Murdoch, a younger man than Auld who was clearly beginning to tire at the end of such a fine season. Murdoch's nerve held good as the team won difficult fixtures at Cappielow, then Dunfermline at Parkhead on Tuesday May 3rd, which more or less won the Championship although it had to be technically confirmed at Fir Park, Motherwell the following Saturday.

It was only the second League Championship since World War 2, and incredibly only the seventh since World War 1 - amazing statistics which show how far Celtic had regressed since the great days of the Edwardian Celts. Things were soon to change and the same Edwardian Celts; Young, Loney, Hay, McMenemy, Quinn et al., although still legends, would soon be eclipsed by Jock Stein's men.

Murdoch had had a fine season, winning the plaudits of most journalists and also silencing any remaining doubters on the Parkhead terracings. Everyone had now been won over to his powerhouse style of play. He had indeed moved from being an indifferent forward to a world class midfielder, and this had been recognised by Scotland with whom he had won four caps that season. His International debut was at Hampden, with Jock Stein temporarily in charge, when John Greig scored a late winner against Italy in early November to give Scotland a slight chance of World Cup qualification.

The defeat of Italy, narrow and late though it was, gave the game in Scotland a tremendous lift and Murdoch had played as well as anyone in this fine victory. But Scotland had previously lost to Poland and were therefore still behind Italy. Yet a win in Italy could see Scotland qualify for the World Cup Finals the following summer in England. Sadly, it was not to be as a sadly depleted Scottish side went down 0-3 in Naples, Italy in December. (In between games, Scotland had defeated Wales 4-1 at Hampden and Murdoch had scored twice!)

The Scotland team for the Italy game was "sadly depleted" because of players' inavailability and injuries picked up in the English League the previous Saturday. The English clubs had refused to release them - and the finger of accusation must here be pointed at one or two English clubs who had Scottish managers. They either would not release them or "encouraged" them to have injuries so that they could not travel to Italy. It hurt later on to hear such managers bleating on about how much they loved their country. It would have brought tears to a glass eye...but it was sheer cant and hypocrisy, revealing the extent to which the imperial power could control the economy and the destiny of a small nation.

*"We're bought and sold for English gold*
*Sic a parcel o' rogues in a nation!"*

It has of course long been this author's contention that Scotland could have won the World Cup in 1966. The conditions in a neighbouring country would have suited them, there would have been no problem of acclimatization, they would have been well supported by the protoype of the Tartan Army - and quite simply, Scotland simply had enough good players to have done it. The talent was certainly there in a way that it has not been since. The Manager would have had to be tough but there can be little doubt that players like Law, St. John, Baxter, Murdoch, Johnstone, Bremner, Greig and others - on their day - would have taken some beating.

Murdoch did make a bad mistake however in April 1966 when England came to Hampden. He played when only half fit, suffering from a flu virus and against the eventual World Cup winners, Murdoch hardly got a kick of the ball. He should of course have been more insistent in declaring himself unfit, but newly appointed Scotland Manager John Prentice was very keen to play him. In addition, the attraction of playing for his country against the Auld Enemy was just too much for Bobby! In any case, on the morning of the game, he began to feel a little better... or so he thought.

Even in 1966 the annual Scotland v. England fixture was still regarded as the most important in the calendar. Granted it was beginning to come under inordinate pressure from rich clubs involved in domestic or European competition who were unwilling to release their players, but it was still the game of the year in the eyes of the fans, particularly perhaps the fans of neither Celtic nor Rangers whose own teams gave them less to cheer about. It is one of life's ironies that Murdoch played this game when only half fit, when nowadays some players give the impression of looking for any excuse (and being encouraged by their club managers to do so!) to avoid wearing their national colours! This sort of thing had certainly occurred the previous December in the World Cup game against Italy - and had had such disastrous consequences for the game in Scotland.

But the Scotland v. England game of 1966 was much looked forward to and anticipated, possibly more so because of Scotland's failure to qualify for the World Cup. Scotland's recent form had been good in this fixture. After the 9-3 thrashing of 1961, Scotland had recorded a hat-trick of victories - 2-0 at Hampden in 1962, 2-1 at Wembley in 1963 and 1-0 at a rainy Hampden in 1964. The 1965 game had been an honourable 2-2 draw at Wembley. Thus Scotland had no need to fear the approach of the English on April 2nd. The game would be on BBC Television (in the mid 1960's only this game and a very few others could hope to have the privilege of being seen live on TV) and the whole nation would be watching and cheering them on!

Scotland lost 3-4, and Murdoch felt as if his legs were detached from his body and just could not get going. England scored twice, then Denis Law pulled one back before half time to give Scotland some sort of a chance. Jimmy Johnstone scored two fine goals in the second half, but each time after England had gone a further goal ahead. It was a close game, and unfortunately for Scotland to have won the game it would have needed everyone to be on top of his game and 100% fit.

In the second half Murdoch, by his own admission, prayed for the full time whistle even though Scotland were down! It is interesting to speculate what a difference a fully fit Bobby Murdoch might have made. Scotland might well have won, (he had certainly been in fine fettle in recent games for Celtic) and England would have entered the World Cup finals in their own backyard with a wheen less confidence. Did England win the 1966 World Cup thanks to the Murdoch flu virus?

As it was, this gross error of judgement by the over zealous Murdoch and the optimistic Prentice would cost Bobby to a certain extent his International reputation, and meant that he was by no means the automatic selection that he should have been. He would return to the International fold, but only sporadically and a total of 12 International Caps is scant reward for his devastating club play.

Yet he had no time or desire in summer 1966 to worry about his International future. Celtic, Scottish League champions and winners of the Scottish League Cup, took their team on a close season tour of the United States and Canada in an attempt to further strengthen the links between them. In this they succeeded wonderfully well, but no-one could quite have predicted what was coming next year.

# Annus Mirabilis

So much has been written (and so well) by so many Celtic historians about the wonderful season of 1966-67 that it is difficult to add to it. In the case of Bobby Murdoch, it was without doubt the most remarkable time of his life when he matured from being a fine team player into quite simply the best midfield player in the world, and as valuable a player as any in the European Cup triumph.

Yet, paradoxically, Murdoch was not the man who stood out in that excellent team. For one thing, the salient factor of the Lisbon Lions was that they played as a team and were a coherent unit. Yet within that proviso, Gemmell was more flamboyant and attention-seeking, Johnstone with his tricky dribbling and red hair was the "tourist attraction", for a football romantic, interest was provided in the resurrected careers of Simpson, Auld and to a certain extent Chalmers, the speed of Lennox resembled that of a greyhound and all sorts of other things prevented Murdoch from being the instantly recognisable figure of the team.

Yet foreign managers showed a surprising unanimity when they stated that Murdoch was the man who made the team. Another group who would share that opinion were an even more knowledgeable and relevant collection - namely those who had watched the team since Murdoch's debut and before. This hard-bitten, gnarled and much enduring group of people would not be slow in nominating Murdoch as the man who made all the difference.

Tactically, Stein had honed to perfection his 4-2-4 formation, the very axis of which was Murdoch and Auld in midfield. It was a very gradual development - and one which began on the very successful 1966 summer tour of America. It had been much discussed by the players themselves along with their manager, and everyone was happy about it.

The very idea of 4-2-4 in the mid-1960's had some traditionalists holding up their hands in horror. This formation was associated with boring Continental defensive football in the minds of most reactionary Scottish fans who love their M and W formations (along with a brown ball, referees wearing black and goalkeepers wearing thick polo neck jerseys). Indeed it came as a shock to the author watching a game in the company of a friend who played professional football for East Fife and therefore knew more about the geometrics of the game than the average punter. My friend pointed out that Celtic were now playing 4-2-4 - and very successfully and very positively in that they were scoring loads of goals.

Murdoch was on the right side of midfield and Auld on the left, but there was more to it than that. While Auld was the subtle and crafty playmaker, Murdoch was the powerhouse, using his massive commanding strength to win the ball and turn defence into attack. This he frequently achieved by chesting a ball down on the edge of his own penalty box, shrugging off a few challenges as he charged forward, then finding Jimmy Johnstone, Joe McBride, Bobby Lennox or Steve Chalmers with an inch perfect pass. It was the length of his passes that were very noticeable as well - 30, 40 yards was by no means unusual for this visionary artist of the game.

Indeed, it was Murdoch's passing of a ball made even the great James McGrory put him ahead of Peter Wilson as a right half. Wilson was the contemporary of McGrory in the 1920's and 1930's and was a legendary passer of the ball. "Peter Wilson didn't pass the ball, he stroked it and caressed it to make it do what he wanted" it was frequently said.

Murdoch, according to McGrory (who knew a thing or two about football - and Celtic!) was even better than Wilson - and he was even able to discriminate between his receivers of the ball. Johnstone, for example preferred the ball at his feet, the greyhound Lennox needed the ball a yard or two ahead of him and the ever ready Steve Chalmers could even cope with the ball behind him, such was his ability to turn, speed up and deliver.

The verdict of McGrory is worth something as well, in that McGrory was in the position to speak authoritatively about both, having played with Wilson and managed and watched Murdoch. McGrory, for his shortcomings as a Manager was a perceptive viewer of the game and knew a good player when he saw one. He certainly saw one in Bobby Murdoch, although the question must surely be asked of the legendary Jimmy "If Murdoch was a better right half than Peter Wilson, why didn't McGrory play him there?"

The seeds for the "Annus Mirabilis" (the remarkable year) had been sown, as we have discovered, in North America. Stein took the team to the U.S. and Canada in late May and early June 1966. 11 games were played, three were drawn against Bologna, Spurs and Bayern Munich, but the other eight were all won - two against Spurs and the rest against local opposition. 47 goals were scored and only 6 lost. The good results however were only half the story. The real value of the tour was to allow Celtic players to get to know each other better and to relax and enjoy each other's company. This was a tremendous success as well, and the team returned to Scotland, having been excellent ambassadors for the game and for their country.

The record of the 1966-67 Celtic side speaks for itself. They won every single trophy they entered - all three Scottish domestic trophies, the Glasgow Cup (still in 1967 a reasonably prestigious competition) and of course the

European Cup, becoming the first British team (in fact the first team from North Europe) to do so.

Yet it was the style of their play that was even more attractive than the actual record. Other teams had won the European Cup (and more would continue to do so) by dour defensive play, scoring a goal typically in the early stages of the second half and then soaking everything up on the edge of their own penalty box. It is effective although somewhat uninteresting football.

This charge could hardly be levelled against Celtic in 1966-67. It was said that they were a team who did not know how to defend. This was hardly true, but it was also true that only on a handful of occasions (notably the League Cup Final of October 1966 and the European Cup Semi Final in Prague) did they have recourse to grim defence. This was usually achieved by pulling Murdoch back into a more defensive role. On other occasions the simple maxim that the best form of defence was attack came into play.

In this respect (as well as others) we can see the value of Bobby Murdoch. Murdoch was nothing if not flexible. He could be an attacker (granted the events of pre-1965 would indicate that this was far from his best position) if need be, he excelled in midfield and could even be deployed as a defender. He was naturally right sided, but could play on the left if he was asked to do so. Occasionally Stein did just that, to fox the opposition.

Yet the team did evolve during 1966-67. It was a growth and developmental process. It was as late as January 14th 1967 at Muirton Park, Perth that the Lisbon Lions of Simpson, Craig, Gemmell, Murdoch, McNeill, Clark, Johnstone, Wallace, Chalmers, Auld and Lennox played together for the first time. Previously, McBride had been in the centre of the forward line, but he was injured at Pittodrie on Christmas Eve. It was sheer serendipity that Willie Wallace arrived from Hearts to replace him, as if

Stein somehow knew that McBride would be injured. Until Hogmanay the full back combination had been Gemmell and O'Neill. In addition, fringe players like Charlie Gallagher, John Hughes, John Cushley and John Fallon - fine players all - were never too far away from a place in the side, and indeed performed creditably when called upon.

There were times when the football was absolutely breathtaking. Possibly the best game for sheer football was at Easter Road, Edinburgh on October 8th 1966. Celtic would eventually win 5-3, McBride scoring 4 goals. The author remembers attending this game and standing towards the bottom of the large Easter Road terracing. A scintillating first half saw Hibs go ahead, then Celtic turn it on, equalize, then take a 2-1 lead. Then Hibs got a dodgy penalty towards half time, and in disgust my companion turned to go to the toilet at the top of the terracing, saying that "Hibs are incredibly fortunate to be going in level". His choice of vocabulary was slightly more earthy than that, in fact, but by the time he had reached the top of the terracing to visit the primitive toilets and do the needful, Celtic and Joe McBride had scored another two!

Another exciting game was at East End Park on November 19th. 3-1 for the Pars at half-time, then Jimmy Johnstone pulled one back only to be immediately countered by Alex Ferguson's 48th minute strike. 4-2 for Dunfermline and things looked all over, but Murdoch was absolutely inspirational and Celtic did not give up until the very last minute when a McBride penalty in the 89th minute earned them a pulsating victory.

Murdoch played one International game for Scotland that season. It was against Northern Ireland at Hampden Park on November 16th and Murdoch played at inside right! He was hardly among strangers for the team consisted of 6 Celts, 3 Rangers, Billy Bremner of Leeds United and Bobby Ferguson of Kilmarnock. Murdoch had been recalled after a lacklustre 1-1 draw in Wales, a game played in an eerie, surreal atmosphere, for it was the day after the Aberfan disaster in which many children were killed at school when a pit bing collapsed on top of them. In fact many people thought that the Welsh game should have been postponed. Murdoch probably did well to avoid that one, but this game against Northern Ireland was a good, if uninspiring, 2-1 victory for the Scottish team.

In their whole domestic campaign, Celtic lost only two games - both, incredibly, to the same opposition of Dundee United. The first was on Hogmanay at Tannadice Park when the team were ahead but careless defending (with Ronnie Simpson having one of his very rare bad games) allowed United to win 3-2.

The other game was a curious one. It was at Parkhead on May 3rd 1967. There was the superficial symmetry of Celtic being 2-1 up, as in the game at Tannadice Park, and losing 3-2, but there were other factors at work as well. Celtic might have won the League that night - but they still had games against Rangers and Kilmarnock to come in any case. They had qualified for the European Cup Final the previous Tuesday and won the Scottish Cup on Saturday. Euphoria was in the air, and of course with euphoria came complacency. Very obviously, one or two players (Murdoch included) took their foot off the pedal, clearly determined to avoid injury lest they miss out on the Lisbon event. This allowed the more than competent Dundee United (who had already beaten Barcelona that season) into the game, and to register a rare Parkhead victory, causing some amazement and consternation, verging on disbelief, in the following day's Courier, the Dundee newspaper.

Cynics thought that the game was deliberately "thrown" in order to set up a title win at Ibrox the following Saturday (as indeed happened) - and certainly this suspicion was much touted about in the disappointed Jungle at full time

- but the probable truth was that some players were jaded, and others had lulled themselves into the belief that everything was going to be all right in any case. It did however make everyone sit up and pay attention to the Ibrox game. A draw was sufficient for Celtic - and that was what was achieved in the Ibrox rain.

Murdoch, a virtual ever present that season - he missed only three games in the League and two in the Scottish Cup - had one moment of disgrace that season when he was sent off in a game with St.Mirren on November 5th 1966 which ended in a dismal draw. Murdoch in fact was captain that day as McNeill was off injured and Celtic were doing very badly. It was a feature of Murdoch, incidentally, in his Celtic years that he was not always a good captain, at least as far as results went. This game was a 1-1 draw and time was running out. The fans, used to constant success, were becoming restive as the gallant St.Mirren kept battling and frustrating Celtic by their offside trap and annoyingly successful defensive play.

The ball went out of play for what Murdoch thought was Celtic's throw. The linesman pointed the other way, Murdoch looked at him, shook his head and ran away. At the same time, another Celtic player, later admitted to be Joe McBride, delivered a mouthful of obscenities at the linesman. The linesman thought it was Murdoch, held up his flag to call over the referee and Mr.R.Henderson of Dundee dismissed the incredulous Murdoch. It was a wrong decision, and apparently Archie Gemmill of St.Mirren (later of Argentina fame - it was he who scored that great goal for Scotland against Holland in 1978) was prepared to speak for Bobby. Bobby was later fined a trivial amount and warned, however. Not that it mattered in that respect. What upset Murdoch more was that if he had stayed on the field, he might well have scraped a winner for Celtic. Stein however seemed to accept Murdoch's side of the affair, and no action was taken from that quarter.

The season had begun with a vicarious cloud of gloom having settled over all Scotland. This was not because of anything that Scotland had done, but rather because on July 30th 1966, England had won the World Cup. Natural feelings of an anti-English kind were sharpened on this occasion by the niggling feeling that Scotland were at least as good. In April, England had beaten Scotland only narrowly and that was with a half-fit Bobby Murdoch who had made an error of judgement in deciding to play. The following April of course Scotland would win famously at Wembley and it remains a matter of anguish almost forty years later that had Scotland qualified for the 1966 World Cup (and there were circumstances beyond their control which prevented them doing this), they might well have won the competition.

Be that as it may, England were the World champions and the following week, Manchester United came to Parkhead. A cosmopolitan team like Manchester United managed by a Scotsman called Matt Busby and containing Denis Law and Pat Crerand as well as Ireland's George Best, hardly represented England, but there were two of England's World Cup winning team in the Old Trafford side.

These were Bobby Charlton and Nobby Stiles. Charlton, being a decent sort, was treated with polite respect by the Jungle that day, but Stiles got a somewhat different reception. His tackling occasionally verged on the robust (as indeed it had during the World Cup itself) and for this he was much and deservedly abused by the unimpressed Celtic supporters. It was not however the main talking point of the game.

Celtic in very impressive mode simply swept Manchester United aside. Murdoch was immense. He scored the second goal as Celtic romped to a 4-1 victory, impressing the English Press and laying down a pointer to what was yet to come. Jock Stein, always a great believer in the value of propaganda, could not have had a better prelude to the season, even though Rangers also beat Arsenal that day. Manchester United would win their own League Championship in 1967 and of course the European Cup itself in 1968, but they could not live with Celtic that day. What Matt Busby and Pat Crerand (both Celtic daft) thought of all this cannot be imagined. Perhaps they regretted the follies of previous Celtic managements in not keeping them to be part of what was about to happen.

Stein was in fact seen that day to put his arm round Pat Crerand as Pat left the field at the end of the game and talk earnestly to him. A few stories (with little in the way of evidence to back them up) began to appear in some papers that Pat might now be on his way back to Celtic Park. He might have been interested if an offer had been made, but Stein was never too keen on attempting to jump into the same river twice, and he knew that Pat possibly still had enemies at Parkhead - but the greatest reason was that quite simply, with Bobby Murdoch in harness, Celtic simply did not need another right half, be he Pat Crerand or anyone else.

The League Cup Qualifying Section was won very convincingly. Hearts put up a little resistance but were ground down and Clyde and St.Mirren were simply swept aside. In the Quarter Final Celtic beat a strong Dunfermline Athletic team 9-4 on aggregate over two legs, and then beat Airdrie 2-0 in the Semi Final.

Rangers were the opponents in the League Cup Final. Celtic had already beaten them twice, once in a Glasgow Cup game and again in the Scottish League, but Rangers, having spent heavily in the close season buying two Smiths, Dave from Aberdeen and Alex from Dunfermline, were steadily improving. But Stein and Murdoch had sussed them out in at least one respect. Kaj Johansen had scored the only goal in the 1966 Scottish Cup Final. Johansen was a full back and his spectacular goal was the highlight of his otherwise fairly dismal career.

His goal was much boasted about by the boys in blue, who had little else to cheer them up in those days. Johansen would therefore be unable to resist the pressure from the fans to try the same again. Celtic's answer was to let him do so, (for Kaj was not a natural goalscorer) thus leaving a gap at the back which an accurate Murdoch pass to Lennox could exploit. This happened several times in the Glasgow Cup game as Celtic romped to a 4-0 victory.

In the League game at Parkhead on September 17th, Celtic ruthlessly exposed and exploited Rangers' "beaten before we start" mentality. In a very real sense, they were in fact beaten by five past three, for Celtic were two goals up and it was Murdoch who had engineered both. In the very first minute a lovely Murdoch through ball found Lennox who beat his marker and crossed to the unmarked Joe McBride. In fact McBride missed the ball totally, but Bertie Auld didn't.

Then with the Celtic End in glorious fervour and the Rangers End wondering what they had let themselves in for, Murdoch scored another, only three minutes later. This time it was sheer genius. A free kick on the edge of the box was conceded by the under-pressure Rangers defence. Murdoch took it and belted it straight at the Rangers wall. It possibly damaged a vital area of some poor Ranger, but the ball rebounded to Bobby. With Rangers rushing at him en masse, he took his time, thought about it and hooked the ball above them and well out of reach of the badly positioned Billy Ritchie. There was no way back for Rangers after that - even though another 86 minutes remained for play!

In the League Cup Final on October 29th however 94,532 saw a close encounter and it would probably have to be admitted that on balance Rangers were the better side.

But it was Celtic who scored a great first half goal - Auld sweeping the ball across to McBride, then a head down for the inrushing Lennox - and had the adaptability to defend well and break constructively. It was in this role that Murdoch was superb, breaking up Rangers attacks before they got to the dangerous areas of the field and putting in a pile of work as he charged about, a positive inspiration to his team mates and a source of strength to us weaker brethren behind the goal.

Once or twice Rangers almost got through and once in particular Willie O'Neill cleared his line when all seemed lost, but as the minutes ticked away, those who were listening to the radio commentary heard the name "Murdoch" again and again. "It's Murdoch who mops up..." " A timely intervention by Murdoch" ... "Yet again it is Bobby Murdoch who wins the ball". The full time whistle came to the delight of the green and white end of the ground, and Murdoch had the satisfaction of another League Cup medal at the end and the feeling of a job well done.

But Celtic were advancing on other fronts as well. By Christmas, Zurich and Nantes had been disposed of in Europe. Zurich were not the most gentle of teams ever to have been seen at Celtic Park and the treatment meted out to Jimmy Johnstone in particular was shocking. On one occasion, Murdoch was quite clearly seen telling a Swiss defender that if he did not lay off Johnstone, he (Murdoch) would do something about it... and the rough treatment visibly slackened after that, for Murdoch was now a big lad. He was also apparently "booked" in the game against Zurich. He was unaware of this, for in these days a yellow card was not brandished, merely a name going down in the note book. The referee said nothing and it was only when a journalist told Bobby at full time that he had been booked that he realised! He appealed against this later and the caution was quietly quashed.

Against Nantes in France, it was Murdoch who was responsible for the key goal with a brilliant defence splitting pass to find the ever ready Bobby Lennox. This gave Celtic a comfortable 3-1 victory, and the result was repeated at Parkhead the following week on December 7th to put Celtic into the Quarter Finals.

By this time another piece of silver had joined the League Cup on the Parkhead sideboard. This was the Glasgow Cup, arguably the most handsome of them all and a fine piece of Victorian craftwork. The timing of this victory was important. The Final was played at Parkhead on Monday November 7th, two days after Murdoch's "mistaken identity" ordering off against St.Mirren. In these days, an ordering off did not automatically mean a missing of the next game into the bargain and Murdoch played that night against Partick Thistle with a point to prove to the 30,000 Parkhead fans, who cheered him to the echo to indicate their acceptance of his side of the story. McNeill, who had been out against St.Mirren, also returned and Murdoch, without the pressures of captaincy, was instrumental in the 4-0 victory over a gallant and gracious Thistle.

In the League, following the win over Rangers at Parkhead in September, Celtic continued brightly and reached Christmas with no defeats and only three draws in the deficit column against St.Mirren (the game in which Murdoch was sent off), Kilmarnock at Rugby Park (a hard game on a hard pitch at a time when Celtic were heavily embroiled in Europe) and Aberdeen at Pittodrie on Christmas Eve. By this time Willie Wallace had joined the club from Hearts and he too very quickly struck up an understanding with Murdoch. Wallace's arrival was timely. He signed on December 6th and on Christmas Eve, Joe McBride was badly injured at Pittodrie and never played again the rest of the season. He had nevertheless scored 35 goals in his half-season, many of them from the visionary play of Bobby Murdoch.

It was after the New Year that Celtic really began to hit top gear, gaining a real boost from extraneous events on January 28th. In the Scottish Cup, Celtic were playing Arbroath and a Murdoch goal started the routine demolition of the brave Angus men. Some other brave men from lower divisions were doing somewhat better that day however. East Fife, for example, beat Motherwell but that paled into insignificance compared with the other one.

Berwick Rangers were hosting Glasgow Rangers. That game kicked off at 2.30 p.m as Shielfield Park, Berwick had no floodlights. They were thus half an hour ahead of Celtic v. Arbroath. Towards the end of the first half at Parkhead, rumours began to circulate round the terracing that Rangers were a goal down at Berwick. There was nothing unusual about that, for any Celtic game always has its fair amount of wishful thinking among the ever optimistic supporters.

But this time the somewhat primitive half time score facilities seemed to confirm this. Scottish radio coverage was nothing like as comprehensive as it is now with its up to the minute score flashes, and apparently it was the English BBC which someone was listening to on a portable radio in the stand which brought the good news. A few people around the lucky man in the stand cheered hysterically. The game on the field had stopped for an injury to an Arbroath player, Murdoch turned round to see what the mini disturbance in the Main Stand was, recognised one of the delirious fans as a man whose judgement he trusted, immediately jumped up and punched the air, telling Tommy Gemmell the joyful news. The crowd immediately picked up what had happened and the whole ground soon was resounding to paeans of delight. Most of the fans however still found it hard to swallow and it was not until they entered pubs that they saw on television screens the unbelievable score of Berwick Rangers 1 Glasgow Rangers 0.

To a Celtic team that hardly needed a boost, this result was yet another shot in the arm to the greatest season of all time. Yet it would be a fool who would say that Rangers' fall from grace did not have some of its provenance at least in the apparent invincibility of Celtic and their ability to do anything about it. The New Year fixture at Ibrox was frosted off, and this was a bigger blow to Rangers than it was to Celtic. Early March saw Celtic's defeat of Vojvodina in the European Cup Quarter Final (who can ever forget McNeill's late winner from a Charlie Gallagher corner?) and for Murdoch, the good news continued with, on Thursday March 16th, the arrival of Bobby Murdoch junior when Kathleen presented him with an addition to the family.

There was a bad game in the Scottish Cup - the Semi Final against Clyde which ended 0-0, although even then a penalty was denied in the last minute. Many reasons were put forward for this poor performance - over commitment, bad refereeing, exhaustion, "you never get a good game between those two, Celtic and Clyde" were all trotted out by the punters, but the real reason was that Murdoch was out, having problems (not for the first nor last time) with his ankle.

He had been taken off injured at Tynecastle in an otherwise confortable 3-0 win over Hearts. Hearts, funnily enough seemed to be the bogey team as far as Murdoch's ankle was concerned, for it was in 1963 at Parkhead in an accidental clash with goalkeeper Gordon Marshall senior that it was first damaged. He had his photograph taken with his ankle in bandages while holding the very tiny baby Bobby in his arms. He was back however in time for the European Cup Semi Final.

This unfortunate injury might well have put Murdoch out of contention for the England v. Scotland International at Wembley. This was of course the famous game of Jim Baxter's keepie-uppie and the general humiliation of the arrogant England side and media. It was a result that was hailed with jubilation in the rest of the world, not least in places like Argentina and Germany, where there was a justified grievance against the way the English had won the World Cup. It was a shame that Murdoch missed this one. He had in fact returned to the first team on the previous Wednesday against Dukla Prague, but had quite rightly not been considered by the Scotland management for the Wembley game. Simpson, Gemmell, Wallace and Lennox however were all in the team, and indeed Lennox scored one of the goals in the 3-2 win.

Murdoch's other games in the latter part of the season were quite simply Celtic triumphant. Europe provided its great moments with two fine Willie Wallace goals and one from Jimmy Johnstone against Dukla Prague at Parkhead. There followed that painfully long second half in Prague against Dukla, the Army team of Czechoslovakia, when Celtic had to defend with ten men and leave Stevie Chalmers on his own up front. It was a strange game played in a strange stadium, not unlike an open-air theatre in Ancient Greece with many of the audience watching from the side of a hill with bushes occasionally in the way!

Murdoch tells of his one awful moment in that game at Prague. Celtic were 3-1 up from the game at Parkhead and defending reasonably comfortably, although this was an alien form of football to the normally attack minded Celts. The second half was progressing and Celtic were beginning to breathe a little easier, while at the back of their mind there still lurked the thought that one goal for Dukla might well bring two. Murdoch tackled a Dukla forward just inside the penalty box. It was a fair challenge, but the Czech forward went down in a heap clearly making the most of it. Murdoch looked in panic at the referee. A penalty here might have made all the difference... but fortunately the referee Herr Gottfied Dienst of Switzerland, one of Europe's finest, said "No", and Murdoch, Celtic and Scotland (most of it listening to the radio) all breathed again.

The author has his own personal reminiscence of that moment. A young man in perfect health, a student at Scotland's ancient seat of learning, the University of St.Andrews, he was pacing the floor of his room while listening to BBC Radio Scotland. Such was the tension that one couldn't sit still and visits to the toilet were a frequent necessity. The commentator said "Penalty!... No!" and the legs gave way underneath this desperate student.

Four days after returning from Prague, (they flew home that very Tuesday night, everyone avoiding Jim Craig who seemed to have picked up a flu virus) there was the Scottish Cup Final - a fine competent triumph against a good Aberdeen side, then the winning of the League at Ibrox with a 2-2 draw against Rangers and finally that glorious day in Lisbon when the European Cup was landed. The supporters had sung all season "We Shall Not Be Moved". Neither we were, and the history of football was changed.

The game itself was played on May 25th 1967, a Thursday night with a 5.30 p.m kick-off. It is difficult to estimate the number of fans who actually went to Lisbon, (it must not be confused with the number who claimed to have done so!) but certain it was that far more watched it at home on black and white television. It was one of the few football games in history which actually emptied the streets in all of Scotland's big cities, medium sized towns and small villages.

Murdoch nearly did not make it. This would have been a grievous, perhaps even a crucial loss. He had aggravated his right ankle injury in training, and played the game with it heavily strapped, so much so that he claimed it looked twice the size of his left. He also claimed to have kicked the ball less than half a dozen times with his right foot in the whole game, favouring quite clearly his left. In this Bobby is being less than fair to himself for video footage does not entirely back this up, although several times in the course of the game he tested the Italian goalkeeper Sarti with his left foot rather than his right! It was like the great Spanish writer Cervantes who wrote the Don Quijote in about 1500. He had been wounded at the Battle of Lepanto in 1471 and lost the use of his left hand "for the greater glory of the right", as he said. It might have been said that Murdoch virtually lost the use of his right foot in Lisbon "for the greater glory of the left"!

Presumably the hard core of extremist Rangers supporters found it extremely hard to take, but quite a lot of the boys in blue gave Celtic some grudging support. Supporters of other teams were likewise pro-Celtic, and we had the pleasing experience of the late Kenneth Wolstenholme of the BBC, notoriously biased normally in favour of English teams, saying quite openly that he hoped Celtic would win. When the much loved Ken died in March 2002, a great deal was made of his "They think it's all over... it is now" remark in the World Cup of 1966. I far prefer his "I'm biased, of course, I want Celtic to win" or even better, "Glory hovers over Parkhead".

It did just that. In a magnificent display of attacking football, Celtic rocked Europe. Inter Milan went ahead with a soft penalty in the 5th minute, and it would presumably have been felt throughout Europe that the Scots were in for a tanking, or at best a sterile performance against boring defenders. But the midfield duo of Murdoch and Auld took a grip of the game, and wave after wave of green and white attacks surged forward.

The snag was that Inter Milan were experts at absorbing all this. Half time came and went with the score still at 1-0, and it was well into the second half (and after loads of near things, including Sarti's famous one-handed save from Murdoch, and more dodgy refereeing decisions) before Gemmell equalized. Five minutes remained when Chalmers scored the winner. Murdoch, of course, was involved in the build up to both goals.

Gemmell's thunderbolt from the edge of the box levelled the score. It had come from a move involving Murdoch and Jim Craig. Chalmers' winner came as Stevie steered Murdoch's left foot effort (which may or may not have been heading goalwards) into the goal. Then came the buttock - clenching agony of the wait for the full time whistle.

A rational detailed look at the footage of the last five minutes will indicate that Celtic were in little danger of losing a goal, and certainly Kenneth Wolstenholme is supremely confident that Celtic will make it. The supporters at the ground and at home did not see it that way. Many are the detailed accounts of atheists on their knees praying to God and promising to be at Church every Sunday for the rest of their lives, of men taking dogs for walks round the block simply because they feared a heart attack if they watched any more, of one veteran supporter (who had seen Patsy Gallacher and Tommy McInally) hiding in his garden shed. His bewildered wife was unaware of where he had gone, until she twigged where he was and shouted the immortal words "They've won!"

Kathleen of course was at the game in Lisbon, but Bobby's parents, Barbara and Bobby senior watched the game in their Rutherglen home. The agonies for any supporter were long and intense, but it must have been so much greater for the parents of one of the players - especially if the player concerned was the star man! Yet what must the rapture and ecstacy have been when the final whistle went, the proud parents saw the Cup being presented and then the neighbours all came in for a party! Glasgow and Scotland belonged to Celtic, and Mr and Mrs

Murdoch had played their part in it.

The Italians were gracious in defeat, although it must have been hard for them, for they were confidently expected to win comfortably. Almost 35 years after the event, in an interview with Scotland on Sunday on May 19th 2002, Inter's defender Giacinto Facchetti and now a respected financier and ambassador for his still beloved Inter, makes a revealing comment. The context is the absence in Lisbon through injury of Luis Suarez, Inter's famous Spanish midfielder. Facchetti says "I cannot stress enough that the absence of Suarez was a major blow to us. He was our playmaker and the most vital member of our team. It would be like asking Celtic to take the field without Bobby Murdoch".

The full time whistle released all tension and unleashed an orgy of celebration the likes of which Glasgow and Scotland had never seen before. The Weekly News supplement (produced specially for this occasion) puts it rather well when it says "It was VE night, Coronation Night, Hogmanay and Central Station on Fair Friday all rolled into one mad, deliriously happy celebration" Murdoch, like the rest of the team, wept. Celtic were the first British team to win the European Cup, and in the context of where Celtic had been in Murdoch's early Celtic career, it was barely credible. Minds of course did go back to that eerie silence of the Celtic End at Hampden that hideous night of the 1963 Scottish Cup Final as 50,000 turned their backs on Celtic. It was only four years previously. Who would have said that that team would be the first to bring the European Cup back to Britain?

But the agonies of the past were all forgotten that night as fans both in Lisbon and back in Scotland went crazy. There is a picture from the environs of Parkhead of four ragged urchins holding up the Celtic dishcloth. Perhaps they were not born with a silver spoon in their mouth, perhaps they had little else going for them, but they now had a European Cup. They would never forget it the rest of their days. They were the risen people!

The Celtic Song, released in 1961 ended with the words

*"... for we only know,*
*There's gonna be a show*
*And the Glasgow Celtic will be there"*

This was surely the much promised "show"!

The return to Glasgow saw unparalleled scenes of joy at Celtic Park. Murdoch and his colleagues were taken round the running track on a lorry, showing off that big ugly Cup which has now became so much a part of the Celtic Park mythology. A generation later, it is still true that this game is lived every day. And so it should be! The replica of the European Cup serves as a reminder that Celtic were (and always will be) the first British team to lift the trophy and it is also a potent spur to future players of the club that this sort of thing can happen again. Awful, barren years like 1978 and the early 1990's cannot be excused. The European Cup will always say "It disnae need tae be like that!"

For Bobby Murdoch, the return to Glasgow with his beautiful Kathleen to his family, young Bobby and young Kathleen was like a dream come true. He had done all this for his family, including his parents - and for the team that he loved. From now on, those who talked about Jimmy Quinn, Jimmy McGrory and Patsy Gallacher would have to include Bobby Murdoch. As the song which became popular at the turn of the century would say

*Oh, they gave us Jimmy McGrory and Paul McStay,*
*Murdoch, Tully, Chalmers, Auld and Hay*
*And most of football's greats*
*Have passed through Parkhead's gates*
*To play the game in the good old Celtic way!*

In 1967 life probably just could not get any better for Bobby Murdoch. It was indeed "The Best Day Of Our Lives".

There were a couple of epilogues to this season. One was the following week when Rangers played Bayern Munich in the Final of the Cup Winners' Cup. Opinions on this one were of course divided among the Celtic support. Some could never have supported Rangers in any circumstances, but Murdoch and most of the players who were friends with the Rangers men were disappointed to see them go down and fail to land both European trophies for Glasgow and Scotland.

And the week after that on June 7th, with full scale war raging in the Eastern Mediterranean and threatening to involve more than simply Israel and the Arabs Celtic ignored some people's advice and returned to the Iberian peninsula. This was to play Real Madrid for the benefit match of Alfredo di Stefano, he whom Celtic had tried to sign in 1964! There in front of Spanish Dictator Francisco Franco, the victor of the bloody Civil War of thirty years previously and erstwhile ally of Hitler and Mussolini, Celtic beat Real Madrid 1-0.

Franco, for all his faults, was a genuine football supporter and a fan of Real Madrid. He had watched Celtic's European triumph on TV, had been mightily impressed and was delighted to see the Glasgow side take on his favourites, congratulating them when a solitary Lennox goal was enough to beat the great Real.

Murdoch, funnily enough, played this game at inside right, John Clark taking the right half position to allow Willie O'Neill a game on the left. The man of the match however was Jimmy Johnstone.

Thus the glory season finished with even Real Madrid graciously acknowledging the triumph of Celtic. Real Madrid, the victors of Glasgow's European Cup Final of

1960, whom Celtic had audaciously organized a friendly against in 1962, who had given Celtic some sort of comfort by beating Rangers in 1963 and from whom Celtic had tried even more audaciously and ludicrously to buy di Stefano in 1964, were now only second best in Europe to the Celtic team which included Bobby Murdoch! Murdoch could never have dreamed as much.

# Marginal Decline

Following the great days of summer 1967, it was perhaps inevitable that what came next would not be quite so good. One Celtic historian said that on Friday 26th May 1967, the day after the European Cup triumph, football should have been closed down, for it was impossible to conceive of anything better. This was, of course, a remark made in jest rather than in any seriousness, but there were times in the next season when quite a few of us would have agreed with it.

At least three times, in fact. Celtic had a poor autumn, both at home and on foreign shores. Several players gave every sign of being unable to cope with the success and constant adulation that Lisbon had brought them. There was little doubt that one or two egos (not Murdoch's necessarily) had swollen to unconscionable proportions and there was also the undeniable fact that some of them felt they no longer needed to bother, particularly in the early part of the season before they received a few nasty shocks. Murdoch himself would admit years later that winning the European Cup was one thing, but living with it was something else.

But 1967 was still a great year. The Beatles, the Hippies, Flower Power and a new Radio Station called Radio 1, dedicated to non-stop pop music encouraged a feeling of well being. The late sixties was probably a time of working class prosperity under the Labour Government of Harold Wilson. The prosperity was being shared as well in a way that had never been seen before with Central Scotland, in particular, booming. Yet all was not as rosy as one would have liked it to be.

The "gnomes of Zurich" as they used to be called - the international bankers - would several times (for naked political reasons) make life difficult for a Left-orientated Government. They organized runs on the pound, withdrew financial support, encouraged inflation and failed to lend as much as they promised - something that if carried to extremes (as happened in Chile in 1973) would have endangered and jeopardised the British democratic system. The people had voted for one thing, but international finance wanted something else.

But there were limits to what the financiers, speculators and get-rich-quick brigade could do and they could not really prevent the general feeling of progress, prosperity and contentment. Roads, schools and hospitals were being built, and unemployment had virtually disappeared. The Glasgow of 1967 was now totally unrecognisable from that of even 20 years earlier.

There was of course inflation, but at the moment it was containable. Inflation was very obvious in footballer's salaries, some of whom made little or no attempt to hide how much they earned. The maximum wage had, of course, been abolished many years ago and the media were not slow to spread the rumours of how much any particular player was raking in. "£100 per week" (whether true or not, no-one knows nor will ever know) was the emotive phrase much mentioned. The three figure sum was probably about five times the average wage. Yet it was a constant gripe from Celtic players that they were paid less than Rangers players were, even at the peak of Celtic's success.

Salary figures should be a matter of confidentiality between employer and employee, but footballers met each other on International outings and exchanged information. Celtic players may or may not have been paid less than others but they were undeniably far from Social Security or the poor house. Such wages of course had to be earned.

Celtic had certainly done that as all Scotland spent summer 1967 listening to Beatles' records, enjoying Coronation Street, protesting about the war in Vietnam and basking in the glory of Celtic's success in Europe, something that had at least taken the edge off England winning the World Cup the previous year. Even a few Rangers fans had to admit that they were able to bask on a Spanish beach under palm trees and earn the admiration of a few women because they were Scottish.

Celtic players were the talk of the nation. Someone would always claim to see Murdoch on holiday in the Trossachs, or Wallace driving his sports car through the streets of Forfar, Craig in Elgin or Clark at Ayr races. Anyone who was small and red-haired was likely to be stopped in the street and asked for his autograph, for he was surely Jimmy Johnstone. Schoolboys in their Higher English class would read Macbeth and there would be a certain competition for who would be allowed to read the hitherto insignificant part of a Scottish nobleman called Lennox. Even at Wimbledon, the Umpire would occasionally say "Bertie Auld" however much the commentators told us that he was really saying "thirty all".

In such a frenzied cult atmosphere, much was expected of the team. Stein was always careful to juggle the forward line so that the 11 European Cup winners (it would be years before they were called the "Lisbon Lions") seldom took the field together for the same game, (it is a myth to state that they never all played together again as a team) but perhaps he made an error in not really adding any new blood to give added competition for places. He could certainly not claim poverty as an excuse, for the club were absolutely rolling in money! Complacency began to set in, and there was the feeling that everything was going to be all right anyway. A team like this could not be beaten, it was erroneously believed.

Yet the fragility and ephemerality of success was shown by one bad week in September. It started with the Old Firm League game at Ibrox in September. Celtic had drawn with and then defeated Rangers in the League Cup in August, thus ensuring their passage to what would eventually be another League Cup victory. Supporters recalled how Celtic had been one goal down to Rangers with fifteen minutes remaining and had won 3-1 after Rangers missed a penalty. They shared the supreme and obvious confidence of the players as they approached Ibrox for the September League clash chanting "Champions of Europe", as indeed they were.

But this September day saw a tough Rangers side, whose tackling was ferocious and robust. To their shame Celtic failed to rise above this and allowed themselves to be dragged into the nastiness. Murdoch in particular, a victim of a bad tackle early on in the game, seemed off colour and lethargic, and as a result Celtic's midfield did not function. Rangers scored early in the second half, something that need not have panicked Celtic, for with players like they had, there was enough time to equalize and possibly even win. Everyone now looked for Bobby to take hold of the game by the scruff of the neck. This he failed to do and paid the ultimate penalty of football criticism - that of not having his name mentioned in newspaper reports of the game. Rangers, although themselves sustaining a few injuries, played better football and possibly deserved their 1-0 victory.

It was one of these victories that was praised "not without cause but without end" by Rangers' apologists in the Press and in the streets of Scotland, whereas all it really meant was that Rangers were two points ahead at the start of a long League race. Hysterical headlines told us that Celtic's glory days were at an end and that Rangers with their new summer signings were about to take over. This was of course moonshine, but Celtic sustained another and more serious blow the following Wednesday night.

It is amazing how often it happens that a defeat by Rangers is a catalyst for another defeat, in sympathy as it were, with the first one. This one however was less easily redeemable than other ones, for it was the visit of Dinamo Kiev to Celtic Park to provide the opposition for Celtic's first defence of the European Cup.

Once again Murdoch went through his own private hell of simply being unable to get going until too late. The whole side was nervous, unsteady and - always a clear sign of a team in trouble - argued with each other, often blaming others for things that were quite clearly their own fault. The Ukranians scored in the fourth minute and then on the half hour mark, so that half time was reached with Parkhead enveloped in introverted silence with the atmosphere reminiscent of a cemetery or a public library. This was in total contrast to the pre-match atmosphere of frenzied and sustained singing and chanting.

Brave efforts early in the second half did bring some reward as Lennox scored on the hour mark, but an equalizer would not come against this superbly drilled and organized defence. Murdoch, who had allowed himself to be too penned back in the first half, surged forward; cajoling, encouraging and exhorting in search of that elusive goal that would have at least given the side a draw and some sort of a chance in Kiev. But it would not come, and the crowd departed Parkhead that night with Celtic's grip on their European Cup appearing to be a very tenuous one indeed.

Bobby's wife Kathleen would always say that "Bobby was his own fiercest critic" in that he knew when he was off form and knew that the problem needed to be addressed. The problem is that, as in other walks of life, bad luck and bad form does not necessarily come in one isolated game. There is often a run of it. It follows you around. Conversely of course nothing succeeds like success and good breaks are often given when they are not required. Twas ever thus!

The return was in Kiev in a fortnight's time, and perhaps the thought of foreign travel was playing a part in worrying the Celtic men. In addition to Ukraine (and the players remembered with horror their problems in getting back from Georgia eighteen months previously after they had played Dinamo Kiev in the Cup Winners' Cup), there was also of course the trip at the end of October to Argentina to play Racing Club in the World Club Championship. These are long trips in the early years of the 21st century. In the 1960's they must have seemed like trips to another planet.

That things were going from bad to worse became apparent on Saturday 23rd September, a few days after the home defeat at the hands of Kiev. St.Johnstone came to town, and although the Perth men were doing very well and would turn out to give Celtic more bother than most teams during the Celtic glory years, no-one expected the European Champions to have any problem with them. In fact it was a fixture to which the support looked to iron out a few frowns and soothe a sorrowing breast or two.

As it happened, it made things a lot worse. It was the forwards who decided to play rubbish that day. After 37 minutes Celtic lost a man when Jimmy Johnstone retaliated against Kenny Aird and was promptly sent off. The referee had little option.

Soon after that the Saints went ahead and it was only late in the game that the equalizer came. In total desperation Murdoch had moved up to the forward line, and it was Bobby himself who scored the goal. Attempts were redoubled to get the winner, but it would not come, and the Sunday papers were totally justified in their banner headlines that Celtic were in trouble.

The chickens of summer time complacency came home

to roost with a vengeance on October 4th in the distant fields of Kiev. Ironically, Celtic played some of their best football since Lisbon and with a little luck and a little self-restraint, might well have won the game. Celtic played brilliantly for an hour, but with no tangible result, then it all happened within two minutes.

First Murdoch, in an almost criminal act of culpable idiocy (as he himself would admit), got himself sent off by fussy Italian referee Antonio Sbardella for throwing the ball away in disgust at a free kick awarded against Celtic. It was not all that bad an offence, but he had been booked previously - again for a fairly innocuous looking tackle - and he really should have known better. In tears he begged the referee for clemency, but off he had to go! He left reluctantly, his head covered with his Celtic jersey which he had peeled off. Murdoch's feeling of remorse for letting the side down was something that would stay with him for the rest of his life.

He was thus in the dressing room in disgrace and having already felt the justifiable wrath of Stein when Lennox scored. It was from an Auld free kick which floated over the defence and Lennox was able to squeeze the ball home. 29 minutes were left for Celtic to win the game. The goals scored were now 2 each, but Kiev had scored more in Glasgow.

Murdoch's feelings as his team mates fought for the equalizer are easy to imagine. There was the normal churning of the innards when any Celtic fan watches his team involved in a close finish. In Murdoch's case, there was a deep sense of guilt, an angry frustration at the officious referee, a feeling of injustice and also, one suspects, a feeling of apprehension for his future. Stein might well decide (and with some cause) to make Murdoch the scapegoat for the defeat and relegate him to the second string, promoting the impressive David Cattenach instead.

Late in the game, John Hughes scored. Celtic had virtually no supporters with them in Kiev, so the goal was acknowledged by only the Celtic bench and some Scottish journalists. There were however 85,000 Ukranians there, and they were able to impose their collective will on the referee and compel him to disallow the goal, apparently for a barely visible push on the goalkeeper. In the absence of film, it is difficult to say whether the goal was a valid one or not, but it was the unanimous opinion of the Scottish journalists and the Celtic players that Hughes's goal was legitimate.

Salt was rubbed into the wound when Kiev scored in the last minute. It had been a brave performance by Celtic, but the fact was that they were out of the European Cup. There was something in this that was typical of Scotland, one feels. Just occasionally, Scotland produces world champions in some sport or other. It does not happen very often, and there is sometimes the concomitant feeling that one should feel guilty about it, and immediately do something to lose this success. It happened to Bonnie Prince Charlie at Derby in 1745, as well!

Murdoch clearly was upset at this turn of events on the European scene, but after a head to head discussion with Stein in which no punches were pulled, Bobby turned it on. The month of October, which saw Celtic lift the League Cup in an excellent Final against Dundee, was a good one on the Scottish scene. The Final against Dundee however, although a fine game, was not Celtic's best performance. That was undeniably the Semi Final when they beat Morton 7-1 in a game which was totally exhilarating from start to finish. Celtic, the strain apparently off them and with a point to prove, began to play the way that they had played the previous season. "Why hadn't we seen this against Kiev?" the supporters asked themselves.

That was fine, until South America beckoned. One of

the unfortunate side effects of Celtic's win in Lisbon was their involvement in this unofficial championship of the world, in this case against Racing Club of Buenos Aires, Argentina. Argentina in 1967 was a little known place. We knew that it was big, they once had a dictator called Peron, they exported beef (a few years ago some contaminated corned beef from either Argentina or Uruguay - did it matter? - had caused typhoid in Aberdeen) but little else was known about that faraway country.

The only recent British contact with Argentina had been a year past summer in July 1966. It was the Quarter Final of the World Cup. Argentina were playing England. As a rule, Scottish supporters (and certainly all Celtic fans) would support Argentina against England. It so happened that England edged through that extremely controversial game, and we all sympathised with the Argentine claims of biased refereeing, cheating etc.

How ironic it was then that the Argentines (who always had a huge chip on their shoulders about Great Britain and its Empire anyway) would associate Scotland with England in this respect, and wish to get their own back in a particularly brutal and violent way! Even more ironic it was that the feelings of hatred against British Imperialism (brought to their logical but absurd conclusion in their foolish, vainglorious and tragic invasion of the Falkland Islands in 1982) should be directed against Celtic - the one team in Great Britain whose supporters openly rejected the values of the British Empire, espousing instead the cause of Irish Republicanism!

The first game was played at Hampden Park on October 18th. Celtic would say that the move to Hampden was an attempt to get the whole country behind them etc. but cynics were convinced that it was to pack in a few more fans and earn a few more bucks to pay for the appalling cost of the flight to South America. At Hampden, the world had an early example of what to expect in South America. Racing Club did indeed arrive carrying the luggage of the 1966 World Cup. Celtic won 1-0, Murdoch playing very well, but the ugly side of Latin football was also exposed in the hacking, spitting, elbowing and punching. It was a salutary lesson, and quite a few alarm bells started ringing about the advisability of going to Argentina with some of the players expressing apprehension. But Celtic were committed to going.

There are times when apparent "cowardice" is the braver course. This is a case in point. Had Celtic withdrawn at this point on the grounds of what happened at Hampden, there is every chance that FIFA would have supported them, and pressure might than have been put on Argentina to clean up their act, or face international isolation. Celtic however felt that they had obligations and went.

They actually flew out hours after winning the Scottish League Cup. The League Cup Final was an excellent example of Scottish football played by two good footballing teams in Celtic and Dundee. The score was 5-3 and those who were at that game remember it as being a thriller. It was ironic however that men like Murdoch now picked up League Cup medals (in Murdoch's case, his third winner's medal) en route, as it were, to other things. It is a shame too that what was about to happen in that distant land would overshadow the good side of Celtic.

Every effort was made by the Argentine authorities to unsettle the Celtic team and their officials. The living accommodation was sub-standard with all the amenities of the average Scottish Youth Hostel, the food was dreadful and the whole atmosphere with armed police surrounding the building was hostile and intimidating. Even without football, Argentina was the land of coups, military dictatorships and people who quite literally "disappeared", so perhaps the high police profile was natural in that country. For

Glaswegians, it was totally alien.

Worse was to happen before the game started. During the pre-match warm-up Ronnie Simpson was felled by a missile thrown apparently from the crowd, although some Celtic players believed that it was done by a journalist, photographer or even a Racing Club reserve. The stunned Simpson had to be replaced by a brave John Fallon. Once again, the idea of refusing to play was discussed, but in that atmosphere, there would have been a full scale riot and possibly even a bloodbath.

Murdoch would admit later to being terrified, but play he did and played well, in so far as he was allowed to by the cynical Argentine tackling and the weak Uruguayan referee. The official awarded Celtic a penalty early on (converted by Gemmell) and clearly felt that that was Celtic's ration for the day. Racing scored twice and as the away goals rule did not apply, this meant a play-off in neutral Uruguay with a Paraguayan referee.

The Celtic party was now openly divided. Chairman Bob Kelly was in favour of the next flight back to Scotland, a view shared by most of the players who did have genuine fears for their safety, but Kelly was outvoted by his other Directors who pointed out that Uruguay, although still in South America, was neutral and likely to be fair. Indeed even on the broader political scene, Uruguay enjoyed a certain reputation for calmness and stability, being called the "Switzerland of South America". Ironically it was one occasion where Bob Kelly's judgement was right, and if Celtic had listened to him, Celtic would have been spared a great deal of anguish.

In fact, the country of Uruguay, if anything, was pro-Celtic and anti-Argentina, but relationships between the two teams and indeed the players had deteriorated to such an extent that constructive football was no longer possible. Murdoch, like everyone else, was homesick and afraid and clearly would far rather have been playing at some place like Rugby Park, Pittodrie or even Ibrox than on this alien and apparently barbaric continent.

The game went ahead on Saturday 4th November 1967. There was no direct radio commentary back to Scotland, although summaries were relayed to the tense and nervous Scottish public. In fact Celtic lost that game, but that was almost incidental to what else went on. John Clark at one point clashed with an Argentinian and was sent off, but the beleagured referee apparently sent off Bobby Lennox by mistake. Bertie Auld was sent off and didn't go! John Hughes and Jimmy Johnstone were also dismissed, and Tommy Gemmell gave the most blatant kick in the privates to a deserving Argentine case that the history of television has ever seen!

The dismissal of John Hughes was probably justified, but the referee, a Dr.Rudolfo Osario, who "didn't know what day of the week it was" according to Bobby Murdoch, said that he had sent off Murdoch. This at least was a pardonable confusion, for Hughes and Murdoch did have a certain resemblance to each other, and occasionally even the Parkhead punters got them wrong! Hughes was bigger and bulkier, but their hair styles were sometimes similar. But Murdoch was innocent and in time was exonerated.

One particular incident however, shown on television, but not highlighted at the time (as there was so much other juicy stuff around!) reflected great credit on Murdoch and earned him the applause of the Uruguayan crowd. One of the tactics used by the Argentinians, particularly after they had gone ahead and were trying to kill the game, was to feign injury. Now there was nothing new about this - the rolling over and over in apparent agony, the screams of righteous indignation etc. But on this occasion when one Argentinian collapsed in a heap of non-existent pain one yard from the touchline, Murdoch merely grabbed hold of him and pulled him over the line so that the game could continue. TV pictures showed quite clearly the approval of the crowd.

This did not hide the fact however that Celtic were by no means entirely the injured innocents in this dreadful business. All this was shameful stuff, and Celtic's reputation suffered immensely. Indeed the club themselves showed their disapproval of some players' conduct by fining everyone a token amount to show that they were taking this seriously and also perhaps to head off further action from elsewhere. In the players' defence it has to be said that the treatment meted out to Jimmy Johnstone in particular was unparalleled in its ferocity and the whole trip was a disaster from the word go, but the Celtic historian has to admit that the faults were not all one-sided.

What is to the team's credit is their recovery from that cataclysm. They returned no longer looking invincible. In fact quite a few of them had been severely mauled by a traumatic experience. Jim Craig, for example, had picked up a bug and was out of the team for some time, and many others did not play as well as they could have, looking lethargic and uninterested. The positive aspect of all this however was that the large heads of the summer had been severely shrunk and the feeling now grew that success did not necessarily come to them on a plate. The Scottish League had to be won - and of course the League Cup was already on the shelf to encourage and remind them of success.

Celtic's play from their return to Scotland until the New Year was not necessarily all that good. This was hardly surprising in view of what had happened, but results were generally ground out - an exception was a great game once again in the tradition of jousts between Celtic and Dundee, when Celtic won 5-4 on December 16th at Dens Park. In these circumstances, the manager looks to players like

Murdoch. Bobby did have a few bad moments, but he seldom had a bad game, and it was noticeable that the supporters who occasionally vented their frustrations on other players never did so with Murdoch. Murdoch showed that as well as having great playing ability, he also had something that was almost as valuable, namely character.

He also showed some sort of ability as a goalscorer. Since he had been moved back to the right half position, he scored fewer goals - but they were often crucial ones. Mention was made of the game against St.Johnstone in September when Murdoch scored the goal that gave Celtic a point after Jimmy Johnstone had been sent off. In similar circumstances, he scored against Dundee United at Parkhead to earn Celtic a draw - this time Willie Wallace was the offender who received the early bath. Also on November 11th, the first game after the fragile Celtic team had returned from South America, physical and mental health shattered and confidence at a low ebb, it was Murdoch who scored the key second half goal at Broomfield to confirm the points against a hard working and determined Airdrie side who were threatening to equalize.

Celtic now approached the January 2nd fixture against Rangers with Rangers two points ahead. Rangers too were winning games (not always convincingly) and Celtic were getting no help from any other team whom they might have expected to beat Rangers. It seemed that Celtic would have to beat them themselves. In 1968 teams only played each other twice, and therefore January 2nd was Celtic's last opportunity to catch Rangers if they were not to "be needing snookers" i.e. to have to rely on other teams doing it for them.

The game was a personal nightmare for goalkeeper John Fallon, and something that haunts the loveable big man to this very day. "Some people talk as if it was the only gemme I ever played there!" he has been heard to say before a game at Parkhead where he is a regular attender. Ironically, John, a great friend of Murdoch, was a last minute change for Ronnie Simpson who had injured himself against Clyde the previous day.

Twice with Murdoch outstanding, Celtic went ahead and were really well on top of Rangers, but twice did John Fallon make mistakes and allow Rangers to get the draw that they did not deserve, his second mistake coming so late in the game that Celtic had no time to address themselves to going for a winner. Murdoch was distraught, both for his friend John Fallon and because he himself had scored the goal that had seemed to win the game. It was a magnificent swivel and turn inside the penalty area and a wonderful left foot shot.

This was bad enough, but things turned serious for Celtic that season when they went out of the Scottish Cup at the first time of asking. It was to the strong going Dunfermline, but it happened at Parkhead in front of 47,000 people, the only possible excuse being the absence of Jim Craig. The Sunday Express carried the headline of "It's a Long Way From Lisbon". The Scottish League was now all that was left for Murdoch and Celtic that season.

In truth Celtic did not really deserve all that much at that stage of the season, and had played particularly badly against the Pars in that Cup tie. Too many players looked sluggish and unhappy and Murdoch himself was dragged down by the general lack of punch. Credit must also be given to Dunfermline who played particularly well that day, although things might have been totally different if an apparently good goal by Jim Brogan in the first half had not been disallowed by the referee for offside against Willie Wallace.

So the Scottish Cup had gone for Celtic. Dunfermline Athletic would in fact win the Scottish Cup that year, but for Celtic all that remained was the League. For Celtic, games (other than the January 2nd shocker) tended to be won, albeit not always too convincingly. But annoyingly, Rangers too kept on winning to maintain the two point differential.

A further feeling of frustration may have been caused in Murdoch that spring by his inability to win back his Scotland place. He had last played in a shocker of a 0-1 defeat in Northern Ireland that autumn and he and others had been made to carry the can. In truth, it had been an awful performance but in Murdoch's defence it must be stated that he had been played in the forward line - somewhere that anyone who had watched Celtic in the early 1960's would have told Scotland's Manager Bobby Brown was not his best position.

Yet from February onwards, the wheel turned slowly but inexorably in Celtic's favour. It all stemmed, according to Tommy Gemmell's book "The Big Shot", from a meeting in the table tennis room at Parkhead on the day before St. Valentine's day. The atmosphere was not about love, but neither was it in the vein of a Caponesque St.Valentine's day massacre. It was Jock Stein at his best. The position was put to the players. They were a better team than Rangers, but Rangers were still two points ahead. Yet Celtic had to put the pressure on Rangers by winning games and by winning them convincingly. Football always has been a game played in the head as much as on the field, and if Celtic could paralyse their opposition, particularly if they could be well ahead by half time, news would reach Rangers and dispirit them.

Murdoch nodded in agreement with this. He was now, more than cver, a key man in the Parkhead team for his midfield colleague Bertie Auld had been injured in a midweek game at Motherwell and would effectively be out for the season. Auld's replacement would be Charlie Gallagher. Charlie and Bobby had been through hard times together. Both had played in the dysfunctional forward lines that disgraced the colours in the early 1960's. Bobby had of course prospered under Stein, whereas Charlie had often given the impression of being a perpetual reserve, even though a very willing one.

Yet Charlie had been capped for Eire, and the feeling persisted among the true connoisseurs of football (particularly those of the older generations who yearned for Patsy Gallacher and Tommy McInally) that we had not yet seen the best of Charlie Gallagher. We were soon to be satisfied. In some ways 1968 was to be the much deserved finest hour for the phlegmatic Charlie whose approach to life seemed to resemble one of the current songs in the Hit Parade that spring "Me, The Peaceful Heart" sung by fellow Glaswegian, Lulu.

The first game of the Gallagher reawakening was a disappointing 2-0 win over Stirling Albion, a team who really should have been hammered much more comprehensively. But that was only a settling-in game to allow Bobby and Charlie to read each other in midfield. After that the team really upped a gear or two, beginning with a 6-0 demolition of Kilmarnock. Rugby Park, heavily sanded that day and an unlucky ground for Bobby as regards injuries, saw him replaced by Jimmy Quinn in the second half, but not before he had destroyed Killie. It was a classic example of co-ordinated midfield play - Murdoch characteristically bludgeoning his way through the right side of the midfield feeding the eager Jimmy Johnstone and buzzbomb Lennox, while the elegant Gallagher sprayed passes on the left. Upfront the forwards were all on song, and Killie were lucky to get off with a 6-0 defeat.

That the corner had been well and truly turned was clearly seen in the way that teams like St.Johnstone and Dundee United were put to the sword, and of course Celtic had the "advantage" (if that is the word) of not having to play in any other tournament. Indeed the way that Celtic, with inspired midfield duo of Gallagher and Murdoch, were playing made supporters regret even more their early exit from other competitions. Rangers, by contrast, were visibly toiling. They would eventually lose to Hearts in the Scottish Cup and Leeds United in the Fairs Cities Cup (as the UEFA Cup was then called) but they still would not drop points in the League.

The psychological war was clearly won when Rangers made the silly decision to pull out of the Glasgow Cup. Apart from being an insult to one of the oldest and most honourable tournaments of them all (words like "cowardice" were being openly bandied about in the Press and public) and it seemed that they did not want to face a Murdoch-inspired Celtic of that spring. Celtic perhaps should have shown a little more cowardice the previous autumn in not going to South America, but this was Rangers afraid, apparently, of Celtic and the Glasgow Cup! The effect on their players must have been considerable. Their own fans were certainly far from impressed - and the Celtic fans would not let them forget it!

It was on March 30th however that pressure mounted on Rangers. They defeated Airdrie at Broomfield by the narrowest of margins, 2-1 to maintain that galling two point lead. Yet they must have been intimidated by the news from Tannadice of Celtic's spectacular 5-0 skelping of Dundee United. In fact it was Dundee United who first chipped at Rangers. United had been so embarrassed by their thrashing at the hands of Celtic that Manager Jerry Kerr tightened up their defence, metaphorically booted a few bums and ensured that they fought a little harder to earn a 2-2 draw against Rangers in the following midweek.

The lead was now only one point and Celtic had a far better goal difference. Five games remained. Celtic had to dig deep into their reserves of character to beat Aberdeen at

Pittodrie - a game which Murdoch would say was one of the hardest all season - but no more so than Rangers had to do against Raith Rovers at Stark's Park the following Saturday in a game where dodgy refereeing decisions played a large part.

But then came Wednesday 17th April. Celtic were playing at Hampden in the Glasgow Cup Final, the tournament which Rangers had run away from - a game they won 8-0 at a canter against Clyde, playing some unstoppable football. Rangers were playing in the League at Cappielow, home of that most quixotic of all teams, Greenock Morton. It was apparently a great game of football with Rangers being twice two goals down and coming back to earn a draw. But it was only a draw, enough to give Celtic the edge on goal average with only two games to go. Round about the time that the Glasgow Cup was being presented to Celtic, the good news reached Hampden.

But Celtic's next opponents were - of all people - Greenock Morton at Parkhead, while the dispirited Rangers went to Kilmarnock. Both of these games were tight, unbelievably tight affairs. After a tremendous reception from the Parkhead fans, Morton dug in to defend. All of the second half was played virtually in the Morton penalty area with Murdoch quite blatantly playing as a forward - simply because there was no midfield battle, Morton having withdrawn to their own penalty area! Yet Morton, eager to draw against both of the Old Firm, held on to their 1-1 scoreline until the very last minute of the game.

Meanwhile Rangers had edged a win at Kilmarnock in a game that had already finished. The transistor radios told Parkhead those grim tidings. It looked as if the pendulum which had swung tantalisingly in Celtic's direction for a few days was to swing back decisively to Rangers. The memory remains of Murdoch surging forward repeatedly throughout the second half, but losing out again and again to a well timed tackle or sending his shot askew. It now looked as if all his good work was going for naught.

But just as those of little faith had decided that Celtic were not going to do it that day (and therefore that season) and were trooping disconsolately towards the exits, Murdoch picked up a ball in midfield, charged towards the corner flag, looked up and saw that the penalty area was full. In these circumstances, a hopeful punt can often get results, for there can always be ricochets and in-offs and goodness knows what.

The result this time was like something out of a Marx Brothers film. The ball came to Hughes, he miskicked, the ball broke to Wallace, he in turn miskicked and this time the ball came to the predatory Lennox. He made the third miskick of the sequence as the ball bounced on the hard ground of the goalmouth, hit him on the shin and was prodded into the net.

It was one of the worst goals imaginable, but Parkhead went wild with delight. The memory remains of the Morton player hanging on the net in chagrin at having lost a goal so late, and in such bizarre circumstances, but it was Celtic's day and, as it turned out, Celtic's Championship, for Rangers were psyched out by that late goal into losing to Aberdeen at Ibrox in their last fixture.

This was on Scottish Cup Final day. Murdoch and the Celtic team were at Hampden watching Dunfermline beat Hearts when they were told that they were effectively champions. The last game was at East End Park Dunfermline that following Wednesday night in a game that did not matter unless Celtic lost 16-0. It was now a gala occasion and broke all sorts of records in that dangerously overcrowded, trim provincial ground who laughed at the sight of Dunfermline's manager George Farm parading the Scottish Cup while Celtic's manager Jock Stein tried to steal it from him. It was a fine piece of clowning from two teams who have always had a good relationship with each other.

Murdoch had been an ever present that season. In some ways, it was the most dramatic of Stein's years. 1967 obviously had more glory, and some would argue that the 1969 team was an even better one, in playing terms, than 1967, but 1968 was the year in which Celtic went to hell - and came back. Phrases like "character building" and "when the going gets tough, the tough get going" were peppered all over the newspapers to sum up that season, and they were all justified.

No-one had shown better than Bobby Murdoch what it meant to be a Celt. Next season would see Murdoch playing even better.

# A Man for all Seasons

Season 1968-69 saw Celtic more or less irresistible in Scotland, (although they were twice defeated by Rangers in the League) and but for a very unfortunate occurrence at Parkhead against A.C.Milan, they might well have won the European Cup again. There are those who say that the 1968-69 side actually played better football than the 1966-67 side; others say that this is blasphemy, for there never could be a better team than that of 1967. Not that it matters. It is a pleasant problem for Celtic historians to discuss.

Before the season got properly under way that year, something happened which illustrated how important a force Celtic were in European politics, let alone European sport. In August 1968, the Soviet Union invaded Czechoslovakia. This was because the Czechs had shown under Alexander Dubceck a tendency towards liberalism. The prickly Moscow tyranny construed this as flirting with Capitalism, and as Czechoslovakia happened to be one of the countries furthest west in the Soviet block - action was deemed necessary. The Soviet response was naked, brutal aggression, by no means dissimilar to that taken by Hitler 30 years previously. The tanks were sent in, the ringleaders were arrested and at one stroke the Cold War which had been slowly thawing the past 10 or 15 years, froze up again. Although the Western countries stopped short of military action (which would have undoubtedly released the possibility of nuclear war), other sanctions were taken. Indeed the US were by no means unhappy about this turn of events for it deflected world opinion away from their own piece of genocide in Vietnam.

By this time the draw for the European Cup had taken place with Celtic due to play Ferencvaros of Hungary, an Iron Curtain (or Soviet bloc country) who had themselves seen Soviet brutality in 1956 in similar circumstances. Bob Kelly now approached UEFA and after a struggle persuaded them to redraw the European Cup so that as few teams as possible had to cross the Iron Curtain. Celtic were to play St.Etienne of France in the revised draw, and it was a sign of how much clout Celtic now carried under Kelly. The British Establishment were mightily impressed and Kelly himself, some would say, got his reward at the New Year - and, as we shall see, it wasn't by a victory over Rangers.

How much Murdoch meant to the Celtic team that season could easily be seen if we examine what happened in the month of September when Murdoch was out with an ankle injury. It was in fact an aggravation of his old ankle injury, and one that was to cause him all sorts of problems in the future, as the aggravations became more frequent and more severe. It was all the more galling for the circumstances in which it had been picked up. It was in Dublin on September 4th in a game for the Scottish League against the League of Ireland. It was becoming rather surprising that such quaintly anachronistic fixtures were still being played in 1968, but they did have a point in that they could give aspiring young Internationalists a trial.

This was hardly necessary in Murdoch's case however, for everyone knew how good he was. Yet Murdoch was desperate to play and indeed do anything to win back his International place. Stein was nevertheless justifiably angry at the injury to his star man in such a comparatively meaningless fixture. Murdoch's withdrawal from the field that night meant that the game petered out into a dull 0-0 draw - a huge disappointment for the Dubliners who had turned up to see Murdoch and other Celtic players in action.

Murdoch missed two League games, a European game and a League Cup game. His absence was hardly noticed in the League Cup game, for Celtic beat the hapless Hamilton Accies 10-0, but September 14th at Parkhead saw Rangers beat Celtic 4-2. It was a game riddled with refereeing mistakes and a draw (at least) would have been a fairer result, but there could be little doubt that Celtic were missing the dominating midfield presence of Bobby Murdoch. Murdoch had been playing for Celtic in the two games in August in which they beat Rangers in the League Cup, and it was hard not to connect a Rangers win with Murdoch's absence.

More alarming still was the trip to France in the European Cup with Murdoch's ankle knock still not yet recovered. Celtic played under par and a 0-2 scoreline raised yet again the spectre of last year's First Round knock out. But by the time the French champions came to Parkhead on October 2nd, Murdoch had played two League games - a 1-1 draw at Dunfermline in which he had looked less than totally fit, then a more convincing 2-1 defeat of Aberdeen - and he was in modern parlance "up for it".

It was just as well that he was, for he was axiomatic to the Celtic team. Jock Stein, writing in the Celtic View of September 25th 1968 in the context of the draw at Dunfermline, has this to say;

" ...and perhaps the most significant reason of all - the loss of Bobby Murdoch. Despite the excellence of the reserve power the Murdoch man has an all round power and influence which is badly missed particularly in vital matches. Take the Dunfermline match for instance - Bobby was not fully tuned up - how could he be? Murdoch is a big heavy lad who needs lots of training after an injury, and this he didn't get for the game against Dunfermline.

"We needed him badly and big hearted Bobby turned out, and despite the fact that several of his passes were misplaced he put in a power of work and helped turn the tide in the second half. Under the circumstances, I thought he did really well, and apart from that, when the Murdoch name appears in the line up - I feel the opposition get an inferiority complex."

It would be hard to find a more complete or public commendation of a player by a Manager, and this quote is an excellent example of how highly Stein rated Bobby's contribution to Celtic F.C.

The St.Etienne game at Parkhead was classic Celtic at their European best. A nervy and frustrating first half had been perked up by a 45th minute penalty when McBride was brought down. Gemmell converted, and following an intensely upbeat and expectant half time interval (in both ground and dressing room), Celtic scored three in the second half to win comfortably. Murdoch simply took charge of the midfield that night, and those who had forgotten that Celtic were champions of Europe a mere 18 months previously, were now reminded of that fact. These few weeks in the autumn of 1968-69 showed how indebted Celtic were to Bobby Murdoch.

From then on that season, Celtic and Murdoch fired on all cylinders. The form of the team steadily improved. October had some scratchy games but November 13th saw one of the finest European performances of the lot as Red Star Belgrade were torn apart to the tune of 5-1. Much was made of Jimmy Johnstone who, because of his fear of flying, was allowed to miss the away leg if Celtic were enough goals ahead. Certainly Jimmy was on top form that night but not far behind him came the great Bobby Murdoch. It was Bobby who scored the first goal, and it was Bobby who kept Jimmy supplied for his constant teasing of the hitherto considered top-class opposition. If Jimmy was the producer, it was Bobby who was the provider.

The first goal was a textbook prototype. A free kick to

Celtic in the early minutes of the game a few yards into the Red Star half. Murdoch took the free-kick, found Jimmy Johnstone with it and immediately charged forward. Red Star detailed two men to watch the dangerous Johnstone. This left a gap for Murdoch on the edge of the box. While the crowd and the Red Star defence expected some Johnstone trickery, Jimmy immediately returned the ball to Bobby who hammered home.

This was typical of the Murdoch - Johnstone combination. Jimmy, arguably one of the greatest ball players of all time, possibly needed two things to bring out the best in him. One was the discipline and guidance of Jock Stein; it was never the smoothest of relationships, but it worked most of the time - and the other was the friendship and support, on and off the field, of men like Bobby Lennox and Bobby Murdoch, men who were perpetually cheery, optimistic and approachable. It was certainly a very profitable relationship that Murdoch and Johnstone enjoyed, and Johnstone was always very careful to praise Murdoch for his inch-perfect passes.

Johnstone would call Murdoch "Sam". This was after the Glasgow contractor Sam B. Allison who had the job of demolishing the hideous slums of the Gorbals, not all that far away from Celtic Park. It was part of the 1960's Urban Renewal project. Murdoch acquired the name "Sam" after an incident one day in training at Seamill Hydro. Pots of paint had been borrowed for players to dribble round and practise their ball control skills. Murdoch, being a little clumsier than other players (which perhaps explains why he was a better wing half than an inside forward) managed to knock over a few, in the same way as Sam B. Allison was knocking over the Victorian death traps of the Industrial Revolution. Amidst laughter and jokes that the paint pots beat Murdoch 2-1, the nickname "Sam" was coined.

He also occasionally was called "Chopper". There are

several reasons why a man could earn that particular nickname, but in this case it was a term of respect for his constant willingness to get involved in the action. Murdoch did not lack courage and would never shirk a tackle, even though in his case he would have had every excuse for avoiding the occasional one. This was the problem with his ankle which flared up every now and again.

Celtic's exit from Europe came in March in tragic circumstances. A.C.Milan were the opponents and the first game was in the San Siro in the snow. One does not normally associate Italy with blizzards, but this was February in North Italy, and it did happen. Celtic played a good defensive game and thoroughly deserved their 0-0 draw, Murdoch nominally in the forward line, yet deployed as an extra defender.

The Second Leg at Parkhead on March 12th began with a fantastic atmosphere, so typical of the great European nights at Parkhead in the late 1960's.

The high floodlights gave off their silvery light, the crowd arrived slowly at first. Half an hour before the kick-off, one wondered if there was really a European game on to-night, but yes, there was that small knot of Milan supporters, good natured and clearly finding the problems of Scottish beer and whisky more difficult to contend with than their normal Italian vino. Then suddenly one looked round and the ground was full of passionate fans singing "It's a Grand Old Team to Play For" and "We Shall Not Be Moved" and on this occasion a chant which went "Attack! Attack! Attack! Attack! Attack!"- so inspiring for the Celtic players, and so intimidating (supposedly) for the opposition.

But not tonight, sadly. It was a mistake by Billy McNeill early in the first half which lost the day for Celtic. Yet as was perceptively pointed out at the time, "Where was the sweeper-up?" to cover for such mistakes, and John Clark, normally so reliable and deservedly called "The Brush" was possibly upset by a strange team selection which saw both himself and Jim Brogan playing in the defence. Murdoch was wearing the number 10 shorts that night, but it meant nothing. He was still in the midfield.

The team buckled to the rescue task, but this time they were up against a really excellent European team who would go on and lift the trophy that year, and all the bustle of Murdoch was of no avail. One or two half chances came the way of the Celtic forwards, but the game finished with the Italians winners by 1-0. The longer the night went on, the more Murdoch was seen as an attacker, for the use of both Clark and Brogan in the defence meant no place for Bobby Lennox whose pace might just have made a difference. There was also a clear reliance, perhaps an over-reliance, on wingers Jimmy Johnstone and John Hughes to break down the defence. Sadly both of them had a quiet night with A.C.'s German full back, Karl-Heinz Schnellinger, outstanding against both, and his blonde hair so ubiquitous at both sides of the defence. The deathly, cemetery silence at full time spoke volumes about the support whose expectations had been so high.

An interesting conversation apparently took place between Jock Stein and Cesare Maldini, the Assistant Coach of A.C. Milan about Bobby Murdoch. It was after the game, and congratulations and commiserations had been graciously exchanged. Maldini, who had won the European Cup for A.C. Milan in 1963 as a player, praised Celtic and singled out Bobby Murdoch. Stein smiled. He could hardly have done otherwise, for he himself had not infrequently described Murdoch as "the best player in Britain", but then Stein went on to add "Yes, and what a player he would be in your match set-up of one game a week". The Italian nodded sagely. In a lengthy career which would see the aged Maldini as the Manager of Paraguay in the 2002 World Cup, Maldini would see many fine players. Few presumably would be better than Bobby Murdoch.

It was Stein's reply that was more interesting however. This was clearly a reference to several things. It was a comment on Murdoch's prolonged, energy-sapping midfield role with the club in a country where playing two games per week happened more often than not, if the player was involved in European and International fixtures. It also perhaps said something about the Scottish climate with its perpetual heavy grounds, particularly at the end of winter in February and March, and it was perhaps an indirect comment on Murdoch's weight problem - something that was going to hit him soon in a big way and perhaps, to Stein at least, the early indications of which were already visible.

The exit from Europe was a major blow to all at Parkhead but Celtic were soon able to say "Sorry" to the support for their European failure, and they did this in a particularly impressive way. The three domestic trophies were decided in the month of April, and Celtic won them all. Celtic had always been ahead in the League because of Rangers' poor start. Even the loss of both Old Firm games did not stop Celtic's consistent play that season. There were a couple of runs of draws - one on the hard pitches in December, and another in April with the flag in sight, but Celtic ended up five points clear.

Arguably Celtic's best game in the League was on St. Andrews Day, November 30th 1968 at Easter Road - a ground which frequently saw Celtic at their best. The strong going Hibs had gone 2-1 up with only 15 minutes remaining. McNeill then equalized five minutes later and Celtic simply entered destruction mode. Murdoch stood on the centre spot, clapped his hands, then in the remaining ten minutes, three more goals were scored to give Celtic a 5-2 victory. It was a typical Celtic and typical Murdoch performance.

A less typical Murdoch performance came at Ibrox on

January 2nd when, for the second time that season, Rangers beat Celtic in the League. Murdoch was played in the forward line that day to allow both Clark and Brogan to play in the centre of the defence. It was a curiously defensive formation - out of character with Stein's normal selections for Scottish games, although he did try it in Europe - and the price was paid in an extraordinarily low key game which Rangers won from a soft penalty after Billy McNeill allegedly handled.

Celtic had a Knight of the Realm in charge of them for that game. Sir Robert Kelly was now the name of the club's Chairman, as announced in the New Year's Honours List. Not everyone was entirely in agreement with this (even among those who did not consider Honours Lists as a patronising, anachronistic sham) for there were those with very long memories of Murdoch's early years at the club and other examples of shocking, stubborn, selfish ineptitude. Sir John Stein might have been a better idea, perhaps - but at least the knighthood of Sir Robert Kelly gave yet another indication of how important Celtic now were. Was there a connection between the Knighthood and his "principled" stand against the Soviet invasion of Czechoslovakia? It certainly was a long way away from that grim August day in 1963 where Mr.Kelly had wisely gone to see the reserves play at Dumfries, thereby escaping a lynching attempt at the hands of an angry mob following a dismal Parkhead draw with Queen of the South.

Celtic soon bounced back from the New Year misfortune at Ibrox however and lost ground was soon recovered. Another fine game that year was on April 1st at Muirton Park, Perth when Celtic were 0-2 down at half time, but buckled to the task and won 3-2 with the last goal coming more or less on the final whistle. Once again it was Murdoch who inspired the team in that glorious second half, finding men with inch perfect passes and inspiring the forwards to greater efforts against a first class side in Willie Ormond's St.Johnstone.

The supporters were thus justified in singing:

*"Aye, Aye, Aye, Aye*
*We are the Glasgow Celtic*
*Wherever we go, we'll fear no foe*
*For we are the Glasgow Celtic!*

*Aye, Aye, Aye, Aye*
*Simpson is better than Yashin*
*Murdoch is better than Eusebio*
*And Johnstone is better than anyone!"*

The League was clinched in all but name in a draw at Kilmarnock on Monday 21st April and confirmed the following night when Dundee beat Rangers at Dens Park. That was in between the two remarkable Cup Finals of April 1969.The League Cup Final came along first on April 5th. It had been postponed because of a fire in the Main Stand at Hampden in October, and in splendid Easter weather, Celtic played magnificent football to beat 6-2 a Hibernian team by no means short of talent. Murdoch, as always, was in great form, but it is no insult to him to say that he did not stand out that day - simply because the rest of the team were equally good!

Three weeks later it was the Scottish Cup Final against Rangers.The team had gone in at half time three goals up against Hibs in the League Cup Final, and lo and behold, the same thing happened here! Stein had apparently had to calm them down at half time in the Hibs game, reminding them that the game had to be won and that "It'll certainly no' be three-nuthing against Rangers at half time" Oh no, Jock?

Even he occasionally got things wrong! Rangers

defensive frailities were pounced upon by the Celtic forwards, and the game finished 4-0. At one point Rangers fans invaded the field looking for a quick way out, but the sadistic Glasgow police pushed them back into the terracing to compel them to watch the rest of the game!

For Murdoch, there was special credit for his lack of retaliation at a crucial point of the game. Alex Ferguson, who has since risen to dizzy heights as a Manager, seemed as if to headbutt Bobby. Contact was not made, and Bobby simply ignored the incident, knowing that Celtic were giving their answer on the field. Indeed they were, and seldom had there been such a one-sided Scottish Cup Final.

The most remarkable Cup-tie however came against Partick Thistle at the end of January. A sloppy defensive performance had thrown away a healthy lead at Firhill and a Replay was called for at Parkhead on January 29th. This game Murdoch (as was his wont) simply took by the scruff of the neck and inspired Celtic to an 8-1 victory, which should have been a lot more. Fearing an injury, Stein took Murdoch off and replaced him with Bertie Auld - and Parkhead simply rose to him for such a brilliant performance.

As if these three domestic triumphs were not enough for Murdoch that glorious spring, he also retained his place in the Scotland team, this time against West Germany in the World Cup. He had been brought back for the game against Cyprus in December and had scored in the 5-0 rout. This game however at Hampden against the World Cup runners up on April 16th was a different matter. Although the Scottish team disappointingly drew against the (unlucky) beaten finalists of 1966, it was Murdoch who scored the late equalizer following a nice one-two with Charlie Cooke of Chelsea. A few days after that, Bobby was named Scotland's Player of the Year and it was totally deserved. Modestly, Bobby would say that it was really for all the Celtic team. Maybe so, but it was Bobby who was making the Celtic team.

It was his friend, goalkeeper John Fallon who told him the news. A golf date had been arranged at Strathaven Golf Club. Bobby had left his house before Kathleen received the phone call. She immediately phoned Fallon who had not yet left, and thus it was that Fallon brought the news. Bobby in his book "All The Way With Celtic" says he cannot remember whether he duffed his first tee shot or not, and John confirms that there was a certain amount of celebration before the round actually started!

Having won the Scottish domestic treble, the defeat by A.C. Milan was made all the more galling. Revealingly, at the Scottish Cup Final in April, the Rangers fans started singing "A.C.Milan, A.C.Milan" to the tune of Auld Lang Syne, for they had no other ammunition left to hurl at Celtic, so complete had been Celtic's dominance in the Scottish League - even although Rangers had beaten Celtic at both Ibrox and Parkhead!

For Scotland, there remained the International Championship, this time played in the month of May and all televised live. Murdoch played in all three games - he was good in the 5-3 goal glut against Wales at Wrexham, mediocre (along with the rest of the team) in the depressing 1-1 draw in the rain at Hampden against Ireland and as he himself would admit, downright awful against England at Wembley in the 4-1 thrashing, and subsequently dropped by Manager Bobby Brown for the World Cup game against Cyprus at Hampden the following week.

He was not of course the only Scottish player to do badly in that game, played unusually (for the benefit of television) on a Saturday evening. In terms of previous and subsequent Wembley doings, the 1969 game was by no means the worst, but it was bad enough. Murdoch played twice for Scotland against England. Neither time did he do himself justice. He played although suffering from 'flu in

1966, and in 1969 he was simply jaded after a long season. He might have felt that he was made the scapegoat when he was dropped for the Cyprus game, but Bobby was always his own greatest critic and admitted that he had played badly.

He could even have claimed "mistaken identity" and said that he was not there at all! After the game he and Kathleen met up with John Hughes and his wife Mary who had been watching the game. They were in a taxi when one disappointed Scotsman came up to John Hughes and said "Hard Lines, Bobby", mistaking Hughes for Murdoch. It was a common mistake, made by supporters, commentators, journalists and even a South American referee in the World Club Championship game! From a distance at least (depending on hairstyles) there was a distinct resemblance. The main difference from a supporter's point of view was the way that they ran. John tended to run head down, while Bobby tended to play straight backed and head up. But John Hughes is convinced that he did not play at Wembley that night, so it must have been Bobby!

The ending was disappointing but it had been a season which had more ups than downs! A domestic treble, Player of the Year, the equalizing goal for Scotland against West Germany, the constant accolade and backing of Jock Stein who would say more than once "Bobby Murdoch is the best in Britain" and defy anyone with that famous withering look of his to disagree with him. Nobody did. There was also a strange attempt by Boca Juniors of Argentina to sign him. There was of course little chance of Murdoch going to the Argentine after what he had seen of their football in that unhappy experience of autumn 1967, and in any case, he had all that he wanted in Scotland - a good job that he loved, a Manager with total faith in him, a loving and attractive wife, two lovely children aged 4 and 2, success in everything. Things, however, were just about to become a little trickier for Bobby.

# The Battle of the Bulge

Life was sweet for Celtic fans in that glorious summer of 1969. The momentous month of April, in which all three Scottish trophies had been annexed, had warmed everyone up. Although the League Cup Final against Hibs had seen the best football played in one single game by Celtic probably since the 7-1 League Cup Final of 1957, it was of course the 4-0 thumping of Rangers in the Scottish Cup Final which produced the most pleasure. The horrors of that dreadful Cup final of 1963 had been more than adequately expunged from the hearts and minds of supporters and players, and it was now Rangers supporters who changed the subject whenever football was mentioned - or more revealingly, launched into an inane and pointless attack on other people's religion.

But in some ways, even Rangers were being left behind by this fabulous football machine. Europe beckoned and continued to beckon. That sad defensive mistake in March which had led to A.C.Milan's only goal had been all that stood between Celtic and another European triumph - a fact admitted by no less people than A.C.Milan themselves. The "rossaneri", incidentally would have been delighted to discover at the Scottish Cup Final that they had apparently acquired about 50,000 new fans! These were the boys in blue who, having no other verbal ammunition to hurl at the triumphant Celtic fans, were compelled to sing to the tune of Auld Lang Syne "A.C. Milan, A.C. Milan, A.C.Milan, A.C.- A.C. Milan etc." The players of that club, good Catholics all of them (one imagines) may have had a good laugh at that one in their dressing room as they prepared themselves for their (successful) European Cup Final.

1969 had proved that 1967 was no fluke. The balance of power in Scotland had changed immeasurable and apparently irreversibly. Moreover, Scotland now had a team whose European credentials had to be taken seriously. 1967 was no fluke in a European context either, and any team that was to win the European trophy would have to consider Glasgow Celtic as one of their more serious rivals.

Yet summer 1969 was probably the summit for Murdoch and for Celtic. From then on, Celtic began slowly to slip and latterly to go downhill with the speed of an express train for the next 30 years before a partial recovery was achieved at the turn of the century. Celtic would reach a European Cup Final in 1970, and two Semi- Finals in 1972 and 1974, but until 2003 virtually disappeared from Europe. From 1980 to 2003, Celtic did not compete in Europe after New Year, a source of major humilation for a club so inextricably linked with continental glory.

All this tends to put into perspective what was achieved by Stein's Celtic at this time. In a sense, a team like Celtic from a small country like Scotland with only a fraction of the wealth and power base of the likes of Manchester United, Real Madrid, Bayern Munich and A.C. Milan have no right to expect success in Europe like they achieved in these glory years ... but they did! For this we had to thank great management and great players - and there was no greater than Bobby Murdoch!

But the decline and fall of Murdoch (inevitable, given what happens irrevocably in Nature) was a slow and still glorious sunset. Season 1969-70 saw the first inklings of Murdoch with a real problem. It was primarily a weight problem, and strenuous efforts had to be made to deal with it. It was not entirely unconnected with another and more familiar problem, that of his ankle which also played him up particularly in the early weeks of the 1969-70 season. His ankle prevented him training to the utmost, and, in the most vicious of vicious circles, the fact that he was therefore carrying more weight meant that his ankle was more likely to suffer because of the weight put on it. Yet Bobby always did have to work hard at his training, as well as taking precautions with his diet. Something else happened that autumn as well however which further threw into confusion Murdoch's dietary and fitness problems.

Bobby's ankle, classed by a court decision in 1995 as an "industrial injury" for which he was entitled to compensation following an accidental clash at Parkhead with Gordon Marshall senior of Hearts in the early 1960's, was a major problem. Before every game, he had to bathe it in warm water and then wrap bandages round it. The result was that he would often take the field looking as if his right ankle was twice the size of his left, and indeed he would frequently ask people to look at footage of the European Cup Final in 1967, slow down the action and look at the comparative size of his feet. He would also aver that he kicked the ball with his right foot no oftener than about half a dozen times that night, such was the pain involved.

The weight problem in Bobby Murdoch (as is the case with most weight problems) was indigenous and genetic. Most people with weight problems are all too aware of this - that no matter how hard they try to lose weight, they will always have this "natural" problem and that there are limits to what they can do. Bobby did try very hard to lose weight, but it always came back to him.

There was too another side to this problem, and it was one that the newspapers, in particular the Sunday Mail, highlighted in a particularly nasty and cruel sort of a way. Bobby was 25 in August 1969. He had now quite clearly filled out and he was a big lad, now commonly referred to by the Celtic punters as "Big Murdoch" "Big Murdie" "Big Boaby" or even just (in the true Glasgow way) as "Big

Man". This was deliberately misinterpreted by some in the media (particularly a few glory hunting cub reporters) as if it were a drink problem. True, Murdoch did occasionally enjoy a pint to the disapproval of the teetotal Stein, but no-body could have said that it was excessive. It did however seem that way from time to time.

It was not helped by the return to Rangers in summer 1969 of Jim Baxter. Jim was anything but the "Slim Jim" of old, and in fact the Celtic End in his first Old Firm game referred to him, as if they were addressing Billy Bunter, as "Fatty! Fatty!". In Jim's case, there probably was some substance to the rumours of his dissolute lifestyle and certainly such rumours were never strenuously denied. Indeed later on in the case of Baxter, in his tragically short life, much capital was made out of them!

But such is Glasgow with its desire to portray one side as being as good or as bad as the other, Celtic too had to have an overfed character who could be lampooned in the Press. It reminded one of the old "BBC Charter" which had to present a balanced picture, even if a "balance" was not appropriate. The high profile Murdoch lent himself to this, and cartoons would regularly appear in the Sunday Mail of two overfed St.Bernard's dogs, one in blue and the other in green and white. They were never exactly called "Murdoch" and "Baxter" but it was clear that this was what was meant.

The return of Jim Baxter to Rangers raised the ante even more in the pre-season hype, creating as it did in the minds of Rangers supporters a few unrealistic expectations that the pendulum was once again ready to swing towards them. For the third year in succession Celtic and Rangers were drawn together in the same section of the League Cup, and on the first Wednesday night of the season, August 13th 1969, Rangers and Baxter won. Celtic had gone ahead early on through a crisply taken Harry Hood goal, but then Murdoch was taken off with yet another injury which added this other sinister new dimension to his fitness and ankle problems. With all due respect to his replacement Bertie Auld, this was yet another clear indication of how much Murdoch meant to Celtic. Celtic lost two second half goals to an apparently resurgent Rangers side, with the loss of control of midfield being an obvious contribution to this state of affairs.

This particular injury was a damaged muscle just above his pelvic bone. It came about after an accidental collision with a Rangers player and the problem was that it caused pain while breathing during exercise. It would have been of no great concern to the average man in the street, but to a professional footballer, particularly a man like Murdoch who simply had to train hard to keep his weight down, it was potentially disastrous.

Murdoch however had temporarily recovered by the return match at Parkhead and it was his thunderous free kick that Rangers goalkeeper Neef could not hold and Gemmell headed the rebound for the only goal of the game. It was a fine game for Murdoch, the only fly in the oitment being his booking by referee Mr.Callaghan for rather too many coarse tackles. Celtic won the Section and duly qualified, but Murdoch missed the last game of the Section and indeed the opening game of the League campaign against St.Johnstone on August 30th.

He returned, but only briefly and he was clearly toiling. After two successive League defeats at the hands of Dunfermline and then Hibs in early September, Stein decided that this particular problem needed to be addressed and addressed quickly, for Murdoch, for whom training was now an obvious source of acute physical pain, was visibly putting on weight - and becoming depressed about it. For Stein the choice was stark. Drastic action needed to be taken before Celtic lost Bobby Murdoch forever. As it was, the team with a half fit Murdoch were going through a lean spell - as was borne out by that particularly spineless defeat at the hands of Hibs at Parkhead.

On September 17th Celtic were in Switzerland playing Basle in the European Cup. Murdoch, now at a low ebb, seemed to pick up a virus in addition to his other manifold problems and did not play in the 0-0 draw. On the plane back, Jock Stein sat beside him, and told him very gently but also firmly and bluntly that a great Celtic team needed a fit Bobby Murdoch, and that he was being sent to a place called Lief's Nature Cure Centre in Tring, Hertfordshire to lose weight.

This was an unusual event in Scottish football, and although Stein tried to play it down, it could not be kept out of the Press, who treated the matter, initially at least, with a mixture of humour, scepticism but also more than a little concern for the welfare of the player. In fact, it was very soon rumoured that this was a hospital for alcoholics and that Murdoch was to be put in "dry dock" for a while, that his Celtic career was over, that he was seriously (even terminally) ill etc.etc.

This was of course complete and arrant nonsense, but certainly the fortnight that Murdoch spent at the Health Farm was a tough one. A rigidly controlled diet (mainly fresh fruit), rigorous exercise (no problem there, for Murdoch was never shy of training), saunas, golf, massages and lectures from physiotherapists, psychologists and others about the evils of over-indulgence. It hardly needs to be stated that there was of course no alcohol.

Physiotherapists were also able to work on Bobby's ankle. He lost a stone in weight. His pelvis problem, without the intensive demands of professional football, improved of its own accord and by the time that he returned in mid-October in time for a Glasgow Cup game against Clyde, supporters could see a tremendous difference in Bobby. Not only was he faster, thinner and fitter, there was a welcome return of his old appetite for the game, something which had been sadly less than apparent at the start of the season. The team for that game was peppered with reserves (Vic Davidson, for example, scored two goals) for only two nights previously, Celtic (with a young Kenny Dalglish in Murdoch's place) had secured their place in their sixth successive League Cup Final.

Jim Craig tells a story about Murdoch's return. Murdoch returned to Seamill Hydro to join his team mates. At lunch, following the dietitians' advice, he told the waiter to take away the white bread and the butter. Well and good! Then he asked for consomme, followed by a piece of fish, cauliflower and no sauce. His team mates, about to tear into their steak and chips were impressed, and indeed somewhat ashamed of themselves. But then the waiter asked Bobby what he would like to drink. Without a moment's hesitation, he said "A pint of Guinness, please!" Needless to say, the waiter was under orders not to oblige!

The team had done well enough in his absence. They were still in Europe having fended off Basle of Switzerland. Several players had had a run in the team in Bobby's absence, and in particular the opportunity was taken to blood the young Kenny Dalglish, but there had been a dismal and prolonged effort to beat Ayr United in the League Cup Semi Final. The eventual painful victory meant however that Celtic were in yet another big Hampden occasion and Murdoch was now back in contention for a place in the team. This game was against the strong going St.Johnstone from the Fair City of Perth who had surprised a great many people and brought a ray of sunlight to an area of Scotland which seldom, in football terms, sees very much brightness.

Murdoch had definitely lost his Scotland place however because of his fitness problems of that autumn. He was not back in time for consideration for selection. This was obviously Scotland's loss, for on October 22nd the team went down to West Germany, once again failing to qualify for the World Cup Finals. Annoyingly, it was by a tantalisingly narrow margin and the game would have a few implications for Tommy Gemmell, sent off for an understandable, although violent reaction to a German called Haller - something which had more to do with frustration and disappointment than outright viciousness.

The League Cup Final was played on the Saturday after the Scotland game and Murdoch was in contention for a place in his first important game since his return. Whether he would have been in the team in normal circumstances is hard to guess, but the dropping of Tommy Gemmell following his sending off for Scotland the previous Wednesday meant that Stein would have to take a risk on Murdoch. He could hardly deliberately choose to face a Cup Final without two of his more experienced players. Yet Murdoch had played only that one Glasgow Cup game since his return - the League game on the intervening Saturday being postponed, given Scotland's game on the Wednesday.

In the event Bobby played superbly in a game which was a great advertisement for Scottish football. The Perth men, playing in their first ever national Cup Final of any kind, were worthy opponents but found Bertie Auld's early goal difficult to counter. Celtic fans were glad to notice the presence of Murdoch, striding up and down the field like a Colossus, taking a firm grip of the game and making sure, particularly in the last desperate moments of the game, that St.Johnstone did not score the equalizer which only hard-hearted Celtic fans denied them.

Murdoch had now won five Scottish League Cup medals and been instrumental in them all. He was quite clearly back with a vengeance, and even re-gained his International place against Austria in Vienna on November

5th. It was however to be his last International cap of 12, for although he tried hard, the heart had clearly gone out of the Scottish team in what was now technically a World Cup qualifier, but in practice, given the defeat in West Germany, a friendly. It was a sad end to an International career.

The question is often asked "If Murdoch was so good, why did he not get more than 12 caps?" There are probably two answers to that one, neither of them the old Parkhead chestnut about discrimination in favour of Rangers players. One that Murdoch himself said was that Celtic were involved in so many competitions that he was not always available for Scotland, particularly given his chronic ankle problem which flared up from time to time, notably at the time when the team was being picked for the 1967 game at Wembley. The other is that with one or two exceptions, Scotland did not see Murdoch play the way he could. In particular, he was embarrassed about his two high profile appearances against England in 1966 and 1969. England were the opponents that really mattered to a Scottish supporter - a sometimes excessive and disproportionate obsession, not dissimilar to the Celtic v. Rangers paranoia - and a Scottish player was usually judged on how he played against England. In neither of his two appearances against the Auld Enemy was Murdoch at his best.

This was reserved for Celtic. Up to the New Year of 1969-70, Celtic now played some remarkable football. Murdoch had taken to scoring goals. He scored one in a narrow 3-2 win at Pittodrie, then two at Somerset Park, Ayr in a 4-2 win. It was a game they could have lost because the defence was distinctly suspect. In fact Ayr United had equalized to make the score 2-2 before Murdoch scored his two goals. Celtic had one bad Scottish game in which they lost to Hearts at Parkhead on November 8th (with some players clearly holding themselves back for the major European clash against Benfica the following Wednesday) but apart from that, Murdoch was once again inspirational as the team turned on some magical football for example in a game at Parkhead on December 17th in which Celtic beat Dundee United 7-2. It is one which will stay in the memory for a very long time indeed.

1969 ended on a very high note for Celtic. There was a 3-1 win over Kilmarnock on December 20th - a game sadly remembered for the broken leg sustained by Killie's great stalwart Frank Beattie. It was a game which saw Celtic at their best in another sense as well, for as Beattie was carried off before a silent and respectful Parkhead crowd, Stein was seen to take off his overcoat and throw it on top of Beattie. The following week, between Christmas and New Year, Celtic blew Partick Thistle out of the water with a glorious 8-1 tanking in which Murdoch excelled.

It was a curious business in Europe, however as the Jekyll and Hyde side of Celtic appeared. At Parkhead against Benfica, Celtic were absolutely unstoppable as they crushed the Portuguese champions (Simoes, Eusebio and all) 3-0 with even the Portuguese journalists apparently gobsmacked at the sheer power of this Celtic team. Benfica, it was generally agreed, were lucky to get off with three. Yet two weeks later, it was a different story. A goal was lost late in the first half and with the Celtic defence still asking themselves what went wrong, another one went in so that it was 3-2 at half time.

It was here that Celtic perhaps made an error in the deployment of Murdoch. He was brought back as an extra defender - an idea which worked well until injury time when a third goal went in. The goal was so late that quite a few Portuguese fans left the ground convinced that the referee had blown for full time before the goal was scored! The few Celtic supporters in the ground would have preferred to see Murdoch playing his more natural game of surging forward trying to get the away goal which would have killed the tie. The result was that, after half an hour of heart-rending extra time, the game went, not to a penalty shoot-out (as would happen now) but to, of all things, the toss of a coin. Billy McNeill proved that he was not just a pretty face and a world class centre half by calling correctly, and Celtic were through to the European Cup Quarter Finals.

Thus ended 1969 with Murdoch back where he had left off in the summer, his health problems at least temporarily solved. The team looking ahead to the 1970's with a great deal of hope and expectation. The decade of the 60's with all its flower power, Beatles, Vietnam, Martin Luther King and other things was a curious and remarkable one for Celtic. At almost the half way stage of the decade, the management of the club changed and so did its fortunes almost overnight. Celtic, instead of being an underperforming rich team whose support and resources were being slowly frittered away, bogged down in a struggle with Glasgow rivals which they always seemed bound to lose, were now a major European and World power. This was all caused by the charismatic and resourceful manager, but if there were any player who symbolised the new Celtic it would have to be Bobby Murdoch.

Without Stein, Murdoch might well have emigrated to Australia, or continued to play fitfully and disappointingly in the forward line of a team which was going nowhere, until eventually being dropped, asking for a transfer, ending up at someplace like Partick Thistle or Bradford City as a mediocre honest journeyman rather than one of the superstars of Europe. One player did not of course in himself turn the club around, but few could deny that the change in Murdoch was awesome in its intensity. Pre-Stein he was enthusiastic and diligent but nervy, insecure, clumsy - and in the wrong position. Post-Stein, Murdoch became world-class, earning tributes from every foreign team that played against Celtic.

Privately, the Sixties had also been good to him with a nice wife and two children. Early in the following year, he was able to produce a book on his experiences up to this point. (Billy McNeill, Tommy Gemmell, Jimmy Johnstone and Ronnie Simpson all did similarly.) It was called "All The Way With Celtic", and although obviously "ghosted" (i.e. written with the help of a journalist) and full of 1960's footballing cliches, it is nevertheless very imformative, and a great deal of Murdoch's character comes through - his gentleness, modesty, determination and total love of his family and of his club.

The decade of the Sixties will always of course be associated with its music and the Parkhead fans, ever adaptable and ingenious, were not slow in copying all the Beatles and anti-Vietnam war songs to their own cause. "We shall overcome" was heard from time to time, but was such a dirge that it did not stay long in the Parkhead hit parade, but "We shall not be moved" was first heard early in 1966-67 and stayed all the way to Lisbon and beyond.

The Beatles would have been dismayed to find that their Yellow Submarine had changed to Green, and they lived under the waves with Jock Stein and not being particularly fond of the Royal Family.

*We all live in a Green Submarine*
*Along with Jock Stein*
*We don't like the Queen!*

"Hey Jude" with the doggerel lyrics became "Na, Na, Na, Na-Na-Na Na Celt-tic" - something that was surprisingly impressive when belted out at a crowded Parkhead. "We love you, Yeah, Yeah Yeah" had also heard since the early 1960's. Other pop songs sung were "The Mighty Quinn" (in memory of the great Jimmy and his grandson who played some 40 games in the late 60's) and of course "You'll Never Walk Alone". This one came via Carousel, Gerry and the Pacemakers and Liverpool F.C.but was never more impressive than at Parkhead.

For the less politically correct, the renewal of the Ulster problem in 1969 (it probably came as a shock even to most Celtic supporters that the Republican propaganda of the early sixties was in fact true, and that Northern Ireland had a similar record on civil rights to most Third World dictatorships) gave an added impetus to Republican songs. A few years before 1969 however had been heard The Merry Ploughboy, although here again the words were altered, so that the young man was off to Lisbon in the green, rather than Dublin! Even less politically correct was the references to the time before 1965 as being B.S (Before Stein)! Given the religious persuasions of very many of Celtic's supporters, the apparent blasphemy of that one might have been a shock, but such had been the upheaval in 1965 of everything connected with Celtic that it was no great surprise that life should be commemorated in that way!

The sixties were such a tremendous decade, and in the same way that Celtic youngsters in the barren 1940's and 1950's were told all about Adams, McNair and Weir;Young, Loney and Hay; Bennett, McMenemy, Quinn, Somers and Hamilton, the great Edwardian Celtic team, youngsters of the 1980's and 1990's were destined to be fed the Lisbon Lions, and one hopes, will continue to hear the deeds of these valiant and immortal men.

The author recalls listening to an old-timer who would wax eloquent about Young, Loney and Hay. If you wished to order three whiskies in a pub, for example, you would say "Young, Loney and Hay". Why? They were three halves of the best! Yet such nostalgia occasionally becames tedious, particularly when one is young and has heard it all before. Riled by the constant references to "Sunny Jim" Young, the right half of that great side, the author bravely and with the impetuosity of youth said "He wasnae as guid as Bobby Murdoch". Surprisingly, the elder statesman stopped his tirade, smiled and said "The wan was as guid as the ither, laddie". That was no mean compliment.

# A Funny Old Year

The year 1970 is possibly the most difficult to analyse in the whole history of Celtic Football Club. There have been good years like 1908, 1967, 1969 and 2001 and some downright bad ones like 1934, 1961 and 1993, but 1970 is difficult for the historian to come to terms with. Three Cup Finals were lost and some of Stein's behaviour was curious and quixotic, but on the other hand, the football played was tremendous from time to time. There was also, without the slightest shadow of a doubt, the club's greatest ever success against English opposition, and the Scottish League Championship was secured for the fifth time in a row.

The League Championship was probably one of Celtic's easiest. As early as March 28th, a draw at Tynecastle was sufficient to see off any challenge from either Rangers or Hibs who had long ago blown up, mesmerised, it would seem, by Celtic and the Murdoch-inspired power play. In fact it was January which decided this Championship. Rangers came to Parkhead on January 3rd to play on a pitch which might not have been deemed suitable had there not been a huge crowd already in the environs of the stadium. Both teams played it safe and bored the public with a 0-0 draw, but it was a draw which suited Celtic more than their rivals, preserving as it did their marginal advantage. Then a fortnight later, Celtic went to Easter Road to edge a 2-1 victory with a late John Hughes winner. Murdoch's fans were distressed to see him being substituted that day, but it was only a precaution after a heavy challenge on his ankle.

In the wake of Celtic's continuing victories in League games, Rangers and Hibs now began to drop points to the distress of their fans who now accepted the inevitability of yet another Celtic League championship. Celtic in fact finished the season 12 points ahead of Rangers and 13 ahead of Hibs. To anyone other than a Celtic fan, the League race was profoundly boring.

The Scottish Cup of season 1969-70 saw many interesting and controversial games. First Dunfermline came to Parkhead, and for a long time it looked as if history was about to repeat itself. Two years previously, as the Parkhead crowd were all too aware, the Pars had defeated Celtic at Parkhead at a similar stage of the competition. Now as this game entered its last ten minutes, Dunfermline were one ahead through a Gillespie goal. It was at moments like this that the value of Murdoch was seen yet again. Bertie Auld had been taken off and replaced by Jim Craig. Murdoch, Hay and Gemmell were urged to go forward leaving Craig, Brogan and McNeill to deal with any breakaways. It was a risky strategy, but times were desperate and it worked. John Hughes, playing one of his best seasons for the club, got an equalizer and just as the euphoric crowd were talking about going to East End Park on Wednesday night for the Replay, Harry Hood was fed by Murdoch and scored a last minute winner.

That Murdoch's ankle was still playing up, however, became evident in the next Round. This was against Dundee United at Parkhead. It was a fairly routine demolition of the Tannadice men, but once again Bobby was taken off. He missed the next League game against Partick Thistle, and fans speculated whether Stein would take a gamble on Murdoch's fitness for the Quarter Final clash with Rangers at Parkhead on February 21st. Youngsters like Connelly and Hay were now making their mark on the team, but Celtic would surely miss Murdoch.

Rangers had an air of desperation about them as they approached this match. They were out of Europe, needed a miracle to get back into the League race and the Scottish Cup therefore represented their only realistic hope of silverware. Manager David White had been compelled to fall on his sword and his place had been taken by Willie Waddell, their famous left winger of 20 years previously, sometime Manager of Kilmarnock and recently scribe of the Daily Express. Jim Baxter, brought back with a blare of trumpets at the start of the season, was on his travels again, and Rangers fans were still waiting for a resurrection of fortunes.

This Quarter Final game at Parkhead would be a severe test of both teams. Rangers had a point to prove to their fans that they were not afraid of Celtic, and Celtic had to make sure that their spectacular European adventures did not make them forget their domestic involvements. In addition, both teams were aware that an Old Firm defeat almost immediately led to newspaper talk of "the pendulum swinging back" and even of "crisis", such was the importance of the issues involved. In these games Murdoch was clearly a key player, (although he was already on record as saying how much he hated these games) but doubts about his fitness were once again emerging.

In the event, Stein did risk Bobby. It was a rough house of a game with Murdoch, it has to be said, no shrinking violet in what rugby commenators would have called the "argy-bargy", but Celtic emerged triumphant. The whole game began nastily and the cause of reconciliation was hardly helped when a couple of Rangers players "congratulated" Jim Craig for scoring an own goal. Alex McDonald of Rangers was sent off by referee "Tiny" Wharton. One or two players on either side were extremely lucky not to join McDonald in an early bath, and bookings were plentiful. Celtic emerged triumphant, thanks mainly to the fast developing Davie Hay whose 85th minute goal was a real cracker, but several players were injured, one of them Bobby Murdoch.

After this game, everyone got a really good, deserved and public ticking off from the S.F.A., the Glasgow Police and many vote-seeking politicians (with an eye on the approaching General Election in the summer) who could not resist the "plague on both your houses" approach - something which can make the critic appear wiser than he in fact is. But this must not disguise a fine performance by Celtic in demolishing their old rivals who were now left towards the end of February with nothing to play for until next season. In any case other, more important matters, were fast approaching.

There is some evidence to suggest that Stein was now genuinely concerned about long term damage to Murdoch's ankle. In this, his worries were far from misplaced, but Murdoch was usually determined to play. There was a kind of compromise. In League games (Celtic were so far ahead that a certain leeway was possible and in any case Stein wished to rotate his squad) Murdoch was either deployed as substitute or played from the start and then himself substituted, whereas he was played from the start in the Scottish Cup Semi Final against Dundee and in the European games.

Europe was now the main topic of conversation that wet and miserable spring. March 4th at Parkhead saw a fine win over Fiorentina, in which the versatility of Murdoch was apparent. The game at Parkhead saw Celtic at their buccaneering best with the midfield duo of Murdoch and Auld showing their prowess in prising open a stuffy Italian defence. 3-0 was the score, and it should have been more than that.

But television viewers saw a different Celtic and a different Murdoch a fortnight later. The second half was beamed live from Florence, and viewers joined the game with Celtic already a goal down. Memories of what had happened at Benfica when a 3-0 lead had been pulled back, came back to haunt those who were gripping their armchairs or wearing a hole in their mothers' carpets as they paced back and forward like a caged lion. But Celtic were composed, with Murdoch this time playing as a defensive midfielder and seldom venturing over the half way line. The game was hardly enjoyable as a spectacle, but time passed and with the sole exception of a shot that beat goalkeeper Evan Williams and hit the post, Celtic were rarely in serious danger of defeat.

Murdoch had shown that he could play a game other than his natural one and still contribute to Celtic's success. He was paid a compliment by the Fiorentina coach Pesaola when the Italian said that "Murdoch is the papa of the team. The rest are the sons around him". Such a statement, typically Italian and redolent as it was of Mafia Godfather imagery, (not to mention a certain touch of the Vatican) must have struck Murdoch as odd. He was, after all, only 25!

And so we came to what the Press inevitably and predictably dubbed the "Battle of Britain". "Battle of Britain" games come up every now and again, and it is basically a good Scottish team against a good English one. The repeated use of the term "Battle of Britain" is, one feels, an insult to the RAF and Douglas Bader and others who fought in the real battle to save civilization. This was a football match, albeit a very important one - the Semi Final of the European Cup, between Celtic and Leeds United.

Leeds United were managed by Don Revie and with men like Johnny Giles, Jack Charlton, Norman Hunter, Alan Clark and others in their team, were a great side. Curiously, for a team which is still a force to be reckoned with in the early years of the 21st century, Leeds in 1970 were a team which had come from nowhere. They had no great pedigree of success, having won their first real honour in 1968 with the Football League Cup and then the Championship in 1969. But this season, full of Yorkshire grit as well as no little talent, they had done well in the European Cup. They had defeated Standard Leige in the Quarter Final at the same time as Celtic were getting the better of Fiorentina. They were going well in defence of their own domestic League Championship as well, although Celtic perhaps had the psychological advantage of already being Scottish Champions by March 28th.

If this were not enough indication of how powerful these teams were at this time, when horns were locked for the first game at Elland Road on April 1st, both teams were also in their respective domestic Cup Finals, Leeds to play Chelsea and Celtic to play Aberdeen. The build-up for this game had seen the media reach dizzy heights in hyperbole and dismal lows in sensationalism with all sorts of attempts to dig up grievances or undermine a player's confidence by stories about injuries etc. In this respect, Murdoch had a certain amount to do to convince himself that he really was fit, for the Press kept insisting, often in a sly and off-hand way, that he was not.

Leeds were an efficient outfit, but generally detested by the rest of England for their somewhat robust approach to the game. Their star man was probably Billy Bremner from Stirling, frequently described as the "Scots terrier" and other such nonsense. His play certainly contained loads of passion, although from time to time he had disappointed when playing for Scotland because of his over-zealous approach. He had been a Celtic supporter in his youth, apparently, but now he was as determined as the other Leeds men to "sort out" the "upstart" Scots.

It would of course be a gross over-simplification to suggest that all Scotland supported Celtic and all England were rooting for Leeds. It simply was not true. What was true however was that Stein gradually and subtly won over the media in the propaganda battle so that Celtic got the lion's share of the publicity - even in the English Press and very definitely in the London based broadsheets, who quite clearly and genuinely admired the football played by Scotland's finest.

Murdoch and his mates were thriving on this. They knew that they had the more skillful players in Johnstone, Auld and Murdoch himself, and that Leeds for all their hardened professionalism lacked any real flair player. Leeds' advantage was that they played in a larger and more competitive League, and therefore played more regularly against top-class opposition, but against that, Celtic had the confident mentality that comes from being on a winning streak.

The Celtic supporters certainly won their particular battle. Even without tickets (Celtic were allowed only a pitiful amount) they travelled down and took Yorkshire by storm, found ways of getting themselves into the ground and possibly even outnumbered the Leeds supporters. Even apart from the area of the smallish stadium set aside for Celtic fans, there was quite a lot of evidence of infiltration into other parts of the ground. Clearly tickets had been "acquired" in Yorkshire by the determined Celtic fans. Leeds supporters in 1970 had not yet earned for themselves the bad name that they would in later years, and eyed this invasion by the green and white bedecked Scots with wide-eyed astonishment and envy.

Don Revie won a minor point of gamesmanship when he made sure that Celtic took the field in orange stockings. Their white stockings would have clashed with the Leeds ones and Revie, ever eager to oblige but totally aware of the nuances of the situation, offered Celtic the choice of orange ... or blue! It was however about all that Don would win that night, for with less than a minute on the clock, George

Connelly put Celtic ahead. He seemed to have done likewise early on in the second half, but the second goal was disallowed for some reason which was less apparent to the crowd and commentators than it was to the referee.

In truth, although it was only 0-1, Leeds had received a shock. The sheer passion of the Celtic supporters had been matched by the power of their team. Murdoch had been immense in midfield, Johnstone had given Terry Cooper more than a run for his money and the Celtic defence had never really been seriously troubled. Things looked good for the Second Leg to be played at Hampden in a fortnight's time. Hampden had been chosen for naked financial reasons, but one must not minimise either the impact that such a huge Celtic crowd in that ground would have on the Leeds men. Leeds frankly had never seen the like of this in their lives. In the event it was a European record attendance, officially given as 135,826 but in practice a lot more than that, given the wholesale climbing of walls and jumping over turnstiles.

But on the Saturday before that game, April 11th, Celtic suffered a serious blow. Yet the players and supporters were not as devastated as they might have been, for there seemed to be good reasons and excuses. It was the 1970 Scottish Cup Final between Celtic and Aberdeen. It was indeed a profoundly unhappy and unfair occasion with Celtic being the victims of three grossly outrageous decisions, the first of these being a penalty to Aberdeen when the ball struck Murdoch on the chest. Murdoch claimed improbably that he had the mark of the ball on his chest for months afterwards, and that he felt the pain where the ball hit him for the rest of his life!

It was however without any doubt at all a dreadful decision. The Scotsman puts it rather well. It does admit that the ball hit Murdoch on the arm (not the chest as Murdoch himself would say) but "it is safe to say that few referees indeed would have decreed intent against Murdoch". The Daily Record says "Aberdeen were awarded the penalty because Bobby Murdoch was said to have played the ball with his arm about shoulder high. A careful study of TV film appeared to confirm that Murdoch, off-balance, had tried to head or bodily smother the ball with his arms outstretched. The nearest Aberdeen player Derek McKay clearly thought that a free kick was being awarded against the Dons".

Matters were made worse when a valid looking Celtic goal was disallowed for offside, and when an obvious penalty claim was turned down. Aberdeen ended up winning 3-1, and were clearly the beneficiaries of some other peculiar refereeing from Mr. R.H. Davidson who seemed to have some sort of personality clash with Jock Stein. Celtic's reaction to the loss of the Scottish Cup was to congratulate and say they were delighted for Aberdeen then to indulge in a few passionate tirades about Mr. Davidson on the Saturday, shrug their shoulders and say "That's life" on Sunday, and buckle down to their preparations for the Leeds game on Monday.

It was not really the way to deal with the situation. A more objective analysis would have shown that there were other factors at work that Saturday as well as strange refereeing. A world class team (as Celtic purported to be) would have been able to deal with bad refereeing as well as this young and incredulous Aberdeen team. For a long time in the second half, it was only 1-0 for Aberdeen... but they held Celtic. The green and white surge did not materialize, the irresistible pressure was not there. Perhaps minds were on the Leeds United game - and if this were so, it was professional dereliction, and a sad comment on Celtic's lack of commitment to the Scottish game.

It is very easy to hide behind an excuse like poor refereeing, but it may be that simply Celtic had peaked.

Stein himself would often say in other contexts that Celtic needed to be several goals ahead, so that "refereeing friction" (i.e. the odd bad decision) could not come into it. Certainly even more tragic events of later on that spring might well have been avoided, if this defeat had been assessed realistically, and action taken in a meaningful way. It was not all the fault of R.H.Davidson.

Murdoch himself was aware that he had not had one of his better games that day and admitted to being upset by refereeing decisions. But the defeat had very quickly to be relegated to the back of the mind, otherwise other disasters might occur in the high prestige Leeds United game which overshadowed it all. Leeds now had a slight psychogical advantage, for they too had played in their own Cup Final on April 11th. They had drawn with Chelsea, so they were still in their Cup, as distinct from Celtic who weren't. Leeds were to lose the Replay to Chelsea, (and the League to Everton) as it turned out, but that was of little immediate concern to them.

So the Scottish Cup disappeared to the North (almost irrelevantly as far as Celtic were concerned) and Celtic forgot it and braced themselves for Leeds. It was an awesome occasion with the huge crowd and intense media attention on Hampden Park. For sheer football it possibly rivals the great night of Real Madrid v. Eintracht Frankfurt of a decade previously at the same ground, and anyone who was there will recall it all his life.

Murdoch thrived on such occasions, and it was appropriate that he should have scored the decisive goal. Leeds had levelled the tie on aggregate through a brilliant Bremner shot, then John Hughes had brought it back to 2-1 before tremendous work by the irrepressible Jimmy Johnstone set up a great opportunity for Murdoch to crash home a blistering shot from the edge of the box. Oddly enough, these goals, four minutes apart, were scored against different goalkeepers! Gary Sprake had been injured immediately before Murdoch's goal and replaced by David Harvey. Murdoch's goal would certainly be remembered by Jack Charlton and was indeed a permanent source of conversation (on Murdoch's part at least) when the two of them met again.

Celtic thus won on aggregate 3-1, and it was a great moment for Murdoch, for Celtic and indeed for all Scotland. The triumph was total and complete and the celebrations went on far into the night. The game itself was possibly even more impressive, in terms of good football, than the Lisbon European Cup Final of 3 seasons previously, and Celtic were now the indisputed kings of Britain, and the media (even those sections of it for whom it must have hurt) unanimously agreed with this verdict. We, players, management and fans were all swept away in a tide of rapture.

Unfortunately, it was the worst thing that could have happened. Such was the euphoria that the rest of the competition was forgotten about. The opponents in the Final were the Dutch side Feyenoord, and the players and Stein himself were almost contemptuous of them. The impression was that all Celtic had to do was turn up in Milan and they would collect the European trophy.

The sad fact was that this last statement would have been, in different circumstances, correct. A good Celtic team would have been able to take on anyone in Europe - but it needed the correct mental attitude. Some three weeks before the Scottish Cup Final against Aberdeen, the Dons had beaten a lackadaisical Celtic team in an insignificant League match at Parkhead. The wake-up call had not been heard nor heeded, and the Scottish Cup was therefore lost. There was now even less likelihood of a wake up call being heard in the midst of the post-Leeds hysteria.

The mental attitude was wrong from Stein downwards.

Feyenoord had been watched but in a very half-hearted way, and Stein talked about some player as if he were a "poor man's Jim Baxter" who would disappear after about half an hour. This was the great Van Hanegem! Tommy Gemmell said that Feyenoord were discussed as if they were some team like St.Johnstone or Partick Thistle.

A joke went around that Celtic were to play with I.R.A. on their crest for this game - nothing to do with any para-military organization, but rather short hand for "I Remember Aberdeen". Sadly, this remained a joke and Celtic failed to take things sufficiently seriously. No-one did remember Aberdeen on that awful night of May 6th. It is a truism that those who fail to prepare must prepare to fail. It was a pity that no-one seemed to take seriously the omens of disaster contained in that Scottish Cup Final. It was very easy to sit back and blame it all on referee Bobby Davidson.

Such complacency achieved its just reward. Murdoch played a bad game - and admitted as much, but did state that the wrong team had been picked. Connelly, one of the heroes of the Leeds games was brought on only after 75 minutes when the damage was done. The team were already shell-shocked by the play of the Dutch and their supporters' horns which effectively drowned out the Celtic faithful. The score was only 1-1 at that point, but the only hope that Celtic had was for a Replay. Even that hope was taken from them at the end as that tragic European Cup Final reached its disastrous conclusion.

Yet Stein was only partly to blame. The players, Murdoch included, were similarly culpable. They took things far too easily, even on the park when they had gone ahead, and then they lost a great deal of their credibility after the game by announcing that they were setting up a syndicate to organise their earnings! The impoverished supporters were anything but impressed by this and rightly turned on them when they saw them at Milan airport the following day.

How Murdoch took all this is hard to gauge. Certainly he would have been as disappointed as anyone, and a guilty conscience for his part in the dismal procedings must have affected him as well. The fact that Celtic were still a better team than Feyenoord (and certainly far superior to Aberdeen) did not in any way compensate for the fact that they had let their supporters and themselves down badly - if anything it made them feel worse.

It was surely a time for a withdrawal and a re-grouping, but there was worse to come that dreadful summer. Anticipating that they would be the Champions of Europe, the club had organized a tour of North America. It should of course have been cancelled the day after the Milan fiasco, but contracts had been signed. It was a total disaster. Jimmy Johnstone, who was afraid of flying (so was everybody else to a greater or lesser extent, one assumes), was excused the trip - something that in the circumstances caused a great deal of resentment. The football was pointless and dull, as no-body paid the slightest bit of attention to the runners-up of Europe. Stein amazed the footballing world by suddenly (literally in the middle of a game in Toronto!) getting up and going home, leaving Sean Fallon in charge of the party, and the said Sean Fallon had to send home Tommy Gemmell and Bertie Auld for bad behaviour!

It was therefore a dispirited Bobby who flew home with the rest of the team at the end of May 1970. For the moment he could enjoy watching the Mexico World Cup, cursing his luck for Scotland not being in it, but compelled to admire the absolute brilliance of the Brazilians who beat Italy in the Final. England went out to Scotland's conquerors - West Germany - and this result was blamed for Labour's defeat in the General Election! The "feel good" factor in England was no longer there, apparently, and Harold Wilson suffered.

And the "feel good" factor had certainly evaporated

from Parkhead as well. It was clear that everything had gone pear-shaped. Would Stein still be the Manager next season? Not for the first nor last time was the media playing its game of trying to persuade a successful Celtic Manager to go to England. They do this by actually stating that he is going to England, and are able to delude many, including a few who should know better, and including, sadly, themselves.

On the playing front Jimmy Johnstone was threatening to go elsewhere, and Gemmell and Auld's future was in doubt. Bobby himself was only too aware that, great player though he was and had been, there was tremendous competition for places among the Quality Street kids as they were known, the new generation of Celtic youngsters, boys called Macari, Dalglish, McGrain and others. Fitness would be crucial.

The immediate threat to Murdoch's future was once again tied up with a weight problem and Bobby had to redouble his efforts and work very hard to lose it. Murdoch in fact missed the first three games of the League Cup campaign, being generally not in the best of condition, but once he came back in the middle of August, he stayed back, even though all around him was in a state of flux.

It was of course a deliberate policy by Stein. Having decided that his future lay in re-building Celtic rather than moving to Manchester United or anyone else, Jock was determined to uproot the spectre of complacency which had caused the damage in the spring. No-body was guaranteed a place, but on the other hand, Murdoch was a favourite of his and much admired. Murdoch therefore retained his place... most of the time.

Without reaching the heights of perhaps a few years previously, Celtic started impressively. Murdoch took part, for example in an exceptionally good Old Firm game, which Celtic won 2-0 at Parkhead on September 12th. Glyn Edwards of the Glasgow Herald says something remarkable about the goal that Murdoch scored (Celtic's second);

"Murdoch came up to put the issue beyond all doubt with a shot from the edge of the box so venomous that the noise of it hitting the stanchion behind McCloy reverberated all round the ground."

If this is true, it must have been some shot to be heard all round a packed Parkhead at an Old Firm game!

The following week however saw an unsatisfactory performance against Hibs at Easter Road where Bobby was distinctly lacklustre and Hibs won 2-0 with goals scored by ex-Celt Joe McBride. And there was another unpleasant moment to round off the enigmatic and difficult year of 1970, and that was when Rangers beat Celtic in the Final of the Scottish League Cup.

This time it was hardly complacency to blame, just simply that Celtic chose to play badly and Rangers well. The Ibrox men got a good goal to launch the career of 16 year old Derek Johnstone and to con the more gullible of their supporters that they were on the threshold of a new era (yet again). On this occasion, the truth was simply that Celtic were the lesser team. Murdoch did try hard, particularly in the later stages but was ill-supported by his forward line who were clearly missing John Hughes.

Thus Celtic lost three Cup Finals in the calendar year of 1970. It was a curious feeling to be on the losing side in not one but three Cup Finals, yet League form at the turn of the year was still good. They were second in the League table having lost to Hibs and Aberdeen, but looked a good bet to overtake Aberdeen, Rangers had all but disappeared from the League race, following their League Cup Final triumph. On a personal level, Murdoch was still in the first team, and there was nothing in his play to make anyone doubt that he would continue there for some time.

And the undeniable fact remained that Celtic were still

officially classed the second best team in Europe. They were making progress in that dimension as well, disposing of Kokkola of Finland and Waterford of Eire (neither of them, admittedly, giants of the European game). The game in Eire against Waterford saw the worst case of hooliganism involving Celtic seen for a long time, but there is evidence to suggest that it was caused by members of the Orange persuasion who had come south for the day with the deliberate intention of discrediting Celtic. 1970 was that kind of a year!

But, those who despaired of Celtic in 1970 had little cause to do so, if they considered what sort of a team Celtic had on the eve of Murdoch's debut in 1962. Yet, 1970 remains a dreadful year with more than one supporter confessing a certain degree of disorientation and bewilderment at events. Murdoch too would have found 1970 a difficult year to analyse and define. Was there a problem in that Scotland was presenting too little of a challenge, the team was betting bored and that success was breeding its own problems?

# In and Out

Celtic by 1971 had recovered from the traumas and roller coaster events of 1970 but Murdoch was out of the picture, clearly not totally fit, still somewhat overweight and apparently out of favour. The more pessimistic of the supporters were beginning to ask themselves whether Bobby Murdoch was finished with Celtic. Yet he was not yet 27.

The year had started with Murdoch not playing in the January 2nd game at Ibrox. It is unclear whether he was carrying an injury or whether he had been dropped in that Stein thought that the hard pitch might cause problems for the notoriously dicky ankle, but in any case it hardly mattered. January 2nd 1971 was the day of the awful Ibrox disaster in which 66 Rangers fans were killed on exiting the stadium - a blow from which Scottish football (and Rangers in particular) would not recover either in playing or any other terms for some time. Murdoch may well have been glad to have missed that game.

The problem was on Stairway 13 after the game. The facts are disputed as to when exactly the railings buckled under the weight of the supporters, but it happened at the end of a 1-1 draw, both teams having scored in the latter stages of the game. Words can hardly convey the sheer horror of it all, but the wonder was that it had not happened previously at any three of Glasgow's big grounds where the safety of spectators was far from paramount, in spite of all the pious words.

Scottish society was shocked and to a certain extent remains shocked, but what was impressive was the sight of

Rangers players at a Roman Catholic mass and Celtic players at a Church of Scotland service, and the unity (sadly only temporary) of the two sets of fans. For a while there was a lull in the hate chanted at each other and some of the Celtic supporters songs like "Derry's Walls Are Falling Down, Falling Down, Falling Down, Derry's Walls Are Falling Down Upon The Orange Bastards" or "They'll Be Jumping Oot The Windaes 'Cause We've Won" (a reference to the multi-storey flats near Ibrox) were relegated to the back burner on the grounds of sheer bad taste.

Yet football went on and Murdoch returned for the next game against Hibs at Parkhead in which, after a one minute silence impressively and impeccably kept, Celtic understandably found it difficult to get going but ended up 2-1 winners. The following week was like old times again, for Murdoch found himself playing alongside the recalled Bertie Auld at Dens Park as Celtic played their best football for some time to beat Dundee 8-1 and leave the Dens Park season ticket holders and the readers of the Dundee Courier shaking their heads at the brilliance of all this.

Dens Park was a marvellous spectacle that winter day as the sun set in the West, symbolising perhaps the end of a marvellous era, for Stein seemed to be intent on breaking up the Lisbon Lions team. Twice in successive Saturdays at the end of January, Murdoch was substituted and thereafter virtually disappeared from the team sheets until almost the end of the season. 'The Scotsman' is too sanguine when it said on February 8th that "Murdoch needs an operation and will be out for six weeks". It would be considerably longer than that.

At that time, however, he was not the only familiar face missing. Others of the more established players were liable to be dropped. On March 6th, for example, John Hughes was left out of the team to play Raith Rovers in a Scottish Cup tie, took umbrage at this and walked out, signifying a serious rupture in the sometimes fragile relationship between Yogi and Jock.

On May 1st 1971 at Parkhead,however, Stein played all the Lisbon Lions for the last time in a game where they walloped Clyde 6-1, (except for Ronnie Simpson who had by now retired, although he did come out with the team only to be replaced later by Evan Williams). This was quite clearly a deliberate piece of theatre. The League had been well won by that time, and this show was designed to get maximum publicity and win the propaganda battle over Rangers whom they were due to meet in next week's Scottish Cup Final.

Any hope that Murdoch might have had of sneaking his way back into the team for the Scottish Cup Final was dashed when he was picked to play in the Glasgow Cup Final against Clyde at Shawfield on Thursday May 6th. It was quite clearly Celtic's "reserve" team in all but name - and in any case Murdoch played badly and Celtic lost 1-2. This nonsense was rewarded by a meagre 3,500 crowd and it is sad to mention in passing the slow decline and death of the Glasgow Cup - at one point a keenly contested tournament, but now a victim of an overloaded calendar and quite clearly small fry in comparison to Europe.

By May 12th, Celtic had won the Scottish Cup in a Replayed Final, but there was no Bobby Murdoch. Since these two successive Saturdays in late January when Murdoch had been substituted, his only contribution was to come on as a substitute in two League games. Naturally he played in that nostalgic last appearance of the Lisbon Lions and he also got a start in a couple of insignificant Glasgow Cup games, but otherwise there was no Bobby Murdoch, and significantly he dropped out of the Press at that time as well. He simply was not mentioned at all. Where he was missed the most of course was Europe. Celtic were blitzed out of the 1971 European Cup at the Quarter Final stage by the eventual winners Ajax, losing 0-3 in Amsterdam and only scoring one at Hampden. In both legs, Celtic could certainly have done with a fit Bobby Murdoch.

There had been reasons for his absence, of course. His ankle played him up and was definitely becoming worse. This time it necessitated prolonged medical treatment. His weight problem saw him make a return visit to the Health Farm at Tring and he also seemed to have lost the confidence that so marked the Murdoch of old. More significantly, he seemed to have lost his appetite for the game, and his general sense of well being cannot have been helped by the very obvious indications that the team, with men like Hay and Connelly playing in his position, were doing very well in his absence.

This is a phenomenon that one finds with professional football players, particularly those who have played at a high level for a number of years. It is quite simply "burn out". It affects other professions as well, notably teaching, law and the priesthood, but then it usually occurs when the patient is in his 50's. He has not necessarily reached the end of the road, but a long period of rest and recuperation is sometimes required.

Murdoch did however come back. He was still not yet 27, hardly too old for the game. Moreover Stein still seemed to have some faith in him, in that he had made no obvious effort as yet to unload him and he was under contract in any case until July 1974. There may have been enquiries for him, but if so, the press and public were not told. Was Stein making the point that no matter how great a player Murdoch was or had been, he was not an automatic selection at Parkhead? McNeill and Johnstone would similarly fall from favour now and again. The question was being asked more and more, however, among the supporters. Was Bobby finished... at least at Celtic Park?

At the beginning of season 1971-72, it looked as if the

question was answered, and positively too, for Bobby had recovered, was back and playing brilliantly. Celtic qualified for the League Cup Quarter Finals by beating Rangers twice (both times at Ibrox because Parkhead's main stand was being renovated) and Murdoch was back, leaner and with as much enthusiasm as ever, being particularly influential in the opening game of the season in which Celtic won 2-0.

Jim Parkinson ofThe Glasgow Herald is very enthusiastic about his return on the opening day of the season;

"On this performance, Murdoch disproved the old axiom that they never come back. He has had his full share of injury and, more seriously, weight trouble, but he is in the team again, fitter than ever and without having lost his immaculate passing skill. When he is directing the flow accurately Celtic are at their peak, and this was how they secured the initiative in their League Cup section. The return of Murdoch and John Hughes to the first team was a refeshing sight."

In the second game, this time a 3-0 victory, Jim Parkinson is convinced that Celtic will be Europe's outstanding team this season and Bobby Murdoch "directed passes with rare judgement". It was Bobby who flighted a long ball up the middle for the young Dalglish to score Celtic's third goal immediately after half time which destroyed any hope Rangers might have had of a come-back.

Murdoch scored in a 9-1 thrashing of hapless Clyde and then played in yet another Old Firm game at Ibrox - this time a closer, more controversial game which Celtic edged 3-2. Celtic then went to Denmark and appalled all Europe by losing to a team of part-timers in the first leg in a game where only Murdoch looked Celtic class.They competently did the necessary at Celtic Park, of course, but by this time injury had returned once again to haunt Murdoch when he sustained a knock in a game against Morton on September 18th and was out until October 9th.

On his return, he did not look totally fit, and on October 23rd he and the team suffered a mental blow from which he took a long time to recover. It was the League Cup Final of October 23rd against Partick Thistle. McNeill was injured, and Bobby was asked to captain the side. He had of course done this job several times before and although captaincy was not the natural role for Bobby, there was no reason to suspect that he would be found wanting on this occasion.

Sadly in circumstances by no means dissimilar to the Milan flop in the European Cup Final of 18 months previously, Celtic grievously underperformed. The circumstances were remarkably similar in that the "serpent of complacency" had taken over at Parkhead once again. Partick Thistle had only recently returned from their first ever spell in the Second Division and looked nothing other than a bunch of enthusiastic youngsters who had every reason to be proud of themselves for reaching this far.

It was a painful exercise in how much Celtic missed Billy McNeill both as a player and as a captain. In extenuation it must be pleaded that Celtic at an early stage lost Jimmy Johnstone with an injury, but if there is any truth in the phrase "Ilka doggie has his day", then October 23rd 1971 was the day of Partick Thistle.

They simply ran at Celtic, and each one of the Celtic defence seemed to have an off day. In circumstances which had all Scotland refusing to believe what was happening, four goals went in before half time and Celtic were simply floundering. Murdoch had one of those days in which nothing would go right, and by the end of the game seemed to be limping again. In these circumstances, Murdoch really needed the reassuring voice of his boyhood idol Billy McNeill, whereas instead it was he who was supposed to be comforting and reassuring others.

Bobby's leadership qualities would be proved to a certain extent when he went to Middlesbrough, but as he would himself admit, he was no Billy McNeill. In fact it was ironic that McNeill had been such an inspirational and successful captain that Stein had never really considered it necessary to train anyone for the responsibilty when circumstances demanded. This was one such day - and a very bitter one for Bobby Murdoch.

It was one of those days when the final whistle could not come quickly enough, and all the cant about "a great day for Scottish football" and "everybody loves Thistle" could not hide the fact that this was a very sad day indeed for Celtic, and one which in different circumstances might have seen a knee-jerk reaction and wholesale sackings of managers and players. As it was, goalkeeper Evan Willimas played very few games after that, and Dixie Deans was brought from Motherwell to spice up the insipid forward line.

As for Murdoch, he may have been feeling a greater sense of loss that day than merely the loss through injury of McNeill and Johnstone. A few days previously, Willie Wallace and John Hughes had been unloaded to Crystal Palace, and given his now recurrent injury and fitness problem, Murdoch may have felt once again somewhat insecure about his future at Celtic Park. As it happened, there was something almost predictable about the fact that he would limp off East End Park, Dunfermline to be substituted on the Wednesday night immediately after the League Cup Final from Hell (as one Celtic commentator would describe it).

Murdoch was now in a lot of trouble. In addition to his physical problem, there was now the psychological one of having been seen to fail when the added responsibility of the captaincy had been thrust upon him. His dream of accepting a trophy as captain of Celtic had come to naught, and there could be little doubt that a great deal of the all-important appetite for the game had disappeared with it. What cannot have helped either was the undeniable fact that the team now began to perform well in his absence. Scores of 5-0 and 5-1 were commonplace as Celtic mounted a very strong challenge for their seventh Championship in a row, and began to apologise, as it were, to their fans for the League Cup Final shocker. The improvement in form was particularly marked when John "Dixie" Deans came into the forward line. He had been signed immediately after the League Cup shocker, but was in the middle of a suspension and could not play for some time.

How injured and out of form players normally react to their absence being almost beneficial, we cannot tell, but a fairly common phenomenon would undeniably be feelings of frustration and indeed jealousy. Human beings are like this. Murdoch might well have felt this way, but Murdoch was a remarkable man and Celtic were a remarkable team. Stein, now buoyed up at the turn of the year by his team's form (especially after a very good win over Rangers at Parkhead on January 3rd immediately after a 7-0 thrashing of Clyde on New Year's Day) and his own obvious good judgement in going for Dixie Deans as well as the developing talent of young Kenny Dalglish, was also very helpful to Murdoch who always had been one of his favourite players.

Unlike other managers such as the legendary Bill Shankly of Liverpool who was reputed to have no time for injured players in that they were drudges and drones in the general set-up of the club, Jock kept encouraging Bobby, saying that he wanted a fit Murdoch back in time for another attempt on the European Cup, talking to him about other players and giving the impression that he was confiding in him. That was how much Bobby Murdoch meant to Jock Stein.

Recoveries from set backs (and to a professional footballer, there is no greater set back than an injury) are frequently psychological and in the mind rather than the body. Footballers down on their luck have to have their egos massaged and their confidence restored. This Stein did so successfully that he was able to bring back Bobby Murdoch for a Scottish Cup game against Albion Rovers on February 5th 1972, and a season which had already turned the corner well (after the Partick Thistle fiasco) became even better.

Life in Britain in early 1972 was dominated by two things. One was a Miners' Strike (the first national one since 1926) which compelled power cuts and horrified public opinion by the thuggery shown on the picket lines, and the other was a catastrophic collapse of any kind of fragile peace in Northern Ireland after internment had been introduced in 1971 and the British Army committed the massacre now known as "Bloody Sunday" on January 30th. But, on a private note, an addition to the family came to the Murdochs on Leap Year's Day 1972 when Barrie was born, a brother to young Kathleen who was now nearly seven and young Bobby a few days away from his fifth birthday.

The only disappointment was Europe, and even then it was bad luck rather than anything else. Ujpest Dosza of Hungary were dealt with in a very competent, professional way. The difficult job was done away from home in the First Leg by this young Celtic side orchestrated by old hands like McNeill and Murdoch. Then came the Semi Final against old adversaries Inter Milan.

The First Leg at the San Siro saw Murdoch as an out and out defender and earning plaudits for a 0-0 draw. At Parkhead, he assumed his mantle of the playmaker, bursting forward, spraying passes and generally controlling the middle of the field to such an extent that the Italians who had always, as a nation, admired Murdoch seemed to have two men on him... but Murdoch still dominated the midfield. Sadly however the Italian catennachio defence could not be breached, no goals came, and the game went to penalties.

It was poor Dixie Deans who was the only player to miss a penalty that sad April night. Murdoch had been given the task of taking the last penalty... but by that time the tie was over and a Celtic team that might just have won the European Cup again failed at the Semi Final stage. Personal feelings of intense disappointment had to be shrugged off, for there were still things to be done in Scotland.

It was the same Dixie who scored the hat-trick in the Scottish Cup Final to equal the feat of Jimmy Quinn in 1904 as Celtic beat Hibs 6-1. It was one of the best ever displays of football by a rampant Celtic side showing the world how football should be played. Murdoch's personal highlight was the devastatingly accurate free kick which found Dixie Dean for Celtic's second goal, but his play had been magnificent throughout. Celtic had already crowned themselves the League Champions at Methil against East Fife three weeks earlier. In one of their easiest campaigns, they won the League at a canter that season by 10 points over Aberdeen who had hardly helped their cause by selling Martin Buchan to Manchester United in February!

This was now seven League titles in a row. It had surpassed the six of Willie Maley's side from 1905 to 1910. That feat in itself convinced even the most inveterate of the Parkhead growsers and mumpers who stood on the terracing to do nothing other than criticise, apparently. Even they would have to admit that this was indeed a great Celtic team... and had been for seven years. How much the achievement owed to Bobby Murdoch no-one can really state with accuracy, but he did play in a key position throughout the seven years, give or take the occasional problem with injury.

Murdoch thus finished this season on a high. He had plummeted the depths after the League Cup Final, but had shown tremendous strength of character to come back. It was hard to imagine what the previous decade had brought to Murdoch. In 1962 he had made his debut in August; in 1972 he was probably the biggest single source behind the relentless and indefatigable strength of this great Celtic team. Murdoch had won 7 League Championship medals, 4 Scottish Cup medals, 5 Scottish League Cup medals, and of course a European Cup medal. He would soon be 28, and seemed to have loads of football left in him. The contrast to what life had seemed like in 1971 could not have been more complete.

But season 1972-73 is considered by Celtic historians to be a failure. Out of Europe before Christmas and losing two (three, if one counts the pre-season Dryburgh Cup nonsense) domestic Cup Finals was "only" compensated for by the winning of the League in exciting style on the last day of the season. One sometimes thinks wistfully that if 1973 was a failure there were times during the 1990's where we could have done with such a "failure". We certainly would have settled for such a failure in the bad old days B.S. (Before Stein).

Bobby was out again for longish spells in the autumn of 1972 (perhaps he might have made a difference in the European campaign), and although fit and available for the League Cup Final on December 9th, was not selected. This may have been a mistake on the part of Jock Stein and it possibly cost Celtic the League Cup. Murdoch had taken part in a massacre of Dumbarton on December 2nd, and was also on the trip that the club had eccentrically arranged to Jersey the week before the League Cup Final. There they beat a local side 11-1 and Murdoch scored from the penalty spot.

So it came as a surprise to read in the morning papers of December 9th that Stein was coy about naming a team and singling out Tommy Callaghan and Bobby Murdoch as having to be pushed in training and that "he was now waiting for a reaction". In the event Callaghan got a game as a substitute but Murdoch did not play at all. Hibs won 2-1 and Stein had to admit to his old adversary Eddie Turnbull that "Hibs were the better team. That's it".

It is hard not to see a connection between a sub-standard Celtic team and the absence of Murdoch. Admittedly this was a fine Hibs team with players like Stanton, Blackley, Brownlie and others. In a few weeks time, they would score their most famous ever victory when they tanked Hearts 7-0 on New Year's Day - but with all due respect to the Edinburgh men, the key factor that League Cup Final was the absence of Bobby Murdoch. With Murdoch on song in the Scottish Cup Final the previous May, Celtic won 6-1. Without Murdoch, Celtic lacked drive.

This failure added to the general air of malaise around Parkhead. It was brought about by the departure from Europe in early November at the hands of Ujpest Dozsa whom Celtic had competently disposed of six months previously. Significantly once more, Murdoch had been playing in March the previous season when Celtic won, but he had injured his ankle again, this time fairly badly, in a game against East Fife on October 21st. Irrespective of Murdoch's injury, however, the Ujpest Dozsa defeat did seem to indicate that although Celtic would still be predominant in Scotland, Europe was now a different matter. The League Cup Final now challenged temporarily at least Celtic's hegemony in Scotland.

Then several things went badly wrong round about the turn of the year. First there was that League Cup Final defeat at the hands of Hibs, something that seemed to betoken a resurgence in the East. This was neither the first nor the last false dawn for the unlucky Hibees, but it certainly had its repercussions on Celtic. Stein possibly blamed himself for not picking Murdoch for this game (Murdoch had played the Saturday before and the Saturday after, showing few signs of injury) and being Stein, took this defeat seriously, so seriously in fact that it had an effect on his health. Stein sustained a mild heart attack and was kept in hospital for a few days. He mercifully soon recovered, but further illness struck Parkhead in the shape of a flu bug which affected several players, Murdoch included. Murdoch was out for the 1-1 draw with Hibs on December 23, and after the flu bug had led to the postponement of a League game against Kilmarnock, Murdoch's continuing absence was a contributory factor in the loss of the Old Firm game against Rangers on January 6th.

It was at that point that Celtic might have felt like Julius Caesar as he was being stabbed by the conspirators in 44 B.C. Great Caesar fell and then saw his friend Brutus stabbing him too. "Et tu, Brute" (You too, Brutus) he said and died. At this point Lou Macari who had been unhappy and causing problems for some time, asked for a transfer and left to Manchester United.

New Year 1973 was therefore anything but happy for Celtic, but the team rallied - and the rallying of fortunes coincided with the return to fitness, form and consistency of Bobby Murdoch. He was in the team against Dundee on January 13th and looked back to his best as Celtic, admittedly without any great conviction, defeated Dundee 2-1. In fact, he was seldom out of the news from then on, although he was clearly, like the rest of the team, lacking confidence and under pressure from a resurgent Rangers team.

On two occasions, for example, he missed penalties - once against Airdrie at Broomfield in bad weather as the team went down to a miserable 1-2 defeat and on another occasion at East Fife when (in some kind of a record performance) he was one of three separate players - Hood and Dalglish being the others - who missed penalties in a game where Celtic were lucky to get off with a 2-2 draw. It was a remarkable game, played on a heavily sanded pitch on a day when most other games were off, but this one was saved by Bayview's proximity to the sea. After this game Bobby was now officially demoted as the club's penalty taker, and would admit to be glad to be free of that responsibility.

In between times, he scored what was touted as Celtic's 6,000th League goal. Not every historian agreed with the calculations, but it was certainly a great landmark. Yet it was a dreadful goal, a scrambled toe-poke, in an equally dreadful 1-1 draw against Partick Thistle, for which he was awarded a china tea set. Some people thought that this award was an insult to a professional footballer, but Murdoch happily accepted it. It might have been more fitting, some thought, if young Kenny Dalglish had scored the goal, but no-one typified Celtic more than Murdoch in these days. Bobby was certainly well worth his place beside other Celtic Greats of history; Adam McLean, Jimmy McGrory and Jimmey Delaney who had scored the other landmark goals.

Meanwhile Celtic visibly toiled and Rangers, undefeated since early December, kept piling on the pressure. Murdoch was injured again in early March against Aberdeen, but this time was only out for two weeks before returning. In his absence the team had struggled. A dreadfully insipid 1-0 win over Morton was followed by the dropping of a point at Dundee United, as Murdoch sat in the stand and visibly winced at some of the things he saw on the field.

Murdoch, however, on his return once again reflected Celtic. This was no great Celtic side in 1973, and it was by no means Bobby Murdoch at his best either, but both Celtic and Murdoch were determined, workmanlike, professional and totally committed. In this way they won back the respect of their support who on several occasions over the past few years accused them of taking things too easy and being complacent. Certainly one or two heads in the team had grown from time to time to be uncomfortably large - and not always with justification.

It was a great climax to the season. The month of April saw Celtic, with Murdoch inspirational once again, on full throttle in both Cup and League. They needed to be good to win the League this year, for Rangers were hot on their tails, unlike previous years where they had given up and disappeared. Early April saw both teams equal on points with Celtic just having the edge on goal difference. On April 21st, the second last day of the season, as Celtic were easily beating Arbroath 4-0 at Parkhead, the transistor radios (one of them even photographed in the Manager's dugout!) told everyone that Rangers were struggling at Pittodrie and eventually were held to a 2-2 draw.

On April 28th, therefore, Celtic went to Easter Road needing to win to guarantee the League, although a draw might just have sufficed. Fortunately, in front of a packed, long-haired crowd with a fair sprinkling of hooligans (this was the 1970's!), Celtic turned it on brilliantly and beat Hibs 3-0 to win the League for the 8th year in a row. It was a hard fought campaign, but the joys of victory were so much sweeter this year in that they had had to fight for it, and they could claim with justification that in 1973 at least they did have worthy opponents in a revitalised Rangers side.

Murdoch was immense that day as the Championship was won, but it was probably his last great Celtic performance. The following week at the Old Firm Cup Final - the Centenary Final as it was erroneously called (the first Scottish Cup Final was in 1874 and because of two World Wars the hundredth Final was not until 1985) Murdoch did not dominate the game. He was an ordinary player, not a brilliant one, and as a result Rangers won this titanic struggle 3-2.Yet, there was so little in this game between the two teams. A younger, fitter Murdoch would surely have turned this one round, but he was noticeably slower and crucially, once again, seemed to have less appetite and relish for the game. There was a lot less of him running into position, harrying for the ball, shouting for it and cajoling others. This year, it was a loser's medal for Bobby.

The wheel had turned full circle. In 1963 at the end of Murdoch's first season, he had picked up a loser's medal. 1973 would turn out to be his last season and once again the team lost to Rangers in the showpiece of the Scottish year.

At full time, Murdoch would have been amazed to see Rangers' Manager Jock Wallace ignoring his own jubilant players and making straight for him to shake his hand. Apparently, on a previous occasion, Wallace had been seen by the TV cameras to ignore Murdoch's proferred hand at the end of a game and had been roundly rebuked by his embarrassed mother! On this occasion, Wallace was more sporting - but it was also a mark of how highly Murdoch was regarded by opponents that apparently small things like this were very important - even to the Manager of his greatest opponents, and at a moment like that!

This was also more or less the end of Murdoch's Celtic career. A few days before the 1973 Scottish Cup Final, Stein had bought Steve Murray from Aberdeen. Murray, of course, was ineligible to play in the Scottish Cup Final, but the clear implication was that Murray, a hard working, industrious player who had played well for Dundee and Aberdeen, was being seen as Murdoch's replacement. Murray, Celtic daft all his life, was not as good a player as Murdoch in his prime (nor would he ever in all honesty, have claimed to be) but he was certainly more mobile and faster than Murdoch was now. There was no place for both men in the Celtic set-up and Murdoch must have known even as he took the field for that disappointing 1973 Cup Final that the writing was on the wall for him.

Sometimes Stein's psychology worked. Sometimes the signing of a potential rival to an established player would act as a jolt for the established player and bring out the best in him now that his position was seen to be under threat. This time it did not work, for Murdoch, already under pressure after a long painful season during which he had more than once felt that his time at Parkhead was running out, was alarmed and upset at the signing of Steve Murray. Ironically, Murray was only a couple of months younger than Murdoch, but was a lot fitter and slimmer.

Murray was indeed in the first team as season 1973-74 started, Murdoch's only outing being in a pointless League Cup game against Arbroath at Gayfield after Celtic had already qualified. At some point, apparently, in the first few weeks of the season Jack Charlton, recently appointed Manager of Middlesbrough and appalled at the singular lack of talent that he saw, phoned Jock Stein, his old adversary but now respected friend, to ask unofficially if there were any good right halves available in Scotland. Stein stated right away "I could give you Bobby Murdoch". Another version of this story is that Stein, in one of his endless trips to England to watch games, found himself watching Middlesbrough. After 20 minutes, he turned to Charlton and said "You need Bobby Murdoch".

Meanwhile Murdoch had approached Stein to ask if he had any sort of future at Celtic. The two men had never found communication between each other particularly difficult, (in that they both shared an open down-to-earth philosophy of life as well as a deep love for the game and the club and respect for each other) but this time Stein was uneasy at such a direct approach. He was compelled to use some diplomatic sophistries to hide the truth.

It so happened that in that season 1973-74, there was in operation in the Scottish League Cup an experiental law whereby a player could not be offside except in his opponent's penalty area or its "lateral extension" - a line being draw from the edge of the penalty area to the touchline. This experiment had been tried in pre-season tournaments like the Dryburgh Cup and was considered by the authorities to be worth a try in the League Cup.

Now Celtic and Stein had made it plain that they were not all that keen on this idea, and indeed the Celtic View stated more than once that Celtic would effectively ignore this experiment. Yet it did give Stein some leeway as far as Murdoch was concerned so that he did not immediately have to tell one of his favourite players that there was no room for him at Parkhead. He made the point that the League Cup would suit Steve Murray, a faster running wing half, more than it would Murdoch for under the new League Cup set-up with less chance of someone being caught offside, Steve could run at defences. In the League, it might be a different story...

This convoluted and specious line of argument did not fool Bobby. He saw it for what it was, namely an attempt to let Bobby down gently. Indeed in his heart of hearts, Jock did not necessarily want to lose Murdoch entirely, for he would be handy in the event of injuries, but he was also realistic enough to grasp that Murdoch needed first team appearances, both in terms of money and indeed professional pride. He may even have nurtured some hopes of Bobby joining him in the backroom staff some day. It is interesting as well to note that Stein did all in his power to encourage the transfer to Middlesbrough rather than to another Scottish team. Stein did not want Murdoch to come back and haunt him! At Middlesbrough, Murdoch and Celtic would never cross swords in anger.

That this fear of ex-Lisbon Lions coming back to haunt Celtic was a real one was brought home with some vigour before the year was out. Celtic would lose the Scottish League Cup that year on a miserable December day to a Dundee team inspired by Tommy Gemmell, who, unlike Murdoch, probably did feel that he had a point to prove to Stein. The Celtic fans, huddled together for warmth, on that awful day, were reduced to using an old Rangers chant "Gemmell's a bastard" at their old hero, who nevertheless had the last laugh. It would have been a tragedy if that sort of thing were to happen to Murdoch.

Bobby, of course, did not want to leave Celtic or Glasgow but he knew that the time had come. He wished Steve Murray well, but did not feel that he should simply hang around Parkhead waiting for Steve to be injured. He might have gone to another Scottish team - Motherwell and Dundee were both reputedly interested - but he probably felt that, at the age of 29, he needed a total change of scene. In any case, Stein did nothing to encourage any other Scottish interest. The Scottish game, indeed, was going through a trough with attendances low and most teams, including Rangers, sometimes almost paralysed into lethargy at the sight of Stein's Celtic. Cups might be lost by Celtic, but it was hard to see them not winning the Scottish League.

Murdoch's mind was made up, and he was given a boost when Celtic gave him a free transfer. This might have seemed to be callous, (or even interpreted as some kind of an insult) indicating that he was being turned out to graze, but in fact, it worked to Murdoch's advantage because he could now negotiate his own terms which would be more generous as Middlesbrough did not have to pay a transfer fee. There is also the undeniable fact that if Middlesbrough had had to pay a large fee, they would naturally have insisted on a medical and Bobby's ankle would never have passed such a test.

The news was still being dominated by the military coup of a few days previously in Chile and its violent consequences, when the great Bobby Murdoch left Parkhead on September 17th 1973. To say that everyone was sad was an understatement. Yet, however distraught and distressed Murdoch was in private at having to leave the club that he loved, there was an absence of any public bitterness, for both Stein and Murdoch knew that as Celtic had made Murdoch, so had Murdoch made Celtic. But this symbiosis could not go on for ever, and it was time to go after 14 remarkable years at the club. There was also the realistic determination to make the most of a new and different challenge. Perhaps Murdoch had stagnated for having been in the same pool for too long.

Years later, Stein would say "As far as I am concerned, Murdoch was just about the best player I had as manager. I only let him move because he had run out of challenges with Celtic" This statement may or may not be the whole truth. There was certainly a feeling that Stein made a little money for himself on Murdoch's departure (the ugly term "kickback" was used among the supporters who thought that Murdoch was good enough to be kept for a little longer) and Murdoch himself certainly denied that he had run out of challenges at Celtic Park. In an interview with Shaun Keogh, he sees it a different way. "I had just signed a two year contract with a two year option, and he (Stein) stuck me in the reserves. I couldn't afford to be in the reserves, because you don't get appearance money or bonus money unless you are in the first team. I didn't ask for a move but I told Jock that I didn't want to play in the reserves and he said he would see what he could do for me. So he told three clubs - Boro, Preston and Sheffield United - that I was available."

Whatever the truth of this matter, Murdoch remained a

Celtic supporter and friend and confidante of Jock Stein until the latter's death in 1985, but for the moment, it was time to say farewell and try pastures new.

# Middlesbrough

To say that the Middlesbrough team that Murdoch joined on September 17th 1973 were perennial underachievers was to state the obvious. They had won precisely nothing (other than Division 2 Championships) in their history and struggled to keep up with the other big clubs of the North East, Newcastle and Sunderland, whose triumphs, if spectacular, were also isolated. Yet if the teams of the Tyne, Wear and Tees had under-performed (and they had, grievously, to the constant disappointment of their fans), there was certainly no lack of interest in the game. In that respect, the North East of England resembled Glasgow with the exception that seldom did both big Glasgow teams do badly. In the North East, seasons and even decades could pass without any great significant mark being made on English football by any of the big three.

The whole area had missed the boat, it was felt, in cultural and every other kind of terms as well. Already in the mid-1970's were the clear signs of the nation out of balance - something that would become even more pronounced during the Thatcher years from 1979 onwards - with the wealth draining steadily southwards. Britain had joined the European Economic Community on New Year's Day 1973, and it was only natural that the south east corner of the country, the area closest to Europe, would become more prosperous than any place else.

But even in terms of the North of England (Black England as it was sometimes called because of the concentration of heavy industry) the Eastern half was losing out to the West, culturally at least. The 1960's had of course seen the Beatles in Liverpool and it is no accident that Liverpool F.C. had had their awakening at the same time. The North East still awaited a revival, as it struggled to shrug off its undeserved image of craggy miners, inadequate housing, incomprehensible accents and general poverty.

The town of Ironopolis (as Middlesbrough was traditionally called in the same way as Manchester was Cottonopolis and Dundee Juteopolis) had had their fine players, but they seldom had a great team. Before Murdoch arrived, their best year had been 1926-27 when George Camsell netted a record 59 goals to ensure the Second Division Championship. This remains the record for the Second Division (First Division as it is now called) but is not a record for all of England. It was beaten the following season by William Ralph (Dixie) Dean of Everton in the First Division who netted his 60th with five minutes remaining of the last day of the season!

There was a certain tradition of Scottish players, although not as pronounced as it was at Newcastle with Hughie Gallagher, Frank Brennan, Jimmy Scoular, Bobby Mitchell and countless others. A famous Scottish player for Middlesbrough was one John Marshall of the 1920's, a full back, originally from Saltcoats, who won 7 caps for Scotland, not all of them as a Boro player for some of them were when he played for Welsh team Llanelly! There was also Jackie Milne who played a couple of games for Scotland on the eve of World War 2, but Boro's most recent successful Scotsman was of course the great Willie Fernie, arguably one of Celtic's best ballplayers of the 1950's.

Middlesbrough's best ever player was probably Wilf Mannion who was one of those unlucky to have lost his best years to the Second World War. But he was still good enough to take the Boro to their best ever League position of fourth in Division 1 in 1938-39 and to win 26 caps for England after the war. In 1946 Middlesbrough had stayed in

Division 1 until 1954. They were relegated that season to Division 2 where they remained, apart from one humiliating season in 1966-67 which had been spent in Division 3!

Yet the deployment of Ayresome Park in the 1966 World Cup showed a certain ambition on the part of the Directors, for they were chosen ahead of a more likely site in St. James' Park, Newcastle. The stadium had been given a facelift, but unfortunately their fans, sickened presumably by being relegated to Division 3 or perhaps not enthusiastic about paying high prices, let them down by not attending in sufficient numbers. The humiliating spectacle of empty seats was seen at Ayresome Park during World Cup games, leading people to ask whether Middlesbrough really was a footballing centre.

But Ayresome Park saw one of the great shocks of World Cup history when North Korea beat the great Italy thanks to a goal scored by Pak Doo Ik, a gentleman who immediately became a Middlesbrough folk hero, leading unkind people to wonder whether he was the greatest Middlesbrough hero of all time!

In 1969 European success came to the North East when Newcastle United won what is now called the UEFA Cup, and just that summer of 1973, the whole of the North East had been set alight by Sunderland's victory in the F.A. Cup when Bob Stokoe's team had defeated the great Leeds United. These sort of things however further depressed the Boro supporters, for although they had had great players in the recent past - Brian Clough, Willie Fernie, Eric McMordie, John Hickton - they were sickened of being reminded by Geordie and Sunderland fans that no great success had ever come their way, they had not seen the First Division since 1954 and that they had not even won the Third Division Championship in 1967! Indeed they finished up 12 points behind Queen's Park Rangers that year and were considered lucky to get promotion.

Manager Stan Anderson and Middlesbrough had parted company in the middle of the 1972-73 season, and following an interim period with Harold Shepherdson, the Middlesbrough Board acted with an unaccustomed degree of initiative to appoint Jack Charlton of Leeds United to the job. This was announced on Monday 7th May at the end of Charlton's testimonial match against, of all people, Celtic. The appointment of a proven winner and someone with whom Boro supporters could identify was greeted with almost Messianic intensity on the banks of the Tees.

Charlton was by no means everyone's favourite person (particularly in the south of England) because of his somewhat robust approach to the game. He also had an unfortunate tendency to say the wrong thing, earning a certain amount of notoriety for example when he said on a television programme that there were certain players that he would like to "do", as he put it. Perhaps he also suffered from the constant comparison with "Our Kid".

"Our Kid" was of course Bobby Charlton, one of the genuine heroes of English football, and deservedly so. Bobby had captured the hearts of the nation because of his survival of the Munich air disaster in 1958, and his immediate rise to stardom in the aftermath. Bobby always interviewed well, coming across as a shy yet likeable boy, as distinct from his more abrasive elder brother Jack. Bobby also ventured into management at this time with Preston North End, but was by no means a success, simply being too nice a man for the job.

But the Charltons were local boys from Ashington near Newcastle. Famously on the night of the World Cup Semi Final of 1966 when England beat Eusebio's Portugal, Mr. Charlton senior had been down the pit doing his shift, rather than watching his two boys doing their stuff! With a background like that, Jack understood the North East better than most. He also gave the impression that he wanted to be part of the local set up, buying a house, for example, in North Yorkshire, in Great Ayton, a charming village, one time home of Captain Cook, the discoverer of Australia. Having been a member of the team which won the World Cup in 1966 as well as having had a long and successful career with Leeds United, Jack was quite clearly a winner.

Jack set about moulding a team that could in the first instance take the Boro back into the First Division, and it was in this context that he contacted Jock Stein. To his surprise, he says, (although the matter may have been discussed when the two men met at a Dinner in May) he was offered Bobby Murdoch. Even more to his delight, he got Murdoch on a free transfer. Amazingly, Murdoch was the only man that was added by Jack Charlton to Stan Anderson's previous squad. Murdoch was sufficiently good to make a difference on his own.

Everyone, not least Charlton, knew that Bobby had serious fitness problems and there is nothing to suggest that Jack saw Bobby as a long term move. Bobby was certainly a little short of pace, but that could be counterbalanced by the pace of other members of the midfield. In addition Jack felt that a man of Murdoch's obvious class and astonishing ability to pass a ball (and Charlton knew from his encounters with Celtic in 1970 how good he was) would be good enough to raise Middlesbrough to the First Division. The long term future could take care of itself, but for the moment a European Cup winner and holder of eight Scottish League medals, even on a free transfer, could surely do the necessary business in the English Second Division.

Boro supporters now could hardly contain themselves with excitement. The streets of Redcar, Thornaby and Guisborough talked about little else. Some of the more pessimistic pointed out that Murdoch was perhaps past it and had chronic ankle and weight problems. On the other hand, 1973 had now brought a World Cup winner and a

European Cup winner (neither of these categories exactly ten a penny) to Ayresome Park both at the same time. The "promised land" (in Boro's case, the much needed and long overdue "promised land") seemed just round the corner!

Yet the Evening Gazette of September 17th 1973 is curiously low key about the business. The headline is that Jimmy Smith (a disappointing underperformer for Newcastle United as he had been for Aberdeen) had been picked by Willie Ormond for the Scotland squad. Bobby's joining the club is a sub-headline. There is a picture of Bobby with Jack Charlton, Jim Platt, Stuart Boam and Graeme Souness about to leave for London to play Leyton Orient that night (Bobby would merely be an observer), but Cliff Mitchell, the reporter, is matter of fact about Murdoch. He does however quote Jack Charlton who is as "chuffed as little apples" (a curious phrase) about Murdoch joining the squad. Charlton also says that Stein had been going to tell "Our Kid" at Preston as well about Murdoch's availability, but elder brother Jack got there first.

When Bobby and Kathleen moved to Redcar in the first instance (they would later move to Normanby) with their young family, the lifestyle would not necessarily have been totally alien. The accents, the industries and the scenery was different from Glasgow, but the passions for things like football were similar, and the people were every bit as warmhearted as those in their native Glasgow. Bobby and Kathleen immediately loved their time in the North East. He would describe the fans in his famous catchphrase as "different class". It was just as well, for the Murdochs would be there for almost the next ten years.

In one footballing respect too there would be a striking similarity with Middlesbrough of 1973 and Celtic of 1962 when Bobby made his debut. They were the dispossessed. Their supporters were loyal but their patience was being gradually ground down and worn away by poor management, incompetent Directors and a general air of depression about the place. Murdoch had, since 1965, contributed in the making of a huge difference to Celtic, transforming them from a third rate team into a global power. It would clearly be a flight of fancy to expect Murdoch at his age and with his fitness problems to move the earth at Middlesbrough but could he and Charlton not do something reasonably similar with Middlesbrough and at least earn them respectability - and most importantly, win some trophy to give the fans something to shout about?

Certainly in some respects, Charlton and Stein were different men. An early example of this came when, one night, Manager Jack Charlton knocked on Bobby's door and asked him if he wanted to go out for a pint! This was in total contrast to the strictly, even obsessively, teetotal Jock Stein who spent most of his evenings on European trips spying on his players, making sure that they and strong drink did not meet! On another occasion Jack, a very keen fisher and shooter, actually persuaded Bobby to come out and do some "beating" for him. As the kindly Bobby did not actually like being a part in the killing of birds, this activity happened only once.

The team had made what could be euphemistically described as an indifferent start to the season, with the most common score being 0-0. Indeed Murdoch's debut on 22nd September 1973 was a 0-0 draw at Blackpool on a greasy surface, a game which the Evening Gazette was clearly finding a problem about getting interested in, (although the reporter does mention a large detachment of red-bedecked "Ayresome Angels" in the crowd) and concentrates its attention on the newly arrived Scotsman whom he describes tactfully as "stocky". Boro's defence was strong enough, but they were in serious danger of boring their punters with lack of creative midfield play and imaginative forwards.

Bobby told the Evening Gazette's Cliff Mitchell on the Monday that he was pleasantly surprised that English Second Division football wasn't "a wee bit quicker". The slower pace would suit him, for apart from anything else, he was short of match practice having played only one game for Celtic that season and a mere handful of reserve games. Jack Charlton, before departing to Portugal to play in Eusebio's testimonial, also said that Murdoch had played well enough to retain his place. "He lacks a lot of understanding with the rest of the lads but that will come."

Murdoch in fact knew little about Middlesbrough, although he had played once at Ayresome Park for the Scottish League against the English League in 1968. It was not a game which contained very happy memories, however, for a poor Scottish team went down 2-0. Nevertheless teaming up at Middlesbrough in midfield with a Scots lad from Edinburgh called Graeme Souness, as well as the more experienced David Armstrong, Murdoch simply took command.

He clearly revelled in his role, and had taken on a new lease of life. Granted some of the opposition was none too demanding, but the team moved to the top of the table on October 6th after Murdoch scored the only goal of the game in the rural atmosphere of Swindon. They then stayed at the top. They did not lose a League game until February 2nd. Admittedly it was a bad one (1-5 to Notts Forest) and came a week after a disappointing Cup exit at the hands of Wrexham, but this was merely a wobble en route to the Second Division Championship.

But the game that endeared the Boro fans immediately to the mighty Murdoch was a game in the League Cup. It was on October 8th 1973 at Old Trafford against Manchester United. Granted, Manchester United were in a trough and far from the great club that they are to-day or had been in the past, but they were managed by Tommy Docherty and contained great players like Martin Buchan, Jimmy Greenhoff, Willie Morgan and Murdoch's old Celtic partner Lou Macari. It was an epic game as far as Middlesbrough were concerned, and although it was Malcolm Smith who scored the only goal of the game from a Souness pass in the third minute, it was Murdoch who masterminded the victory.

Where Murdoch's experience showed was in the second half when the desperate Manchester United threw everything at them. Murdoch knew how to win balls in midfield, to waste time, to slow things down, to take the sting out of the attack, and although even Boro supporters admitted that it wasn't always pretty, the media were impressed by the new professionalism of Charlton and Murdoch's new Boro. The following day, one national newspaper "The Daily Mirror" proclaimed "There was only one First Division club out there and it wasn't Manchester United". The Yorkshire Post (more than a little biased one suspects) used a chiasmus - "they were simply superb, superbly simple".

Middlesbrough had developed a three man "running" midfield of the two Scotsman, Murdoch and Souness, and the Durham boy David Armstrong. The idea was to run at the defence, draw them out of position, then flick the ball to Alan Foggon. It was very successful, but it was nothing new to Murdoch, for he had always been encouraged by Stein to run at the defence in his Celtic days. Now at Middlesbrough, there were three men who did this.

In their charge towards the title, the Boro occasionally picked up the reputation of being a hard team. This charge was not entirely without foundation, for men like Souness, Boam and Craggs (and Murdoch himself if truth be told) did not always hold back, and in addition, Jack Charlton did have the habit of being perhaps more verbally aggressive than was wise, but there was now far more steel in their play than previously. The crowds respected this approach and shortly began to love it, and attendances rose to an average of about 26,000 as distinct from 18,000 before Murdoch arrived.

On Boxing Day 1973, for example, a massive crowd of 37,038 packed Ayresome Park to see Middlesbrough beat Sunderland 2-1. It was like the good old days again, and the remains of the Christmas turkey and the plum duff must have been sweet for the Boro fans who saw their team beat local rivals and the F.A. Cup holders. The winning goal came about a minute and a half from time. David Mills picked up a ball and made as if to pass to Murdoch. Bobby's run took a couple of defenders with him, leaving Stuart Boam in space. Mills then found Boam who controlled the ball well and scored.

October 1973 however had seen an event which shocked England. They failed to qualify for the World Cup, whereas Scotland had done so in September. No doubt, Murdoch had enough tact to hold his tongue and look slightly glum when the subject was mentioned, but it cannot have been easy! More seriously, so well were the veteran Murdoch and the young Souness playing that the possibility of both of them joining the Scotland squad was mentioned.

Winter 1973-4 was a difficult one for Great Britain. Internally inflation was soaring and industrial unrest was the order of the day. Abroad, Israel and the Arabs once again crossed swords in the Middle East when the Arabs attacked Israel on Yom Kippur day, October 6th 1973. The attack had been planned for some time but caught Israel by surprise, coming as it did on Israel's holiest day of the year. This war, although eventually settled by the superpowers, was not the rout that the 1967 war had been, and lasted a little longer. It also had more repercussions for the Western world.

In early November nuclear war was briefly threatened

by the U.S. President Richard Nixon, himself under pressure because of the Watergate scandal, which eventually forced him to resign. He saw external affairs as a way of taking pressure off himself, even if it meant risking the world's security. Oil prices had risen steeply as the oil moguls took a little revenge on industrialized nations for their perceived siding with Israel and petrol therefore became scarce. There was an added dimension to all this in Great Britain for the miners imposed an overtime ban which eventually caused a three day week in some industries. A General Election was called by a panicky Conservative Government in February 1974, they were defeated for having let inflation get out of control and a minority Labour administration took over.

In these circumstances, concentration on football was not easy, but Middlesbrough did just that. On March 2nd, just as Edward Heath, two days after the General Election, was trying to do a deal with the hitherto despised Liberals in order to keep himself in power, the Boro travelled to Roker Park where over 41,000 saw Mills and Foggon score the goals to give them victory... and a double over Sunderland. But the architect was Bobby Murdoch with his visionary distribution.

In the middle of March, with Harold Wilson's Labour Government now back in Downing Street, West Bromwich Albion and Fulham were each thrashed 4-0 and the Boro gained promotion on March 23rd. Oxford were the opponents at Ayresome that day, and it took a long through ball from Murdoch to Armstrong to break the deadlock. The Evening Gazette on the following Monday has a picture of Jack Charlton doing a passable impression of Sir Winston Churchill with a V sign and a cigar for what was the greatest moment of Boro history for 20 years.

And as Churchill would have said "it was not the end. It was not even the beginning of the end. But it was perhaps the end of the beginning". Boro became Champions of the Second Division as early as March 30th at Kenilworth Road when they beat Luton 1-0 - a Murdoch pass for Foggon to cross to Mills to do the needful - and finishing up 15 points ahead of their nearest rivals. This was no mean feat when one considers that only two points were awarded for a win in those days! The League well won, the Boro celebrated by beating fellow Yorkshiremen Sheffield Wednesday 8-0.

Incredibly, they were occasionally called "Boring Boro" by jealous journalists from the south of the country. This name was much resented and rightly so, for a grand total of 77 goals does not seem to be all that boring! The tag owes its origins to envy but also to Boro's ability to get ahead of a team and to stay ahead, even if it meant a little defensive play. It was of course something that Murdoch had learned with Celtic, for it was occasionally necessary in Europe and it certainly taught Souness a trick or two that he would use with Liverpool. "Defensive minded", "Boring Boro" they may have occasionally been called but this does not alter the fact that the 1973-4 side was probably the best Boro team in its history.

Deservedly then did the Teesiders celebrate their victory, looking forward to their encounters with the big boys next year. In fact they avoided Manchester United who had been humiliatingly relegated that season, but great was the feeling of expectation for the following year. Murdoch felt he had a great season. His injured ankle had occasionally played up and once or twice he had been substitued and missed a game or two, but his play in the number 7 shirt had been immense, and he had became a folk hero to the success starved Middlesbrough supporters almost overnight.

Graeme Souness would describe Murdoch's first season with Middlesbrough in the following terms; "He came along at just the right time, not only for me but for the whole team. His experience settled us down as we went for promotion and he also proved to be a big influence on my career. Bobby was a great passer of the ball and he had an excellent attitude. He would always pull me to one side to pass on advice or to tell me when he thought I was acting wrongly." Souness however also stresses that Murdoch led by example. His advice to youngsters like Souness was always tactful and constructive, and Murdoch was his own greatest critic if he himself had a bad game. Such occurrences were a rarity in 1973-4.

As well as winning the Championship, Middlesbrough won their highest ever number of points in 65 (not quite beating the record of Tottenham Hotspur in 1919-20), went 20 home games without defeat, went 24 League games without defeat and conceded only 30 goals. The 15 points margin by which they won the League was also a record. They now felt ready to "lick the Division 1 cream" as the Evening Gazette put it.

Holland would reach the Final of the World Cup in Germany that year, and most people would consider them unlucky not to win the trophy itself. They played a concept called "Total Football" and were fortunte enough to have the players who could implement that. Basically it meant that all the players were all over the place and they were more or less impossible to mark or to tie down because of their ability to interchange so rapidly. Middlesbrough played that sort of thing as well, and, although Alan Foggon, one time of Newcastle United scored 19 goals, every other player apart from goalkeeper Jim Platt managed to score at least once! Great days indeed at Ayresome Park, although everyone was aware that next season in the First Division, it would be a different story altogether. Yet, with new hero Bobby Murdoch no-one feared the future.

Bobby himself was enjoying life. His young family (Kathleen was 8 when they moved, Bobby 6 and Barrie a toddler) had settled in the North East, and he was revelling in the pleasure that success brings. His ankle and fitness problems were now temporarily in remission, and he was looking foward to the challenges that the next year would contain. Murdoch would not have been Murdoch, however, if he had not kept an eye on what was happening at Celtic. A Cup and League double (the League for the 9th year in a row) had been won, but Murdoch must have felt that he did well to avoid the European Cup Semi Finals against Atletico Madrid in which the unacceptable side of Hispanic football was once again shown to the world, and Celtic were, not to put too fine a point on it, kicked off the park.

In a Celtic context as well, it must be recalled that Murdoch once apparently upbraided himself for having in season 1973-4 made Graeme Souness what he was. "I sometimes wish I hadnae bothered" he would say as Rangers, under Souness, won Championship after Championship in the 1990's!

# Big Jack's Pride

Summer 1974 was thus spent in great excitement in the North Yorkshire area. Clashes with the big guns, a local derby with Newcastle United, encounters with other Yorkshire teams like Leeds United and Sheffield United were much looked forward to. The World Cup in Germany generated less excitement in England than in Scotland - for the obvious reason that England were not there! - but Murdoch would have been delighted to see Scotland perform creditably. Scotland beat Zaire, then drew with Brazil and Yugoslavia, being the better team on both occasions. They were thus eliminated on goal difference, but returned undefeated. Unlike four years later, they came home with honour.

The super-optimists of Middlesbrough were far less concerned about that than they were with the rebirth (or perhaps even the birth!) of their team. Some were even talking about the club winning the League Championship itself, such was the enthusiasm generated by the Scottish midfield of Murdoch and Souness. Questions were even asked of Willie Ormond (Scotland's team manager) why neither of them were in the Scottish team. One of them, of course, had had his day in the Scottish team - and the other's opportunity was yet to come.

The First Division of the English League enjoyed the same mystique and magnificence that the Premiership does today. There were one or two subtle differences however. Today's Premiership possibly is the strongest League in the world, given the wealth and earning potential of some of the teams. 1974's First Division claimed to be the best in the world, but wasn't. There were a couple of TV programmes at lunch time on a Saturday (annoyingly both on at the same time, one on each of the two main channels) which fostered this myth. They did this by the technique of showing the highlights - the great goals, the superb penalty saves of all the best games and giving the impression that every game was like this. They also had the ability (TV being somewhat less critical then than it is now) of elevating the most ordinary of players into superstars.

This was the scenario into which Middlesbrough entered in 1974. Being newcomers and a northern team, they were of course patronised by the media, but there was a determination about them to show that they were not simply there to make up the numbers. Pre-season entertainment took place in the shape of the Texaco Cup against the other three Northern teams in Carlisle, Newcastle and Sunderland. It was a severe disappointment and included a 4-0 thrashing at the hands of Newcastle, but failed in anyway to dim the enthusiasm. It was put down to experience. If you are going to play badly, it was said, where better to do it than in pre-season meaningless rubbish?

When the League season proper started on August 17th, the first game saw a good away victory at St.Andrews. The following midweek brought First Division football to Middlesbrough for the first time since 1954 but the large crowd was severely disappointed with a defeat at the hands of fellow "parvenus" from the North, Carlisle United, who had also beaten them in the Texaco Cup. After that, however, the team soon settled to play good football and earn consistent results.

Charlton had added to the squad by bringing in his old Leeds team mate Terry Cooper to fill the left back slot. Murdoch remembered Terry as the man mercilessly roasted by Jimmy Johnstone in both games in 1970, and had a certain respect for him in that Terry did not resort to foul tactics to get the better of Jimmy. The cynics however simply said that it was only because Terry couldn't even get within fouling distance of Johnstone!

But the main talking point of the first half of the season on Teeside was a good run in the League Cup. Wednesday September 11th 1974 saw one of Middlesbrough's greatest ever results when they went to White Hart Lane and thrashed Tottenham Hotspur 4-0. Normally, North East teams do not do particularly well in London, but on this occasion, Murdoch simply ran riot (Souness wasn't playing) feeding Smith, Mills, Hickton and Armstrong to score the four goals which stunned the London side. At the end of the month, they would beat poor Spurs again in the League at Ayresome Park. It was indeed a weak Tottenham team who would face relegation at the end of the season.

There followed in the League Cup a narrow 1-0 win over Leicester City at Ayresome on October 8th, and then on November 12th, Middlesbrough once again made everyone sit up and take notice by beating Liverpool at Anfield. It was a gruelling contest on heavy ground, and the winner only came in the 92nd minute following a fine one-two involving John Hickton and Willie Maddren, but it is never easy to win at that particular venue. Indeed, when one considers that this Liverpool team would end up 2nd in the League, were less than three years away from winning the European Cup and contained men like Emlyn Hughes and Kevin Keegan in their side that night, the achievement was little short of marvellous.

Thus the Boro were in the last eight of this competition. The excitement continued when Manchester United were drawn at Ayresome. Manchester United, who suffered in these days from an image problem of an under-performing side (they were this season in the Second Division) and hooligan supporters, were still a mighty team and a great attraction. Managed by Tommy Docherty, that most charismatic and quixotic of Scotsmen, they had a young team and were slowly re-grouping. An all-ticket crowd of 36,000 at Ayresome saw a great but goalless game. Sadly, Murdoch was not playing, having suffered a recurrence of his chronic ankle injury against Queen's Park Rangers on November 23rd.

He was back however for the Replay a week before Christmas at Old Trafford, but this time Murdoch, arguably less than 100% fit, had a poor game as the Boro went down to a fine, developing Manchester United side full of (as often happens in Manchester United history) youngsters. It was a bad night for the North East as Newcastle shocked their fans by going down to Chester as well, but for Boro, this Old Trafford shocker was an isolated one. Form in December was actually very good, and following a 1-1 draw at Goodison on December 28th, the Boro were astonishingly 2nd in the League, their best ever position!

In truth, this was a slightly misleading phenomenon because other teams had games in hand, but it did nevertheless show how far the team had come in the short time (15 months) since Jack Charlton had signed up Bobby Murdoch. It would have been interesting to know the feelings of Jock Stein at about this time. Murdoch had always been a favourite of Jock's, but quite clearly Jock had thought in 1973 that Murdoch was finished. Jock could perhaps have done with Bobby back, for midwinter 1974-5 was when Celtic at long last began to lose out to Rangers who would deny them 10 League titles in a row.

Murdoch on the other hand had been far from convinced in 1973 that he was finished, although he had possibly felt that he was getting a little bored in Scotland. Certainly he was now thriving in England, having rid himself of the negative aspects of Scottish football. He certainly did not miss Celtic v. Rangers games, (for which he admitted a hearty dislike) and with a Protestant wife, had no time for sectarianism. He was now far away from that. There was also the fact that he had maybe gone as far as he was likely to go in Scottish football, which in truth, given Celtic's clear superiority over everyone else, was becoming more than a little boring.

He had clearly needed a new lease of life. He now had one, and the early months of 1975 saw a good run in the F.A. Cup for Boro. With one exception, the football was mediocre, but the Boro did reach the Sixth Round, something that they historically did not do very often. The glorious exception to the comparatively dull football was the 4th Round on January 25, when in a pulsating local derby, Middlesbrough beat Sunderland 3-1 before 39,000 spectators, Murdoch leading the way and scoring one of the goals.

Before that they had beaten Wycombe Wanderers after a Replay and a struggle. Wycombe were in these days a part time, amateur team, and had done very well to hold the mighty Boro to a draw at their own Loakes Park ground on January 3rd 1975. It was in danger of becoming seriously embarrassing for Boro however when it took them until the 89th minute of the Replay at Ayresome Park before they scored. And what was significant about the Boro team on these occasions? Why did they play so badly? Why, Bobby Murdoch was out injured!

A similarly pedestrian performance (even though Murdoch was back) was seen in the Fifth Round against Peterborough, but Boro did win through to earn a Sixth Round spot against Birmingham City. Boro had never reached the Semi Final of the F.A.Cup and this seemed to be as good an opportunity as ever before. Birmingham, like Middlesbrough, were traditional underperformers given the size of their catchment area, but on this occasion they attracted 47,260 to St.Andrews to see them. Boro fans were there in strength too (an estimated 10,000 of the astonishingly large crowd) and must have been very disappointed to see them lose by the only goal of the game, scored by Bob Hatton immediately after half-time. The Boro faithful were thus deprived yet again of a chance to see their team play in a Semi Final.

It was a shame because this came in the middle of a great run of form for Boro in which they won four straight League games in a row in the month of March. It was enough to ensure that they finished 7th in the League, a highly creditable performance. It was not, however, quite good enough to qualify for Europe, but it did get them into a piece of meaningless nonsense (now long abandoned) called the Anglo-Scottish Cup. Some good players had emerged and Alan Foggon, who had scored goals in the promotion season, showed that he could also do it in the more rarified atmosphere of Division 1. Yet again Murdoch, although disappointed in the defeats in both Cups, had shown that he had what it took, even at the highest level in England. He was now almost 32 and as yet gave no indication that he was finished.

But Jack Charlton blamed Bobby for Middlesbrough failing to qualify for Europe. It is an interesting story because perhaps it says a little about the character of both men. It was a Wednesday night game at Ayresome Park (April 5th 1975) the fifth last game of the season. Interest was high, for Derby County were going for their second Championship in four years and 30,000 had seen Boro go in one up at half-time with a crisply taken David Mills goal.

Time was slipping away from Derby and Boro won a corner on the right. Murdoch trotted up to take it. Jack sprinted down the touchline and told him to play a short corner and keep the ball in a safe place. Whether Murdoch did not hear or deliberately disobeyed is not clear, but he clearly felt that a second goal would kill the game and fired his corner in. It missed the Boro heads, hit a defender's shoulder and went out for a corner kick on the other side of the ground for another corner.

Murdoch trotted across to take it and this time Jack was in no position to repeat his instruction loudly enough for Bobby to hear. Once again, Murdoch chose the aggressive course and fired in his corner, only this time it was intercepted by Derby's ace goalscorer Kevin Hector who ran the length of the field to equalize. The final whistle went immediately afterwards. Hector's goal was probably instrumental in the eventual winning of the Championship for Derby a few weeks later, but Charlton was furious at Murdoch for losing a point.

It is hard to believe that Murdoch, consummate professional that he was, wilfully disobeyed the Manager. He simply felt that a goal was a possibility from a corner kick ... and it is unfair, surely, for Charlton to claim that this cost the Boro a place in Europe. In any case, Jack has got his facts wrong, for he seems to think that this game was the last of the season. It wasn't, and Boro did lose their next two games after that to Leicester City and Wolves.

It was these defeats that were probably the reasons for Middlesbrough's failure to qualify for Europe and their participation instead in the benign rubbish called the Anglo-Scottish Cup! In any case, perhaps, not qualifying for Europe was no big deal. Unless you have the players to capitalise on the experience, playing in Europe is not always the Shangri-la that some folk would have you believe. A trip to Albania or Bulgaria and a defeat in the First Round are not always the most positive of experiences. Middlesbrough had done well in 1975, but they were something short of good European standard - something of which both Charlton and Murdoch, given their European pedigree, would have been all too aware.

In Scotland, 1975 was the year that Celtic lost the League Championship to Rangers at last, even though they did pick up both the Scottish and the League Cups. Murdoch would have noted that McNeill retired on May 3rd immediately after the Scottish Cup win over Airdrie, and that now only Lennox and Johnstone of the Lisbon Lions were left at Celtic Park. Times certainly were changing, but he himself was still going strong, although becoming more and more aware that relentless age was catching up with him and his ankle in particular.

That summer, Bobby and Kathleen went on holiday to Minorca. There they met old Manager Jock Stein and his wife along with Glasgow bookmaker Tony Queen. Bobby was quite amused to "get a row" as he put it from teetotaller Jock for drinking a pint of beer beside the pool, as distinct from Jock's perennial pot of tea. Jock tore into him about fitness, weight and the general effects that alcohol had on people's system. "You're far too good a player to allow drink to get the better of you!", he told Bobby, not, one imagines, for the first time. Yet Bobby found this quite amusing. He no longer played for Jock, and in any case it was his summer holiday!

Neither Jock nor Bobby were to know this, but on Jock's return to the United Kingdom, he was involved in a horrendous road accident on the notorious A74 road near the English-Scottish border. He might well have lost his life, and in any case required prolonged hospital treatment. He was out of action for a year. This meant that Sean Fallon would be in charge for the 1975-76 season. Sean of course might have done worse than bring back Bobby from Middlesbrough (a possibility that was at least mentioned once or twice in the Scottish Press) given Bobby's experience and the fact that both Stein and McNeill were no longer at Parkhead, one temporarily, the other permanently. Murdoch's expertise might have been of great benefit and prevented Celtic having a totally barren season. Whether Murdoch would have wished to return, however, is a different matter.

Middlesbrough finished half way up the League at 13th in 1975-76, and did well in two of three Cup competitions. They went out anonymously to Bury in the Third Round of the F.A. Cup, but reached the Semi Final of the League Cup and actually won the Anglo-Scottish Cup, a curiously half-hearted affair devoid of the big teams (who were playing in Europe) but nevertheless another medal for the Murdoch cabinet.

The Boro qualified from the North of England section in a virtually unprecedented and gimmicky format whereby a bonus point was awarded for scoring three or more goals in a match! It is awarded the ultimate humiliation by being mentioned only in summary form in the otherwise very comprehensive Rothman's Football Year Book for the following year. The Boro subsequently got the better of a lacklustre Aberdeen, then Mansfield in the Semi Finals, then Fulham in the Final by 1-0 at Ayresome Park and a goalless draw at Craven Cottage on December 9th 1975. It was an achievement of sorts (and certainly much appreciated by the more enthusiastic Boro fans) but attendances of 15,000 and 13,000 in the Final tended to indicate how seriously this tournament was taken.

The tournament survived for a few more years and is notorious in Old Firm circles for the fact that Celtic managed to lose to Burnley one year, and Rangers went one better after that by losing to Chesterfield! St.Mirren won it one year, but the tournament did not last long into the 1980's.

The League Cup on the other hand was more demanding and was a recognised tournament. It had successfully shed its Mickey Mouse image of the 1960's, had now persuaded all clubs to enter and had not yet reached the stage where the big clubs quite deliberately rested their star men for European commitments in the interests of "squad rotation" or "bringing on the youngsters".

Middlesbrough did well before the turn of the year to reach the Semi Finals by beating Bury, Derby County (League Champions of 6 months previously), Peterborough and then Burnley. Excitement once again ran high in the North East for Newcastle were also in the Semis, and an all North East Final at Wembley was envisaged. On January 13th, an all-ticket crowd of 35,000 saw John Hickton score the only goal of the First Leg against Manchester City, but then eight days later Boro unaccountably and irrationally blew up at Maine Road, losing 0-4 to the almost tangible disappointment of the large travelling support.

Everything had gone wrong that night. The team bus was late, the players were therefore out of sorts and had not had time mentally to attune themselves to the game. Murdoch, who had not played the previous Saturday, was not really fit for the game but was pressed into service for his experience and commitment. He was substituted before the end, having sustained an additional knock and clearly suffering from an inability to keep pace with the strong Manchester City team. City were of course an excellent side and would go on to beat Newcastle United in the Final.

It was probably this game more than any other which was responsible for the decline and fall of Middlesbrough F.C. Any Cup Final, even if not a successful one, would have convinced the North East that they had a worthwhile team at Ayresome Park. As it happened, the indigenous, in-built depression which had permeated Teeside all its life, now returned. It began to be believed that Middlesbrough simply did not win trophies, at least not real ones. The Anglo-Scottish Cup perhaps, but that was all. They did not expect to win, therefore they didn't. Once that attitude takes root among management, players, press and supporters, it is difficult to shake off. Murdoch knew this very well, for he had seen the same problem at Parkhead.

In any case, the sands of time for Bobby Murdoch's football career were rapidly running out. His season effectively ended on February 7th when he was substituted with his ankle playing up again. He made a comeback for the reserves soon after that but he only played one more game that season for the first team against Sheffield United on April 17th, feeding young Tony McAndrew for a hat-trick in a 3-0 win. Few people would have realised that this was the last game of Bobby Murdoch.

Murdoch himself certainly did not necessarily think that the end would come so soon. He was training hard in summer 1976 for the next season when he suddenly realised that he couldn't handle the pain any more. 1976 was a particularly fine summer, much remembered by cricket fans for the visit of the all conquering West Indies that year and the sight of the Oval for the Final Test which looked like the Sahara Desert - such had been the lack of rain. Murdoch was therefore training at the Hatton Road ground for the following season on a dry, bone-hard, unyielding surface when suddenly, and with devastating clarity, realised that he could not go on suffering this pain, and that he was therefore finished at the age of 32.

The pain was so intense in spite of his heavily strapped ankle that he stopped running and told coaches Jimmy Greenhalgh and John Coddington and Manager Jack Charlton that his career was over. Charlton was disappointed with this, although it was hardly a surprise. One look at Murdoch's ankle would have been enough to convince anyone that his playing career had been on borrowed time for some while. In fact his whole Middlesbrough career was a bonus - and what a bonus! Jack was convinced that Bobby Murdoch was far too good a man to be lost to football and to Middlesbrough. Within a matter of days, and before any counter attraction from north of the border could manifest itself (Celtic had experienced their first trophyless season since 1964) Murdoch was offered a job as a coach at Middlesbrough. He had little hesitation in accepting.

# On the Bench

Bobby Murdoch was coach to Middlesbrough from 1976 until 1981, working under Jack Charlton for one year then, when Jack became frustrated at the club's lack of ambition in signing new players, under John Neal until 1981. The role of a coach at a football club is not an easy one to define. One is nowadays quite mystified and perplexed at the sheer amount of men one sees on the bench. Presumably they all have a job to do, but it is occasionally difficult to figure out why a club needs quite as many. Terms like "social co-ordinator" or "director of football" are often heard by a mystified public, and the term "physiotherapist" is also heard. He seems to be what we used to call a "trainer", but the difference is that whereas the trainer used to confine himself to a bucket of water, a towel and smelling salts, the physiotherapist now has a suitcase with loads of paraphernalia inside.

Yet what is a coach? The job seems to be to act as assistant to the Manager (but is not to be confused with the Assistant Manager!) basically being in charge of the reserve and the youth teams and reporting to the Manager on the progress of youngsters. It is not always an easy job, for not all youngsters make it in the game. In fact, proportionately, very few do. Often indeed there is a fine line between a player making it and not, and sometimes the coach has the melancholy job of telling a young player that the club will not be requiring his services the following year. This would be something that Murdoch would know about from his years at Parkhead. Murdoch himself (and a few others) certainly made it to the big time, but whatever happened to the likes of Ian Lochhead, Bobby Jeffrey and Samuel Henderson?

An even more nightmarish scenario can unfold if a youngster does not make it, not through lack of ability - there are after all other things one can do with one's life and football can still be played for recreational purposes - but because of an injury. Murdoch's own career was certainly foreshortened by injury (and a bad one at that) but it only really became manifest after he had made it to the top, and had a European medal, many Scottish domestic medals and several Scottish caps to his name. How does one tell a 19 year old that a cartilage or ligament problem has effectively ended his career before it has started, and that persisting in playing football, even at an amateur, recreational level, may cause permanent damage and a limp?

Another side to a coach's repertoire of activities must be the ability to pick players up. They may be going through a bad spell, possibly even unconnected with football - perhaps their marriage or their children - and the coach must be a guide, philosopher and friend. Footballers' lives are transient, unsettled things sometimes, and a player does not always settle well into a new environment. A footballer does not always have a wide choice of career opportunities, even within football. Very few footballers can actually choose where they want to work and live - it all depends on which Manager thinks he can "do a job for us" in the words of that most horrible of football cliches. A move to a particular area or a particular club may well not suit the family - but there are times when it has to be done.

Of course, professional football is not the only walk of life in which this happens - but it is the only walk of life in which every move will be, by its very nature, short term, for, with a few exceptions, professional football is not very often played by anyone over the age of 35.

Most wives are anything but the bimbos and airheads

that are portrayed on the TV series "Footballers'Wives". This does not mean however that everything at home is going to be easy. A player's wife may well be causing trouble to the sensitive soul who is anything but the "hard man" that the terracing punters think he is. Because of the time of life that they are at, professional footballers are likely to have wives and young children. Children of course bring pressure to the most ordered of households, and footballers are sometimes away from home at crucial points, living their high profile, intense existence.

The Press can be nasty. If a journalist takes a dislike to a player, there is a great deal that he can do to undermine the player's confidence in terms of character assassination, or more subtly and tellingly, by what he doesn't say in his weekly report of a game. A footballer who is ignored by the Press i.e mentioned only in the team lists at the end, will gradually find his confidence being sapped.

A coach must understand all this. In particular, after a blasting from the Manager, a player will be down. The coach must be there to nurse him along and without in any way being disloyal to the Manager, support the player, telling him for example that there is no point in a Manager tearing a strip off a bad player. Only the good ones are worth losing one's temper about. "I mind at Parkheid, big Stein used to shout at Billy (McNeill) and Jimmy (Johnstone) - because he knew they could do better." "He left me alane" he would add with a laugh. It wasn't true of course, but Murdoch was a master of psychology, and did have the ability in the true "gallus" Glasgow style to make people laugh - particularly at themselves.

In addition a coach has to organise training sessions. In this respect Murdoch was a huge success, because he had seen training done badly at Parkhead before 1965 and then in an excellent example of the difference between chalk and cheese, done outstandingly well thereafter. Training at

Parkhead in Murdoch's early years seemed to consist of little other than running round the track. Ball work was not encouraged, even apparently not allowed. ("To make them all the more determined to get the ball on Saturday", it was said!) This was bad enough, but even the running round the track was not adequately supervised. Stories are told of players nipping into the empty Jungle to smoke cigarettes, tell dirty jokes and indulge in the mindless politics of any organization - the activity commonly known as "bitching" about each other! The result was that such factionalism was not even hidden - and Celtic fans were frequently treated to the sight (and if you happened to be at the front of the terracing) the sound of Celtic players shouting, bawling and swearing at each other.

In 1964 Neil Mochan arrived as trainer, however, and in 1965, Stein. Training immediately became fun. It was varied and interesting with special routines devised for special circumstances. Weaknesses were highlighted and worked on. Tommy Gemmell tells the story of the aftermath of a game at Muirton Park, Perth in 1968. Celtic had won 6-1, but the goal conceded came with the Celtic defence in "relax" mode (they had just gone 4-0 up) and after a free kick was needlessly given away. Hours and days were then spent on how to clear free kicks! Tommy says that he hoped the St.Johnstone players didn't have as much bother with the six goals that they had conceded in comparison with what Celtic had for their one!

The result was that the Celtic team who won the European Cup in 1967 and achieved immeasurable and almost unbelievable domestic success not only contained no slouches or under-performers, but had a recognisable team spirit about it. They all knew each other, got on well together and although there were the inevitable professional rivalries for positions in the team, there was a distinct lack of cliques and factions - or if there were any, they were well hidden.

Such was the atmosphere that Murdoch endeavoured to create at Middlesbrough. The circumstances were vastly different of course, but it is to Murdoch's credit that he was able to build up a coterie of youngsters and older professionals who never gave less than their best for the club.

In some ways Murdoch's years as coach were the happiest of his life. He was under very little pressure (of the kind that one experiences as a player and as a Manager) and being naturally good with youngsters, he played a large and very rewarding part in the development of future stars like Mark Proctor, David Hodgson, Darren Wood, Craig Johnston, Stephen Bell and Tony Mowbray.

It was a very important job at this time in Middlesbrough's history. 1977 was a pivotal year for the club, with things clearly on a downward slope following the League Cup Semi Final of the previous season. Mediocrity in the League and a certain reputation (based not entirely on fact, but more on the Leeds "credentials" of men like Jack Charlton and Terry Cooper) of being a hard team, rather than a skillful one were forgotten one glorious late winter day on February 26th at Ayresome Park when the Boro, playing fluent football, put Arsenal (Malcolm MacDonald and all) to the sword in the F.A.Cup and defeated them 4-1, with David Mills scoring a glorious hat-trick.

The future looked good, but sadly the Boro were drawn at Liverpool in the next round and obeyed nature's law that everyone must lose at Anfield! Liverpool would of course win the English League and the European Cup that season, and only narrowly lose the Final of the F.A.Cup. The defeat at Anfield happened on March 19th, then the week after that tempers were lost and the red mist descended in the shape of an ordering off at St.James' Park, Newcastle as Newcastle won 1-0. All this was too much for Jack Charlton who resigned a month later. He may or may not have been correct in leaving the Boro citing "lack of ambition" on the part of the Directors but he had repeatedly asked for money to buy players to boost the squad and had been refused. Finances were certainly tight, but perhaps a little investment might have worked well for the club.

The new manager appointed in May 1977 was the little known John Neal who had apparently done well with Wrexham. This appointment put Murdoch in a difficult position. He had always worked well with Jack Charlton but he may have felt his position to be under threat from the new Manager who may have had his own ideas for the coaching staff. Any fears that he may have had on this score were dismissed from the start however when John Neal made it clear that he wanted to work with the talented and famous Scotsman.

There were other problems. The financial situation had now taken another turn for the worse and the Boro were now clearly on a downward spiral. Certainly the Boro supporters found themselves more and more in agreement with the belief that the Middlesbrough Directors lacked ambition. Once again we see the effects of a "never having won anything" tradition, and a lack of appreciation of the big time or any great burning ambition to stay in it. To the despair of all Teeside, for example, Graeme Souness went to Liverpool for £352,000 in January 1978.

Ironically it was the Liverpool capture in almost parallel circumstances six months earlier of another Scottish player that led directly to the demise of Jock Stein. In August 1977, Kenny Dalglish left Parkhead for Liverpool. There was no need for this transfer as far as Celtic's coffers were concerned, and Celtic fans saw this, quite rightly, as lack of ambition. Stein went into a steep decline (although whether through a guilty conscience or general depression or indeed genuine "burn out" at the age of 55 is not clear) and season 1977-78 was a shocker as far as Celtic were concerned and Stein's last. So with Middlesbrough also. As far as most fans were concerned, the transfer of Souness merely proved what Jack Charlton had said. The club did indeed lack ambition. The fans therefore stayed away and with less and less gate revenue, the plain fact was that little money was available to buy players. Therefore a youth policy was even more essential.

Murdoch of course knew all about this. In fact he seemed to be the ideal person for this job. He was himself the product of the Celtic youth policy of the late 1950's and early 1960's. It was arguable whether it was a success or not. Those who thought it was, could point to the European Cup of 1967; those who disagreed would claim that it was only through Jock Stein's return in 1965 that any success at all was brought to Celtic Park. The truth is that youth policies do work, provided they are well thought out and organized - not the result of panic because there was nothing else they could do - and also there must be a sensible balance in any team of youth and experience.

Whatever one felt about that issue, Murdoch was now being asked to replicate the Celtic idea at Ayresome Park. He was not necessarily ill-equipped for the task, for he was a natural at working with youngsters and bringing out the best in them, giving them the benefit of his experience without necessarily patronising them or boring them too often with sentences containing words like "Lisbon" and "Stein". Occasionally he may have had reservations about a youngster being given, perforce, a run in the first team (because of lack of other viable options) but he would keep his opinions to himself and give the youngster every possible encouragement.

Yet he was up against it as well. The club did not really spend a lot of money on its youth policy, and although Murdoch was given every apparent encouragement and indeed enjoyed the favour of those at the top of the club, the lack of finance at Ayresome Park was an almost insuperable problem. But this did not stop the sometimes crazy buying and selling of players. In fact the "silly money" that went about English football at that time gave another impetus to the transfer "inflation" and militated against any possibility of getting the club back onto a permanently stable financial footing.

In January 1979, for example, David Mills went to West Brom for £482,222 and in August of that same year defender Irving Nattrass joined the club from Newcastle for £475,000. It is a shame that the club indulged in this playing Monopoly with these men for with all due respect to them, they were not worth that sort of money and all this did was undermine the credibility of the club who now seemed to be a money making concern first (albeit a none too successful one), then a football team after that. The club would pay a heavy price for all this a few years down the line.

However the likeable John Neal had four tolerably successful seasons against the odds, it must be said. In both 1978 and 1981, they might have made it to their first ever Semi Final of the F.A. Cup but lost in Replays to Leyton Orient and Wolverhampton Wanderers respectively. Life might have been different - in terms of profile and "feel good" if a Semi Final and perhaps even a Final had been reached, but it was not to be. Yet again one felt that the Boro were the victims of their own under-performing history. Sometimes they did not expect to win ... and of course, they didn't. Usually League form was mediocre, but (although relegation was avoided) attendances were dropping, basically in protest at the spineless selling of Souness to Liverpool which tended to prove Jack Charlton's point about lack of ambition - but in 1979 something else happened which had an adverse effect on the North East of England.

On May 3rd 1979 the General Election returned the

Conservatives under Margaret Thatcher. This had followed several years of weak Labour rule and a certain amount of silly, bloody-minded Trade Union activity which had included such high profile and bizarre things as the picketing of a cemetery seemingly to prevent a funeral! This sort of thing was of course gleefully picked up by the tabloid press (sadly in those days in the hands of Tory sympathisers and able to exert an appalling influence on the less well educated of Britain's population). The Conservatives claimed that they would sort the country out. They were clearly in 1979 given a mandate to do so and set about their task with a grim and remorseless determination. The consequence was a rise in unemployment, deliberately created, one felt, to castrate the Trade Union movement and teach a lesson to the working classes - something that was so reminiscent of the vindictiveness of the 1930's. It was a particular blow to the North East. Middlesbrough and the surrounding area did not generally vote Conservative. They could therefore expect no mercy from the relentless rounds of the guns!

There was thus even less money around for people to go to football matches, even if there had been an ambitious team for them to go and watch. The final straw for John Neal was the transfer of a talented Australian called Craig Johnston. This young man had arrived at Ayresome via Australia, had been worked on by Murdoch and had played 64 times for the first team. He felt that he was being undervalued by the club and chose to make his dispute public and prolonged. The fans understandably turned against him, feeling betrayed yet again and in very unhappy circumstances Craig Johnston joined Liverpool in April 1981, a month before Neal himself departed.

It is of course difficult to evaluate and judge the value of Murdoch's five seasons as a coach. Certainly he was much valued by the club and by the fans, and it was a job that he himself liked. Above all else, it involved him in football. Football was the only business that Bobby knew anything about. He had indeed been a sheet metal worker for a short time as an apprentice twenty years ago, but that would have been of limited value to him now if he wanted to get a job outside the game. Like many other great footballers, he was ill equipped for a job in the 'real world'. Yet that was not a problem as long as he had the job in football as coach at Middlesbrough.

It was just a shame that he did the job at such a difficult time in the history of the club. It would have been interesting to see how he and Middlesbrough would have fared at other times in their history, notably in the late 1990's when the club were by and large successful but still lost "big" games. Certainly, Murdoch was not blamed by the angry fans for the problems at the club in the late 1970's. Of course, as the coach, Murdoch was not in the public eye as much as Neal and the Directors who "noblesse oblige" had to take the flak for things that were not entirely of their own making.

On the other hand, Murdoch remained popular with the fans, cheered whenever he took his seat on the bench or in the stand at a game. He was always willing to help out with the local Press as well. The Evening Gazette knew that, even when things were going badly with the club, Murdoch would be good for a quote or a story on some young reserve or how someone's injury was improving. This was of course something that he had learned from Jock Stein. Stein knew how to manipulate the media, and it was noticeable that, although he had the odd disagreement with a particular journalist from time to time, he never antagonized the whole corps of journalists. The time was fast approaching for Murdoch to court the journalists even more.

Occasionally from time to time the Scottish Press ran stories about Murdoch coming home. In 1978, Billy

McNeill became Celtic's Manager to replace Jock Stein and it might have been thought that Bobby, so long McNeill's lieutenant on the field, might have made a good Assistant to Billy. But it was to John Clark that Billy turned for an Assistant first at Aberdeen and then at Celtic - and it was a good partnership. They were in charge at Parkhead for five seasons and won one honour in every season. This was acceptable.

Shortly after Scotland's fiasco of a World Cup in Argentina in 1978 Jock Stein, having spent only a few unhappy weeks with Leeds United, was appointed to the Scotland job. Once again, sections of the Press did their best to persude Jock to approach Bobby, but nothing ever came of this. No doubt however, Jock would unofficially place Murdoch on his list of contacts if he ever wanted an opinion of how a young Scots lad was playing in England.

But Destiny was soon to point the finger at Murdoch.

# The Hotseat

Books have been written on what makes a successful manager. It is a difficult, if not impossible job and unless you are a Bill Shankly, a Jock Stein or an Alex Ferguson, the sad fact is that you are going, sooner or later, to be considered a failure. Quite a few famous managers have been quoted as saying "The only one thing certain in life is that you are sooner or later going to get the sack". And even the three named gentlemen have had their moments in which the supporters were on their backs!

Supporters are difficult people to please. It is often necessary to ask why some supporters turn up every Saturday. Obviously things like family tradition are very important, and there does burn deep in the heart of every supporter a desperate love of his club. It is often said that there are two things in life that no-one can change - one is who his/her mother was, and the other is the beloved football team. Perhaps a better parallel is with the love of one's life, the wife or the husband. Although they can be changed, feelings about them can't - or at least not very easily. Like your football team, they annoy, frustrate and anger you more often than otherwise, but you cannot really alter your feelings for them.

The manager has all this to contend with in so many thousands of cases. He is the man ultimately responsible for whether people have a good weekend or not. It is an awesome responsibility, for on Monday, he is the man who will be lambasted or lauded, exalted or execrated, praised or pilloried, depending on how the team have done.

One is also reminded of the U.S. President who had on

his desk a placard which said "The buck stops here". The manager has no-one ultimately to blame but himself. If he blames his players, the question is rightly asked "Then why did you pick them?". Your normally totally reliable penalty taker suddenly balloons one over the bar. That is your fault. Key men get injured. That is also your fault. The referee has a crazy game and gives everything against you. Yes, that too is your fault.

Middlesbrough and John Neal parted company in May 1981. With the benefit of historical hindsight, it is possible to say that in the circumstances Neal deserves a great deal of credit for keeping Boro in the First Division at least. It did not look like that at the time though and Neal's departure was ill lamented on Teeside. Murdoch, who had been an excellent coach for the past five seasons was invited by Middlesbrough Chairman Charles Amer to assume the mantle of responsibility. Bobby phoned a few friends in Scotland, including Billy McNeill and Jock Stein before accepting the job, but he did not really hesitate for very long. The job was a gamble, but he felt up for it.

He seemed ideal for the job. He knew and loved the club, the town, the area, the supporters. He had produced one or two youngsters for the team, and he had been in the game long enough to know what was required. He had good assistants in Cyril Knowles and Micky Burns. Apart from anything else, he knew football - and he was a winner. He knew how to win things. His early career had taught him a great deal about losing, but he had then worked under a great manager called Stein and a good one called Charlton, and seemed to have learned the trade.

Yet, Bobby's year and a bit was a disaster, albeit one in which there were mitigating and extenuating circumstances. His career as a manager recalls the career of the Roman Emperor Galba in 68 A.D. Galba's career lasted even shorter than Murdoch's tenure of the manager's chair, but he had seemed ideal for the job before he was appointed. The Roman writer Tacitus summed up Galba by saying "omnium consensu capax imperii, nisi imperasset" - "in everyone's eyes, capable of being an Emperor ... if he had not become one".

Bobby's problems on taking up the job in summer 1981 were manifold and possibly greater than they seemed. The team had established themselves as a First Division side, but things had slipped since the days of Jack Charlton. In addition the chill winds of the Thatcherite recession hit the North East of England hard, for the Conservatives had no reason to support or help the Labour voting areas of North Yorkshire. Middlesbrough had never had a huge support (althought their gates had reached comparatively dizzy heights under Jack Charlton) and supporters gave up on supporting a mediocre team, whose Directors had twice in recent years betrayed them badly by selling two players, Graeme Souness and Craig Johnston, to Liverpool. They still however venerated the name of Bobby Murdoch. But was the veneration enough?

Another factor was the very potent one of the media. In the same way that Thatcherite Britain generally worshipped money, so too did the media, the Press and the TV companies worship the larger and more powerful teams to a greater extent than previously. The result was that Liverpool, Arsenal and Manchester United factions began to appear in places like Middlesbrough to a far greater extent than previously. There was of course nothing new about this in Scotland. Teams like Motherwell, Kilmarnock and Falkirk had all suffered from having inside their own town a vocal and obvious "Trojan Horse" or "Fifth Columnist" element which rejected the local team in favour of Celtic or Rangers. It was however a comparatively new phenomenon in England.

Before a ball was kicked that season, Middlesbrough

received a good example of how the law tends to favour the rich. It concerned the Transfer Tribunal of Mark Proctor, a good midfield player whom Murdoch had done a great deal to nurture, but who had now under new contract regulations gone to Notts Forest. This had not been done without a certain amount of dirty work at the crossroads. It concerned Brian Clough, once a playing hero at Ayresome Park but now the outspoken and generally disliked Manager of Notts Forest. Brian was obviously well known and a great attraction for the media circus. Middlesbrough Directors would allege that Proctor had been tapped-up illegally, but this was of secondary concern to the issue of the transfer fee.

The cash strapped Boro valued Proctor at £750,000, by no means an inordinate sum in 1981 for such a good player. Forest said £250,000. One might have expected the Tribunal to split the difference, but in fact they came down closer to Forest's valuation, and said £425,000. Boro needed every single penny of that, for debts were beginning to spiral. The Directors could only see their way out of this mess by further asset stripping, and there was a certain amount of evidence to suggest that there was a great deal of in-fighting as well.

As far as Murdoch was concerned, he needed to make a good start as Manager. He certainly started off with loads of good will, for his personal popularity stayed constant and Boro supporters, although now lower in numbers, were still loyal. A good start would be a real boost for the club in the somewhat limited objective of staying in the First Division. Sadly, things started badly. By the end of October, only two victories had been registered against the none too demanding Birmingham City and Stoke, and it would be March before another three points were gained. By the turn of the year, rumblings were being heard, but there was little that Murdoch could do, for he knew that there was little money with which to buy quality players.

More basically, it was becoming apparent that management was perhaps a job too far for the good natured Bobby. Putting it crudely, he was not enough of a "bastard". Putting it more politely, Murdoch lacked the temperament to be a really good manager. A football manager must be firm and have all the man management skills necessary in other walks of life, but he must be more than that as well. He must be able to lie, to be brutal, to be downright nasty. There must be a mean streak in him somewhere - there certainly was in both the managers that Murdoch played for and was successful for, namely Stein and Charlton, but Bobby himself was not like that.

Jock Stein would often say that players sometimes got complacent and that the Manager had now and again to lose his temper, employing a wide repertoire of foul language, stamping his feet, advancing threateningly to players - or at least pretend to. He should pick a fight with one of his better players over something fairly trivial, like a boot being left on the dressing room floor, or someone whistling as he came in. The wilder spirits would then hear this and fear what would happen to them if the Boss discovered that they had been on the booze or at it with someone else's wife! The story is told of how, when the players were too happy about a good result, Stein would slap his own face before entering the dressing room so that it would be even redder than normal and look as if he were really angry. He would then tear in with "What's the meaning of all this?"

There was also a streak of obsessive paranoia in Stein's character which was not in Bobby's. Once on a European trip with alcohol, of course, forbidden, Stein had listened outside the door of the room that Bobby shared with Billy McNeill. They had both been given their sleeping pill, but it was not having any great effect. If anything it made them ever so slightly light headed, and the two stars were lying on their beds making up silly games and quiz questions for each other along the lines, for example, of "What are the five Scottish teams which begin and end with the same latter?". The answer to that question is of course Celtic, Kilmarnock, Dundee United, East Fife and East Stirlingshire.

The two friends found this quite amusing. Stein was not impressed. He assumed that drink must be the reason and suddenly the door burst open as he and Neil Mochan charged in to look for alcohol! He even appeared slightly disappointed not to find any! It was really rather ironic to think that a sleeping pill is possibly more harmful to anyone than a limited amount of alcohol.

Such paranoia was simply not in Bobby's gentle character. Bobby was kind hearted, laid back, amiable - in many ways like his first manager at Celtic, Jimmy McGrory. The parallel extends further when we consider that both McGrory and Murdoch were outstanding players (Stein and Charlton perhaps less so) and often assumed that players knew how to play the game as well - and as fairly - as they did. They were great ambassadors for their clubs, but failed, at managerial level to bring success.

The failure of Middlesbrough in season 1981-2 lay principally in the forward line. Murdoch would try more than once to sign a young Scotsman called Ally McCoist, but when that did not happen, he failed to find any kind of credible goalscorer. Only 34 goals were scored in the League (considerably less than one a game) and the highest goalscorers both scored 4 each! Ignoring Tony McAndrew for a second who also scored four goals (but his were all penalties!), the equal top goalscorers were Billy Ashcroft, and Dutchman Heine Otto. Yet the Rothman's Yearbook for the following season describes Ashcroft as a defender and Otto as a midfielder!

Some newcomers had arrived - Mick Baxter from Preston North End, Joe Bolton from Sunderland and Bobby

Thomson from Greenock Morton. With all due respect to these men who did their best, none of them was a personality player, the sort of man who could set the supporters alight or move the struggling team up the League. This was for the obvious reason that they were cheap. In no way could they replace the talent that had been lost, nor could they boost the average attendance to much above the 13,000 mark. Against their arrival, Middlesbrough were compelled in March to cancel the contracts of five players - Jeff Peters, Graeme Hedley, Andy McCreech, Mark Robinson and Colin Blackburn. Granted, they were all fringe players, but they might have provided an extra option or two in the run in.

Murdoch did have one imaginative idea however, but it came to nothing. Towards the end of 1981, George Best was available, having been a soldier of fortune in recent years including a spell in Edinburgh with Hibs where he had been brilliant on occasion but unreliable more often than not. He had been seen more than once in parts of Edinburgh where wise and respectable football players didn't go. Now the Irishman claimed to be wanting a English First Division club as a platform to impress Northern Ireland selectors with a view to being selected for the 1982 World Cup in Spain, however unlikely that might seem.

Murdoch offered George terms and for a while it looked as if the talismanic Irish wizard would accept them. It certainly would have given the club a much needed shot in the arm, although there might have been more problems than answers in the long run. In the event, Best decided to go to America instead. Murdoch was disappointed, for he had invested a great deal of effort in trying to get George. Whether it would have been a good move or not, remains open to question, but it was the manner of Best's saying "No" that angered Murdoch.

What had happened was that Bobby and Kevin Amer

(the son of the Chairman) had gone to London to meet Best. Best never turned up and in a somewhat cowardly move, phoned his girlfriend Angie in the U.S.A. to ask her to phone his agent Bill McMurdo in Scotland to say that he was not interested in joining the Boro. Murdoch was rightly upset at all this round-about method of negotiation, if it could be called that.

Murdoch was compelled to persist in the forward line with a Gateshead boy called David Hodgson in the no 9 shirt. It wasn't entirely Hodgson's fault, but he spectacularly and repeatedly failed to deliver and played particularly badly in the home games. The team lost 1-4 to Liverpool in the League Cup (no disgrace in that) and then to Q.P.R at home in the F.A. Cup following a draw on Loftus Road's synthetic pitch. They were unhappy about playing on the synthetic pich, but there was no excuse, for it was at Ayresome Park that they lost. The F.A. Cup defeat was possibly what led to the demise of Murdoch. A good run in the F.A. Cup could have produced for the club a great deal of much needed money, which could have led to new - and quality - players.

A victory over local rivals Sunderland at Roker Park on April 3rd 1982 (on the very day that the House of Commons met in emergency session on a Saturday for the first time since Suez in 1956 to discuss what to do about the Argentine invasion of the Falkland Islands) might have given them a lifeline. It certainly gave the fans something to cheer about, for any victory over local rivals is a good one, but in truth it was a hollow victory over a team who themselves would struggle to avoid relegation, and the crowd of 19,000 told its own tale of a depressed region. The halcyon days of even 6 or 7 years earlier would have seen a crowd of double that amount.

But for Boro it heralded the glimmering of a fightback for there followed two very creditable draws with fellow strugglers Leeds United ( 0-0 at Ayresome and 1-1 at Elland Road) and a 3-0 victory over Notts County with goals from Wood, Bolton and Bailey showing that there was a certain amount of fight, if not talent, left in the Middlesbrough team. There was then a narrow and frustrating 0-1 defeat at the hands of eventual European Cup winners Aston Villa at Villa Park before a couple of good home performances - a 2-1 win over Brighton and a 0-0 draw with Coventry, in which vital chances were missed in the dying minutes and a penalty claim turned down. Had that game been a victory rather than a draw it might have been a different matter.

Early May saw a crucial defeat at Ipswich on May 1st, and then a defeat at home from Arsenal more or less relegated the Boro. Ironically, then the team won two games away from home, and in a moment of supreme agony for Murdoch, the Boro, the hard working players and the long suffering fans, it was after a fighting last minute victory at Swansea on May 15th that relegation was confirmed. This was thanks to results elsewhere, for Sunderland, West Bromwich Albion and Birmingham City all won that day. It would scarcely have helped Murdoch's melancholic condition to be told that Celtic, managed by his old mate Billy McNeill, had won the Scottish League by beating St.Mirren at Parkhead that day. Irony and agony were then piled upon Middlesbrough when, now relegated, they held the new Champions Liverpool to a goalless draw at Ayresome Park in the last game of the season on Tuesday 18th May.

Middlesbrough thus returned to the Second Division. Sadly Murdoch, who had done so much to bring them out of that Division in 1974, now had the melancholy task of taking them back in 1982. Normally football managers do not survive relegation. The blow to finances and pride usually means that the Board meet, a Press Conference is arranged for 10.00 a.m the following morning and the

Manager is on his way with a golden handshake after promising not to talk to the Press. For some reason that did not happen with Murdoch. He had of course only had one year in the job and it was perhaps felt that he deserved another chance. Besides, the name Bobby Murdoch still meant a great deal on Teeside.

But the axe was not long delayed. Murdoch lasted only seven games into the new season in the Second Division. No victory was recorded, although there were respectable away draws at Derby County and Newcastle United. But a 1-4 defeat at home to Fulham on September 18th followed by a 0-3 defeat at Crystal Palace saw only 5,929 fans turn up to Ayresome Park to see Grimsby Town. Long before the end of this 1-4 defeat, the fans made their feelings plain about what was happening to the club, and the hitherto sacrosanct head of Bobby Murdoch was called for.

Murdoch, his wife and his family (Kathleen was 17, Bobby was 15 and Barrie was 10) had been suffering hell for some time. School mates would not have been making life easy for them. On Thursday 29th September, Murdoch was summoned from the golf course and went to Ayresome Park to be asked to "tender his resignation", a newspaper euphemism for being sacked. He was very upset at all this, because he was a genuine man and had developed a genuine love for the club. It was a sad end to a magnificent contribution to football, but Murdoch in taking the manager's job had gone one step too far. He was a fine player and a fine coach (something he continued to do on an unofficial basis after his return to Scotland) but as a manager, history must suspend judgement.

It is of course easy to point to season 1981-2 and say that this was the year that the Boro were relegated and that the manager must take the blame. Yes, but there were other circumstances as well. The decline of the Boro had started long before that - some might argue since the departure of

Jack Charlton - and there was not a great deal of leeway in terms of transfer possibilities. The decline would continue spectacularly after Murdoch's departure as well. His successor was Malcolm Allison who had already been a failure at Manchester City and Crystal Palace and events spiralled out of control until the dreadful day in Boro's history in 1986 when the liquidators moved in.

Murdoch himself was refreshingly honest about his managerial career. The team was mostly youngsters and money was tight. The club needed to sell, and it was particularly disheartening for Murdoch to see men that he had reared like Mike Proctor leaving the club. Stephen Bell had ability but lacked temperament, and he too was a loss to the club. He was more successful with Tony Mowbray who had a lasting effect on both Middlesbrough and Celtic. Tony was all set to give up the game when he was 16 but Murdoch talked Mowbray and his mother in Redcar out of that idea. He made his debut at the age of 18 against Newcastle's Kevin Keegan.

"The players that I did sign" said Murdoch "no disrespect for them, but they were mostly patchwork". He quotes Ray Hankin and Dave Thomas who were acquired from Vancouver Whitecaps, and his old friend Bobby Lennox in Kansas gave him Paul Sugrue - but these men were indeed patchwork and Murdoch had neither the financial resources nor latterly the emotional power to address the problem.

His departure from Middlesbrough to his native Rutherglen was full of sadness and depression but such was the man that there was no bitterness nor recrimination. The family had enjoyed themselves in the North East, where they had been made to feel welcome among people who were by no means dissimilar to Glaswegians, and Bobby's death in 2001 provoked as much grief and regret in Middlesbrough as it did in Scotland.

The author recalls watching a cricket game on a

gloriously hot day at Acklam Road, Middlesbrough some time in the mid 1980's. Two craggy elderly Yorkshire men were talking about Geoff Boycott, Ray Illingworth and the interminable problems of Yorkshire Cricket Club. Taking his life in his hands, the author bravely and presumptuously ventured an opinion on this difficult subject, and his Scottish accent immediately gave away his country of origin. He was immediately asked "Did you ever see Bobby Murdoch?", as if the only virtue of being Scottish in Middlesbrough was sharing the same nationality as Bobby Murdoch!

Cricket was immediately shelved in the minds of these spectators for a whole session between lunch and tea while the subject of Bobby Murdoch in his glory was dissected and the author held court about what Bobby Murdoch was like in his prime. His exegesis was interrupted only for some occasional applause as a half century was reached or a wicket captured.

# Life as a Legend

The departure of Murdoch from the manager's job at Middlesbrough in September 1982 effectively marked the end of Murdoch's footballing life. He may have dabbled with the idea of becoming a manager in Scotland, but Jock Stein warned him against it saying that "he kicked with the wrong foot" i.e that his Catholic background might count against him.

Perhaps this was just Jock being tactful and trying to tell Bobby that football managing in Scotland was a tough game, and that his unsuccessful spell as manager of the Boro should be a warning to him never to try it again. Funnily enough, Andy Lynch in an interview with The Scotsman on May 4th 2002 tells that he too was given similar words of caution from Jock Stein, and it was certainly true that there was at that time a paucity of managers and coaches in Scotland of the Roman persuasion. But not being a manager in Scotland (for whatever reason) may well have turned out to be a blessing in disguise. It is hardly the job with the best long term career prospects.

Yet what was Bobby to do? He was just 38 when the family returned to Scotland, and although during his playing and coaching career hitherto, he had accumulated a reasonable amount of money, some other source of revenue would come in handy. His children were now growing up, Kathleen being 17, Bobby 15 and Barrie 10 - and Bobby Murdoch was very much a family-orientated man.

He did try a variety of jobs, notably running a public house but that was not a success. He helped out with hospitality from time to time at Celtic Park on matchdays and Shaun Keogh tells the story of how he once interviewed Murdoch at Celtic Park.

'I am waiting in the Parkhead reception area when Murdoch hobbles across from the car park with his son and two of his small grandsons. Within seconds he is surrounded by young autograph hunters, all of whom born 20 years or more after he left Celtic, but who all know his name and now rugged features as if he were a member of the current Celtic squad. Murdoch offers me a firm and friendly handshake, then whisks his family and me through security reception. Without me even asking, he immediately takes me for a tour of the Celtic museum, trophy room, boardroom, dressing rooms and finally to the heart of this awesome stadium - pitchside. We talk animatedly, and he patiently poses for photographs, even though his ankle is giving him pain after being on his feet for ten minutes.'

Murdoch continued to suffer from his ankle injury which caused dreadful problems for him. The problem was that he had no ligaments. Following an operation in 1994 in which some material was taken out of his hip and fused into his ankle, he did get some relief. He described it as a "permanent ache" now rather than "searing pain". For example, some nights he had to sleep with his ankle outside the bedclothes, for he could not stand anything on it. Some days he could hardly walk and latterly became totally dependent on his stick. Some nights if he had to go upstairs to the toilet at any point during the night, he would simply go to bed because he could not face the pain of coming down and going up the stairs again.

All this meant that he could have no real footballing commitment, but he did occasionally help his old friend Jimmy Johnstone to coach youngsters. He certainly had a talent for that with loads of patience and a genuine interest in children and young people, and of course a love of the game which had lasted all his life.

He remained a deeply religious man, going to Mass every Sunday. Even the Saturday before his death, for example, he wanted to go to his granddaughter's first Communion, but was too ill to attend. Because he was a genuine Christian man, he despised the Catholic v. Protestant sectarianism that still was present in Scotland at the time of his death. Even if now in an emasculated and discredited form thanks to Rangers eventual departure from their "No Catholics" policy (and the apparent fact that some weeks in the 1990's Rangers had more Catholics playing for them than Celtic did!), the bigotry could not entirely be ignored.

Murdoch's religion seemed to include something about humility. Once he met someone he never forgot them (there were no gradations in his friendships). He was a frequent visitor to Parkhead, even when there wasn't a game on. His first port of call would often be not the Manager, not the players and certainly not the Directors, but the laundry lady called Angie who would share tea and gossip with him.

His religion also included something about charity. He would do anything for anyone if it were for a charitable cause. He was aware that Celtic had been founded for charitable purposes, even if this seems on occasion to have been forgotten in the mega buck era of the early 21st century. Murdoch would be conspicuously present at any function for charity, and the story is told about how he found himself looking at TV and seeing starving African children. Bobby had to leave the room, fearing that he might embarrass everyone by shedding tears.

He retained his love for the two teams he had played for, Celtic in particular. The author remembers meeting him at Celtic Park in February 1998. 1998 was a vital year for the club, because if Rangers had won the League, it would have destroyed for ever Celtic's "9 in a row" from 1966 to 1974 (something obviously very close to Murdoch's heart), for it would have been 10 in a row for Rangers. Celtic had been playing Hearts at Tynecastle the previous Sunday afternoon and it had been shown on terrestrial TV. Celtic should have won by a barrow load, but Hearts in fact equalized through a Quitongo goal late into injury time. Bobby discussed the game in detail than admitted candidly "I couldn't eat my tea after Herts (sic) equalized". In that he was no different from most Celtic supporters.

He still retained his love for music, liking Dean Martin, The Mavericks and U2 as well as his traditional Elvis Presley and Buddy Holly, while Kathleen was fond of Barry Manilow. His particular favourite song was "Unforgettable", a song which featured at his funeral and which in so many ways summed up the man.

He was given a Gold Disc by Jim Kerr and Charlie Birchell of Simple Minds. Jim Kerr in fact has an Inter Milan shirt, thanks to Bobby Murdoch. Bobby had this souvenir of Lisbon, but generous as always, he gave it for auction on behalf of a small girl with a brain tumour. Jim Kerr bought it, and treasures it to this day.

He retained many friendships from his life in football, especially the Lisbon Lions whom he met with regularity, but he was also friendly with old opponents like Jim Baxter whom he visited when Jim was ill. He remained devoted to his beloved Kathleen who continued working at her Rutherglen's lawyer's office. Like many a couple, they had their storms but the way in which they resolved one such "squall" speaks volumes for the pair of them, and casts further ridicule on Glasgow's absurd divide which masquerades in turn under the twin guises of football and religion.

It concerned a Rangers player called Davie Provan, with whom Murdoch had many a doughty duel in the 1960's. This Davie Provan is not of course to be confused with the Celtic player of the late 1970's and early 1980's who now commentates for Sky Television. The Murdochs had been very friendly with the Provans (as indeed they had been with many Rangers players) and sadly Davie's wife died of cancer at an early age. Bobby and Kathleen decided at that funeral that human life was too short for acrimony and separation and that it was time to mend any holes in their marriage. As it is, their son and Provan's daughter currently exchange text message with none too complimentary remarks about the relative merits of the teams that their fathers played for!

Other Rangers players that Bobby remained friendly with were Sandy Jardine, Willie Henderson, Alec Willoughby and a gentleman called "Scrambled". This was of course John Greig. "John Greig" rhymes with "Scrambled Egg", so John has this nickname. Those who watched John Greig play in the 1960's and 1970's would be surprised that he is now friendly with Celtic players, for there was certainly "no holds barred" in the actual games. Yet John is remembered with affection by both Celtic and Rangers supporters for the years in which he commentated and summarized for BBC Radio Scotland in which he was always scrupulously fair without in any way denying his Rangers background. And certainly, in no way does he have the slightest resemblance to a scrambled egg.

Opinions will differ about what Bobby achieved in his life, but there will be no disputing the contention that he was a very fine football player indeed. One hesitates to use the word "best" and indeed it is not something that he would have claimed himself. He was certainly however a member of the "best" ever Scottish football team. The team that he played for, the Lisbon Lions (sometimes one feels that this concentration on the 11 men who actually won in Lisbon is a little unfair to the peripheral players and those who came later or earlier) was undeniably the greatest football team in Scottish history, replacing quite comprehensively the previous best team, the Wembley Wizards - the Scotland team which beat England 5-1 at Wembley in 1928.

Yet many of the Lisbon Lions themselves will state that Murdoch was the best of the lot of them. Murdoch's friend Pat Rolink recalls on many occasions organizing "Meet the Panel" events for supporters. People like Bertie Auld and Jiimmy Johnstone, given their cheeky, pawky, essentially Glaswegian humour were in great demand. Naturally, questions like "Who is your favourite Celtic player" were asked. With a surprising consistency, the players would nominate Bobby Murdoch, the powerhouse of the team.

In the context of British and indeed World football, it is also hard to deny the Lisbon Lions an honoured place. Other teams may have won the European Cup oftener, but very few have done so by playing better and more exciting football. They were the team that put Scotland on the map, well worth a mention among great Scotsmen over the centuries in other fields - William Wallace, Robbie Burns, Alexander Graham Bell and John Logie Baird. They won a cherished place in the hearts of all Europe for Celtic, Glasgow and Scotland. To paraphrase what Padraig Pearse said of the men involved in the Easter Rising of 1916 - "You have redeemed Glasgow from many shames and made her name splendid among the names of cities".

And where did Bobby Murdoch fit into all this? It is of course invidious to say who was better than whom, and the historian must beware of falling into the trap of not comparing like with like. Gemmell for example was a great overlapping full back, Johnstone was the trickiest winger in the world on his day, McNeill was a commanding centre half and captain etc. They cannot and should not however be compared with Bobby Murdoch who was quite simply the engine of the team and recognised as such by most of the people who knew something about football.

There can be little doubt that "The Shamrock" fanzine of 1963 and the more discerning of the support had a point when they said that Murdoch was in the wrong place in the forward line. Stein spotted this almost instantly (he may even have been aware of it while he was still Manager of Dunfermline and Hibs) and it was his move of Murdoch to the right half position which changed the pedestrian Celtic team of early 1965 into the world beaters of a few years down the line.

It possibly worked to Murdoch's benefit that he also saw the down side of football as well. He lived through the dreadful days at Parkhead in the early 1960's, the disastrous loss of what would have been the second European Cup in 1970, a few major disppointments while playing for Scotland and finally the cash-strapped necessity of a hand-to mouth existence at Middlesbrough, leading inevitably to relegation and the sack. Life is not always a bed of roses in football. Murdoch's life certainly was not that, but he did have the strength of character to fight back from adversity. It made him a better footballer and a better man.

Celtic have always had great right halves (or right sided midfield players as they would now be called). There was Sunny Jim Young from 1904 until 1917 whom Eugene MacBride in his excellent "An Alphabet of the Celts" places as the greatest Celt of all time for his play and captaincy. There was also the silky passing of Peter Wilson of the late 1920's and early 1930's - a player much loved by those who recall him. But Jimmy McGrory in "A Lifetime in Paradise" puts Murdoch marginally ahead of Wilson in his team of the greatest Celts of all time. McGrory says "There is little between them in ability. Both could pass the ball well but Murdoch could score goals and spectacular ones at that, and he gets my vote because of that"

McGrory thus goes for Murdoch, and he had seen the pair of them. There were very few people who actually saw both Sunny Jim and Bobby Murdoch (they were after all 50 or 60 years apart) but one veteran supporter who would always claim that Jimmy Quinn and Patsy Gallacher were untouchable, when pushed on the relative merits of Young and Murdoch would not commit himself other than to say allegorically that his grand-daughter was as nice looking as her grand-mother had been! In truth, it is difficult to compare players of different ages, because the game was so different.

It remains a touch unfortunate that Murdoch only got 12 caps for Scotland and never had the opportunity of representing his country at World Cup Finals. There were very few players better than he, although it must be admitted in all honesty that Scotland did at that time have very many good midfield players. Murdoch was unfortunate in that both games that he played against England in 1966 and 1969 were shockers, and significantly, Scotland lost both games. In 1966 he ill-advisedly played when suffering from an illness and in 1969, he was simply jaded at the end of an incredibly long and hitherto successful season.

Yet, there remains a dream scenario which might have happened. Suppose, just suppose, that Scotland had qualified for the 1966 World Cup Finals in England. (In fact, a dreadfully understrength team lost to Italy in December 1965 in the Qualifying Section). The games would have been played in good British conditions with Scotland presumably based at Middlesbrough and Sunderland with a large Scottish support to see them play North Korea, Russia and Chile. Spearheaded by a fit Murdoch, managed by Jock Stein and containing Law, Bremner, Greig and Baxter, it would have been difficult to see Scotland not qualifying from that group. After that, who knows? There might have been a Wembley Wizards Mark 2. No goals that weren't over the line, no thinking it's all over. The abiding memory would have been that of the Queen, putting a brave face on it and trying to think of Balmoral and Glamis rather than Sandringham and Windsor as she handed over the World Cup to a sweaty but smiling Billy McNeill! It might and indeed could have happened!

Murdoch remained a very warm character, a point made by all those who paid tribute to him. It would be difficult to find anyone whom one could class as his enemy - and this in spite of having spent his life in professional football where enemies are notoriously easy to acquire. He was simple and unpretentious, frequently seen in his later years walking about his native Rutherglen with his stick, talking to anyone and everyone. The fact that he had once been one of the best footballers in the world made no difference. In the Vogue Bar in Rutherglen which he frequented and where there is now a memorial to him, he was just an ordinary punter. One is reminded of the story of the great Jimmy Quinn. He looked, walked and talked like "an ordinary man". That could also be said about the great Bobby Murdoch.

Referees, the traditional bane of the professional footballer? Bobby did share the Celtic paranoia about R.H.Davidson, particularly with reference to his appalling decision to award a penalty to Aberdeen in the 1970 Scottish Cup Final. He did not rate Alastair McKenzie of Coatbridge particularly highly, but he respected most others like Hugh Phillips and Tom Wharton, while accepting of course that they could make mistakes. He tells the story of how he once made a polite protest to Tom Wharton on a day when things were not going very well for Celtic or Murdoch. He said "I think you might have got that one wrong, Mr.Wharton." The reply was equally charming "Ah, but you're not having a great day yourself Mr.Murdoch, are you?"

One thing however that may have counted against Murdoch was his apparent acceptance of pain. He had been in pain for nearly 40 years with his ankle (although it did grow and lessen in intensity from time to time) and therefore he did not moan about anything being sore. When he suffered pain in other parts of his body, he did not as a reflex action, run to his doctor to complain. Had he done so, quicker action might have been taken when his health took a serious turn for the worse.

Murdoch died after a short illness (although it was true to say that he had been in poor health for some time) in the early hours of Tuesday May 15th 2001. He had hoped to be able to attend his grandaughter Rachel's first communion on Saturday 12th, but was too ill to attend. He was admitted to Victoria Hospital, Glasgow suffering from a stomach hernia complaint on the Sunday. His condition soon deteriorated and very early on the Monday morning of May 14th Kathleen received a phone call to say that he had "thrown off a stroke" as it was somewhat unusually put. The stroke effectively rendered impossible any attempt to deal with the strangulated hernia, and in the early hours of Tuesday morning, Bobby Murdoch passed away. He was 56. His funeral was held at St.Columbkilles Church in Main Street, Rutherglen on Friday 19th May.

He was survived by his mother Barbara, his wife Kathleen, his three children Kathleen, Bobby and Barrie, and five grandchildren Bobby, Rachel, Paul, John and Neve and on June 6th 2001 (what would have been his 37th wedding anniversary) his wife and family buried his ashes in front of the Jock Stein Stand at Celtic Park.

Of the many tributes paid to Bobby, there was one which linked him to his old rival but latterly firm friend Jim Baxter who had died about a month before Bobby did. It was a banner which said quite simply "Murdoch R.I.P. Baxter R.I.P. God's got some half back line now!" There was something very Glaswegian about it - in that it combined both teams with religion, but not in the despicable, sectarian way that does credit to no-body. It also implied two things about God - one being that he likes football and the other being that he has a sense of humour. Perhaps He does. Indeed one hopes so.

Soon after his death a ballad was produced by a group called "Charlie and The Bhoys" called quite simply "The Ballad of Bobby Murdoch" and goes to the tune of "Bold Robert Emmett", the Irish patriot who belonged to a union called "United Irishmen" who opposed the 1801 Act of Union. Emmett was executed in 1803. Emmett very soon acquired martyr status, but he was hardly any more mourned than Bobby Murdoch

*A soft day in the springtime, a lark in the morning*
*The 15th of May, news I switched on,*
*the radio told me, of my boyhood hero,*
*He told me that Bobby to heaven had gone*

*Bold Bobby Murdoch the darling of Parkhead*
*Bold Bobby Murdoch died with a smile*
*He was the heart of the great Lisbon Lions,*
*To Bold Bobby Murdoch we say Slan Go Foill*

*The news travelled over a stunned Scottish people*
*Gone was the man who loved Celtic so well*
*A family man both loving and caring*
*And all of your friends bid a fond farewell*

*So goodbye to Ronnie, to Jim and to Tommy,*
*To Billy and John I must close my eyes,*
*Farewell to Jinky, to Willie and Stevie,*
*To Bertie and Bobby in dear Paradise.*

★

The generation of Celtic (and Middlesbrough) supporters who saw Bobby Murdoch in his prime are now well into middle age with expanding waist lines and receding hair lines in many cases. They have a great deal to be thankful to Bobby Murdoch for. Football will continue to be played for a very long time, possibly for ever. Every generation will have its heroes. The author recalls for example having great bother persuading his father that anyone was better than Patsy Gallacher. Any attempt to sing the praises of Puskas or Pele was always rebutted with "Look, I've seen Patsy Gallacher".

Arguments about who was the best player of all time are futile and pointless. Football, the beautiful game, for all its simplicity and complexity, does change and adapt to different circumstances, different climates, different times, different geographical locations and different tactics. There is no point in claiming that one player is the best of all time, for it can never be proved. I would however claim the right at all times whenever football is being discussed and argued about to say "Look, I've seen Bobby Murdoch".

He was indeed "Different Class".

# Career Statistics

## Glasgow Celtic

## 1962-63

### League Cup

| | | | | |
|---|---|---|---|---|
| Hearts | Parkhead | 3-1 | 1 | 11/08/62 |
| Dundee | Dens Park | 0-1 | 0 | 15/08/62 |
| Dundee U | Parkhead | 4-0 | 0 | 18/08/62 |
| Hearts | Tynecastle | 2-3 | 1 | 25/08/62 |
| Dundee | Parkhead | 3-0 | 0 | 29/08/62 |
| Dundee U | Tannadice | 0-0 | 0 | 01/09/62 |

### League

| | | | | |
|---|---|---|---|---|
| Rangers | Parkhead | 0-1 | 0 | 08/09/62 |
| Aberdeen | Parkhead | 1-2 | 0 | 22/09/62 |
| Raith Rvrs | Stark's Park | 2-0 | 1 | 29/09/62 |
| Kilmarnock | Parkhead | 1-1 | 0 | 06/10/62 |
| Dundee | Dens Park | 0-0 | 0 | 17/11/62 |
| Partick Th | Parkhead | 0-2 | 0 | 24/11/62 |
| Hibernian | Easter Road | 1-1 | 1 | 01/12/62 |
| Hearts | Parkhead | 2-2 | 0 | 08/12/62 |
| Falkirk | Parkhead | 2-1 | 0 | 29/12/62 |
| Rangers | Ibrox | 0-4 | 0 | 01/01/63 |
| Airdrie | Parkhead | 3-1 | 0 | 02/03/63 |
| St.Mirren | Parkhead | 1-1 | 1 | 09/03/63 |
| Q. South | Palmerston | 5-2 | 0 | 16/03/63 |
| Dundee | Parkhead | 4-1 | 0 | 23/03/63 |
| Partick Th. | Firhill | 5-2 | 1 | 02/04/63 |

| | | | | |
|---|---|---|---|---|
| 3rd Lanark | Parkhead | 2-1 | 0 | 20/04/63 |
| Dunfermline | East End | 1-1 | 0 | 27/04/63 |
| Clyde | Parkhead | 2-0 | 0 | 06/05/63 |
| Dundee Utd | Tannadice | 0-3 | 0 | 11/05/63 |

**Scottish Cup**

| | | | | |
|---|---|---|---|---|
| Hearts | Parkhead | 3-1 | 1 | 06/03/63 |
| G. Fairydean | Parkhead | 6-0 | 3 | 13/03/63 |
| St.Mirren | Love Street | 0-1 | 0 | 30/03/63 |
| Raith Rvrs | Ibrox | 5-2 | 0 | 12/04/63 |
| Rangers | Hampden | 1-1 | 1 | 04/05/63 |
| Rangers | Hampden | 0-3 | 0 | 15/05/63 |

**Glasgow Cup**

| | | | | |
|---|---|---|---|---|
| Rangers | Parkhead | 3-2 | 2 | 22/11/62 |
| Ptk. Thistle | Firhill | 3-1 | 0 | 03/12/62 |
| Trd. Lanark | Hampden | 1-2 | 1 | 08/04/63 |

**Played 34 goals 14**

# 1963-64

**League Cup**

| | | | | |
|---|---|---|---|---|
| Rangers | Parkhead | 0-3 | 0 | 10/08/63 |
| Kilmarnock | Rugby Park | 0-0 | 0 | 14/08/63 |
| Qn. South | Parkhead | 1-1 | 0 | 17/08/63 |

**League**

| | | | | |
|---|---|---|---|---|
| Dunfermline | Parkhead | 2-2 | 1 | 05/10/63 |
| Aberdeen | Parkhead | 3-0 | 0 | 12/10/63 |
| Dundee Utd | Tannadice | 3-0 | 1 | 19/10/63 |
| Airdrie | Parkhead | 9-0 | 1 | 26/10/63 |
| E. Stirling | Firs Park | 5-1 | 0 | 02/11/63 |
| Partick Thistle | Parkhead | 5-3 | 0 | 09/11/63 |
| Hibernian | Easter Road | 1-1 | 1 | 16/11/63 |
| Kilmarnock | Parkhead | 5-0 | 0 | 23/11/63 |
| Dundee | Dens Park | 1-1 | 1 | 30/11/63 |

| | | | | |
|---|---|---|---|---|
| St.Johnstone | Parkhead | 3-1 | 3 | 07/12/63 |
| Hearts | Tynecastle | 1-1 | 0 | 14/12/63 |
| Motherwell | Parkhead | 2-1 | 0 | 21/12/63 |
| Qu. South | Palmerston | 2-0 | 0 | 28/12/63 |
| Rangers | Parkhead | 0-1 | 0 | 01/01/64 |
| Falkirk | Parkhead | 7-0 | 0 | 04/01/64 |
| St.Mirren | Parkhead | 3-0 | 0 | 18/01/64 |
| Dunfermline | East End | 0-1 | 0 | 01/02/64 |
| Aberdeen | Pittodrie | 3-0 | 0 | 08/02/64 |
| E. Stirling | Parkhead | 5-2 | 2 | 29/02/64 |
| Ptk Thistle | Firhill | 2-2 | 1 | 11/03/64 |
| Hibernian | Parkhead | 5-0 | 2 | 14/03/64 |
| Kilmarnock | Rugby Park | 0-4 | 0 | 21/03/64 |
| Motherwell | Fir Park | 4-0 | 1 | 28/03/64 |
| Dundee | Parkhead | 2-1 | 0 | 01/04/64 |
| St.Johnst'ne | Muirton | 1-1 | 1 | 04/04/64 |
| Hearts | Parkhead | 1-1 | 0 | 18/04/64 |

**Scottish Cup**

| | | | | |
|---|---|---|---|---|
| Morton | Cappielow | 1-3 | 0 | 25/01/64 |
| Airdrie | Parkhead | 4-1 | 1 | 15/02/64 |
| Rangers | Ibrox | 0-2 | 0 | 07/03/64 |

**European Cup Winners' Cup**

| | | | | |
|---|---|---|---|---|
| Basle | Parkhead | 5-0 | 1 | 10/10/63 |
| D. Zagreb | Parkhead | 3-0 | 0 | 04/12/63 |
| D. Zagreb | Zagreb | 1-2 | 1 | 11/12/63 |
| S. Brat'lava | Parkhead | 1-0 | 1 | 26/02/64 |
| S. Brat'lava | Bratislava | 1-0 | 0 | 04/03/64 |
| M.T.K. | Parkhead | 3-0 | 0 | 15/04/64 |
| M.T.K. | Budapest | 0-4 | 0 | 29/04/64 |

**Glasgow Cup**

| | | | | |
|---|---|---|---|---|
| Partick | Firhill | 1-1 | 0 | 11/11/63 |
| Partick | Parkhead | 2-1 | 0 | 23/11/63 |
| Third Lanark | Parkhead | 1-1 | 1 | 08/01/64 |
| Third Lanark | Cathkin | 3-0 | 1 | 21/01/64 |

| | | | | |
|---|---|---|---|---|
| Clyde | Parkhead | 2-0 | 0 | 25/03/64 |

**Played 44 goals 21**

# 1964-65

## League Cup

| | | | | |
|---|---|---|---|---|
| Partick | Parkhead | 0-0 | 0 | 08/08/64 |
| Hearts | Tynecastle | 3-0 | 2 | 12/08/64 |
| Kilmarnock | Parkhead | 4-1 | 0 | 15/08/64 |
| Partick | Firhill | 5-1 | 0 | 22/08/64 |
| Hearts | Parkhead | 6-1 | 3 | 26/08/64 |
| Kilmarnock | Rugby Park | 0-2 | 0 | 29/08/64 |
| East Fife | Parkhead | 6-0 | 0 | 16/09/64 |
| Morton | Ibrox | 2-0 | 0 | 29/09/64 |
| Rangers | Hampden | 1-2 | 0 | 24/10/64 |

## League

| | | | | |
|---|---|---|---|---|
| Motherwell | Fir Park | 3-1 | 1 | 19/08/64 |
| Clyde | Shawfield | 1-1 | 0 | 12/09/64 |
| Dundee Utd | Parkhead | 1-1 | 0 | 19/09/64 |
| Hearts | Tynecastle | 2-4 | 1 | 26/09/64 |
| Aberdeen | Pittodrie | 3-1 | 1 | 10/10/64 |
| Morton | Parkhead | 1-0 | 0 | 12/10/64 |
| St.Mirren | Parkhead | 4-1 | 1 | 17/10/64 |
| Kilmarnock | Rugby Park | 2-5 | 0 | 28/10/64 |
| Airdrie | Parkhead | 2-1 | 0 | 31/10/64 |
| St.John'tn | Muirton | 0-3 | 0 | 07/11/64 |
| Dundee | Parkhead | 0-2 | 0 | 14/11/64 |
| Falkirk | Parkhead | 3-0 | 0 | 21/11/64 |
| Third Lanark | Cathkin | 3-0 | 1 | 28/11/64 |
| Ptk Thistle | Firhill | 4-2 | 0 | 12/12/64 |
| Dunfermline | Parkhead | 1-2 | 0 | 19/12/64 |
| Motherwell | Parkhead | 2-0 | 0 | 26/12/64 |
| Rangers | Ibrox | 0-1 | 0 | 01/01/65 |
| Dundee Utd | Tannadice | 1-3 | 0 | 09/01/65 |
| Hearts | Parkhead | 1-2 | 0 | 16/01/65 |
| Morton | Cappielow | 3-3 | 0 | 23/01/65 |

| | | | | |
|---|---|---|---|---|
| Aberdeen | Parkhead | 8-0 | 1 | 30/01/65 |
| St.Mirren | Love Street | 5-1 | 1 | 13/02/65 |
| Kilmarnock | Parkhead | 2-0 | 0 | 27/02/65 |
| Airdrie | Broomfield | 6-0 | 0 | 10/03/65 |
| St.Johnst'ne | Parkhead | 0-1 | 0 | 13/03/65 |
| Dundee | Dens Park | 3-3 | 0 | 20/03/65 |
| Hibernian | Parkhead | 2-4 | 0 | 22/03/65 |
| Third Lanark | Parkhead | 1-0 | 0 | 03/04/65 |
| Hibernian | Easter Road | 4-0 | 1 | 07/04/65 |
| Falkirk | Brockville | 2-6 | 0 | 14/04/65 |
| Ptk Thistle | Firhill | 1-2 | 0 | 17/04/65 |
| Dunfermline | East End | 1-5 | 0 | 28/04/65 |

**Scottish Cup**

| | | | | |
|---|---|---|---|---|
| St.Mirren | Love Street | 3-0 | 0 | 06/02/65 |
| Queen's Pk. | Hampden | 1-0 | 0 | 20/02/65 |
| Kilmarnock | Parkhead | 3-2 | 0 | 06/03/65 |
| Motherwell | Hampden | 2-2 | 0 | 27/03/65 |
| Motherwell | Hampden | 3-0 | 0 | 31/03/65 |
| Dunfermline | Hampden | 3-2 | 0 | 24/04/65 |

**Inter Cities Fairs Cup**

| | | | | |
|---|---|---|---|---|
| Leixoes | Portugal | 1-1 | 1 | 23/09/64 |
| Leixoes | Parkhead | 3-0 | 1 | 07/10/64 |
| Barcelona | Barcelona | 1-3 | 0 | 18/11/64 |
| Barcelona | Parkhead | 0-0 | 0 | 02/12/64 |

**Glasgow Cup**

| | | | | |
|---|---|---|---|---|
| Rangers | Parkhead | 2-1 | 0 | 30/04/65 |
| Clyde | Parkhead | 3-0 | 0 | 03/05/65 |
| Queen's Pk. | Hampden | 5-0 | 1 | 11/05/65 |

**played 54 goals 16**

# 1965-66

## League Cup

| | | | | |
|---|---|---|---|---|
| Dundee Utd | Tannadice | 1-2 | 0 | 14/08/65 |
| Motherwell | Parkhead | 1-0 | 0 | 18/08/65 |
| Dundee | Parkhead | 0-2 | 0 | 21/08/65 |
| Dundee Utd | Parkhead | 3-0 | 0 | 28/08/65 |
| Motherwell | Fir Park | 3-2 | 0 | 01/09/65 |
| Dundee | Dens Park | 3-1 | 0 | 04/09/65 |
| Raith Rvrs | Stark's Park | 8-1 | 0 | 15/09/65 |
| Raith Rvrs | Parkhead | 4-0 | 1 | 22/09/65 |
| Hibernian | Ibrox | 2-2 | 0 | 04/10/65 |
| Hibernian | Ibrox | 4-0 | 1 | 18/10/65 |
| Rangers | Hampden | 2-1 | 0 | 23/10/65 |

## League

| | | | | |
|---|---|---|---|---|
| Dundee Utd | Tannadice | 4-0 | 0 | 25/08/65 |
| Clyde | Parkhead | 2-1 | 0 | 11/09/65 |
| Rangers | Ibrox | 1-2 | 0 | 18/09/65 |
| Aberdeen | Parkhead | 7-1 | 0 | 25/09/65 |
| Hearts | Parkhead | 5-2 | 0 | 09/10/65 |
| Falkirk | Brockville | 4-3 | 1 | 16/10/65 |
| Dundee | Dens Park | 2-1 | 0 | 27/10/65 |
| Stirling Alb | Parkhead | 6-1 | 1 | 30/10/65 |
| Ptk Thistle | Parkhead | 1-1 | 0 | 06/11/65 |
| St.Johnst'ne | Muirton | 4-1 | 0 | 13/11/65 |
| Hamilton A. | Parkhead | 5-0 | 1 | 20/11/65 |
| Kilmarnock | Parkhead | 2-1 | 0 | 27/11/65 |
| Hibernian | Parkhead | 2-0 | 0 | 11/12/65 |
| Dunfermline | East End | 2-0 | 0 | 18/12/65 |
| Morton | Parkhead | 8-1 | 1 | 25/12/65 |
| Clyde | Shawfield | 3-1 | 0 | 01/01/66 |
| Rangers | Parkhead | 5-1 | 1 | 03/01/66 |
| Dundee Utd | Parkhead | 1-0 | 0 | 08/01/66 |
| Aberdeen | Pittodrie | 1-3 | 0 | 15/01/66 |
| Motherwell | Parkhead | 1-0 | 0 | 22/01/66 |
| Hearts | Tynecastle | 2-3 | 0 | 29/01/66 |
| Falkirk | Parkhead | 6-0 | 0 | 12/02/66 |
| Stirling Alb | Annfield | 0-1 | 0 | 26/02/66 |

| | | | | |
|---|---|---|---|---|
| Dundee | Parkhead | 5-0 | 0 | 28/02/66 |
| St.Johnst'ne | Parkhead | 3-2 | 0 | 12/03/66 |
| Kilmarnock | Rugby Park | 2-0 | 0 | 29/03/66 |
| St.Mirren | Love Street | 3-0 | 0 | 05/04/66 |
| Hibernian | Easter Road | 0-0 | 0 | 16/04/66 |
| Morton | Cappielow | 2-0 | 0 | 30/04/66 |
| Dunfermline | Parkhead | 2-1 | 0 | 04/05/66 |
| Motherwell | Fir Park | 1-0 | 0 | 07/05/66 |

**Scottish Cup**

| | | | | |
|---|---|---|---|---|
| Stranraer | Parkhead | 4-0 | 1 | 05/02/66 |
| Dundee | Dens Park | 2-0 | 0 | 23/02/66 |
| Hearts | Tynecastle | 3-3 | 0 | 05/03/66 |
| Hearts | Parkhead | 3-1 | 1 | 09/03/66 |
| Dunfermline | Ibrox | 2-0 | 0 | 26/03/66 |
| Rangers | Hampden | 0-0 | 0 | 23/04/66 |
| Rangers | Hampden | 0-1 | 0 | 27/04/66 |

**European Cup Winners' Cup**

| | | | | |
|---|---|---|---|---|
| G.A Deventer | Deventer | 6-0 | 0 | 29/09/65 |
| G.A Deventer | Parkhead | 1-0 | 0 | 07/10/65 |
| Aarhus | Aarhus | 1-0 | 0 | 03/11/65 |
| Aarhus | Parkhead | 2-0 | 0 | 17/11/65 |
| Dynamo Kiev | Parkhead | 3-0 | 2 | 12/01/66 |
| Dynamo Kiev | Georgia | 1-1 | 0 | 26/01/66 |
| Liverpool | Parkhead | 1-0 | 0 | 14/04/66 |
| Liverpool | Anfield | 0-2 | 0 | 19/04/66 |

**played 57 goals 11**

# 1966-67

## League Cup

| | | | | |
|---|---|---|---|---|
| Hearts | Tynecastle | 2-0 | 0 | 13/08/66 |
| Clyde | Parkhead | 6-0 | 0 | 17/08/66 |
| St.Mirren | Parkhead | 8-2 | 0 | 20/08/66 |
| Hearts | Parkhead | 3-0 | 0 | 27/08/66 |
| Clyde | Shawfield | 3-1 | 0 | 31/08/66 |
| St.Mirren | Love Street | 1-0 | 1 | 03/09/66 |
| Dunfermline | Parkhead | 6-3 | 0 | 14/09/66 |
| Dunfermline | East End | 3-1 | 0 | 21/09/66 |
| Airdrie | Hampden | 2-0 | 1 | 17/10/66 |
| Rangers | Hampden | 1-0 | 0 | 29/10/66 |

## League

| | | | | |
|---|---|---|---|---|
| Clyde | Shawfield | 3-0 | 0 | 10/09/66 |
| Rangers | Parkhead | 2-0 | 1 | 17/09/66 |
| Dundee | Dens Park | 2-1 | 0 | 24/09/66 |
| St.Johnst'ne | Parkhead | 6-1 | 0 | 01/10/66 |
| Hibernian | Easter Road | 5-3 | 0 | 08/10/66 |
| Ayr United | Parkhead | 5-1 | 0 | 24/10/66 |
| Stirling Alb | Parkhead | 7-3 | 0 | 02/11/66 |
| St.Mirren | Parkhead | 1-1 | 0 | 05/11/66 |
| Falkirk | Brockville | 3-0 | 0 | 12/11/66 |
| Dunfermline | East End | 5-4 | 1 | 19/11/66 |
| Hearts | Parkhead | 3-0 | 0 | 26/11/66 |
| Kilmarnock | Rugby Park | 0-0 | 0 | 03/12/66 |
| Motherwell | Parkhead | 4-2 | 1 | 10/12/66 |
| Ptk Thistle | Parkhead | 6-2 | 1 | 17/12/66 |
| Aberdeen | Pittodrie | 1-1 | 0 | 24/12/66 |
| Dundee Utd | Tannadice | 2-3 | 0 | 31/12/66 |
| Dundee | Parkhead | 5-1 | 0 | 07/01/67 |
| Clyde | Parkhead | 5-1 | 0 | 11/01/67 |
| St.Johnst'ne | Muirton | 4-0 | 0 | 14/01/67 |
| Hibernian | Parkhead | 2-0 | 0 | 21/01/67 |
| Airdrie | Broomfield | 3-0 | 0 | 04/02/67 |
| Ayr United | Somerset | 5-0 | 0 | 11/02/67 |
| Stirling Alb | Annfield | 1-1 | 0 | 25/02/67 |

| | | | | |
|---|---|---|---|---|
| St.Mirren | Love Street | 5-0 | 0 | 04/03/67 |
| Dunfermline | Parkhead | 3-2 | 0 | 18/03/67 |
| Falkirk | Parkhead | 5-0 | 0 | 20/03/67 |
| Hearts | Tynecastle | 3-0 | 0 | 25/03/67 |
| Aberdeen | Parkhead | 0-0 | 0 | 19/04/67 |
| Dundee Utd | Parkhead | 2-3 | 0 | 03/05/67 |
| Rangers | Ibrox | 2-2 | 0 | 06/05/67 |
| Kilmarnock | Rugby Park | 2-0 | 0 | 15/05/67 |

## Scottish Cup

| | | | | |
|---|---|---|---|---|
| Arbroath | Parkhead | 4-0 | 1 | 28/01/67 |
| Elgin City | Parkhead | 7-0 | 0 | 18/02/67 |
| Queen's Pk. | Parkhead | 5-3 | 1 | 11/03/67 |
| Aberdeen | Hampden | 2-0 | 0 | 29/04/67 |

## European Cup

| | | | | |
|---|---|---|---|---|
| Zurich | Parkhead | 2-0 | 0 | 28/09/67 |
| Zurich | Zurich | 3-0 | 0 | 05/10/67 |
| Nantes | Nantes | 3-1 | 0 | 30/11/67 |
| Nantes | Parkhead | 3-1 | 0 | 07/12/67 |
| Vojvodina | Novi Sad | 0-1 | 0 | 01/03/67 |
| Vojvodina | Parkhead | 2-0 | 0 | 08/03/67 |
| Dukla Prague | Parkhead | 3-1 | 0 | 12/04/67 |
| Dukla Prague | Prague | 0-0 | 0 | 25/04/67 |
| Inter Milan | Lisbon | 2-1 | 0 | 25/05/67 |

## Glasgow Cup

| | | | | |
|---|---|---|---|---|
| Rangers | Ibrox | 4-0 | 0 | 22/08/66 |
| Queen's Pk. | Parkhead | 4-0 | 0 | 10/10/66 |
| Partick Th. | Parkhead | 4-0 | 0 | 07/11/66 |
| **played 57** | **goals 8** | | | |

# 1967-68

### League Cup

| | | | | |
|---|---|---|---|---|
| Dundee Utd | Parkhead | 1-0 | 0 | 12/08/67 |
| Rangers | Ibrox | 1-1 | 0 | 16/08/67 |
| Aberdeen | Parkhead | 3-1 | 0 | 19/08/67 |
| Dundee Utd | Tannadice | 1-0 | 0 | 26/08/67 |
| Rangers | Parkhead | 3-1 | 1 | 30/08/67 |
| Aberdeen | Pittodrie | 5-1 | 0 | 02/09/67 |
| Ayr United | Parkhead | 6-2 | 1 | 13/09/67 |
| Morton | Hampden | 7-1 | 0 | 11/10/67 |
| Dundee | Hampden | 5-3 | 0 | 28/10/67 |

### League

| | | | | |
|---|---|---|---|---|
| Clyde | Parkhead | 3-0 | 0 | 09/09/67 |
| Rangers | Ibrox | 0-1 | 0 | 16/09/67 |
| St.Johnstone | Parkhead | 1-1 | 1 | 23/09/67 |
| Stirling Alb. | Annfield | 4-0 | 0 | 30/09/67 |
| Hibernian | Parkhead | 4-0 | 2 | 07/10/67 |
| Partick Th. | Firhill | 5-1 | 0 | 14/10/67 |
| Motherwell | Parkhead | 4-2 | 0 | 24/10/67 |
| Airdrie | Broomfield | 2-0 | 1 | 11/11/67 |
| Kilmarnock | Parkhead | 3-0 | 0 | 15/11/67 |
| Falkirk | Parkhead | 3-0 | 0 | 18/11/67 |
| Raith Rvrs | Stark's Park | 2-0 | 0 | 25/11/67 |
| Dundee Utd. | Parkhead | 1-1 | 1 | 02/12/67 |
| Hearts | Parkhead | 3-1 | 0 | 09/12/67 |
| Dundee | Dens Park | 5-4 | 0 | 16/12/67 |
| Morton | Cappielow | 4-0 | 0 | 23/12/67 |
| Dunfermline | Parkhead | 3-2 | 0 | 30/12/67 |
| Clyde | Shawfield | 3-2 | 0 | 01/01/68 |
| Rangers | Parkhead | 2-2 | 1 | 02/01/68 |
| Hibernian | Easter Road | 2-0 | 0 | 20/01/68 |
| Partick Th. | Parkhead | 4-1 | 0 | 03/02/68 |
| Motherwell | Fir Park | 1-0 | 0 | 10/02/68 |
| Stirling Alb. | Parkhead | 2-0 | 0 | 14/02/68 |
| Kilmarnock | Rugby Park | 6-0 | 0 | 02/03/68 |

| | | | | |
|---|---|---|---|---|
| Aberdeen | Parkhead | 4-1 | 0 | 06/03/68 |
| Airdrie | Parkhead | 4-0 | 0 | 13/03/68 |
| Falkirk | Brockville | 3-0 | 0 | 16/03/68 |
| Raith Rvrs | Parkhead | 5-0 | 0 | 23/03/68 |
| St.Johnst'ne | Muirton | 6-1 | 0 | 25/03/68 |
| Dundee Utd. | Tannadice | 5-0 | 0 | 30/03/68 |
| Hearts | Tynecastle | 2-0 | 0 | 06/04/68 |
| Aberdeen | Pittodrie | 1-0 | 0 | 10/04/68 |
| Dundee | Parkhead | 5-2 | 0 | 13/04/68 |
| Morton | Parkhead | 2-1 | 0 | 20/04/68 |
| Dunfermline | East End | 2-1 | 0 | 30/04/68 |

**Scottish Cup**

| | | | | |
|---|---|---|---|---|
| Dunfermline | Parkhead | 0-2 | 0 | 27/01/68 |

**European Cup**

| | | | | |
|---|---|---|---|---|
| Dynamo Kiev | Parkhead | 1-2 | 0 | 20/09/67 |
| Dynamo Kiev | Kiev | 1-1 | 0 | 04/10/67 |

**World Club Championship**

| | | | | |
|---|---|---|---|---|
| Racing Club | Hampden | 1-0 | 0 | 18/10/67 |
| Racing Club | Buenos Aires | 1-2 | 0 | 01/11/67 |
| Racing Club | Montevideo | 0-1 | 0 | 04/11/67 |

**Glasgow Cup**

| | | | | |
|---|---|---|---|---|
| Clyde | Hampden | 8-0 | 1 | 17/04/68 |

**played 50 goals 9**

# 1968-69

**League Cup**

| | | | | |
|---|---|---|---|---|
| Rangers | Ibrox | 2-0 | 0 | 10/08/68 |
| Morton | Parkhead | 4-1 | 1 | 14/08/68 |
| Partick Th. | Parkhead | 4-0 | 0 | 17/08/68 |
| Rangers | Parkhead | 1-0 | 0 | 24/08/68 |
| Morton | Cappielow | 3-0 | 0 | 28/08/68 |
| Partick Th. | Firhill | 6-1 | 0 | 31/08/68 |
| Clyde | Hampden | 1-0 | 0 | 09/10/68 |

| | | | | |
|---|---|---|---|---|
| Hibernian | Hampden | 6-2 | 0 | 05/04/69 |

**League**

| | | | | |
|---|---|---|---|---|
| Dunfermline | East End | 1-1 | 0 | 21/09/68 |
| Aberdeen | Parkhead | 2-1 | 0 | 28/09/68 |
| Dundee Utd | Parkhead | 2-0 | 1 | 05/10/68 |
| Morton | Cappielow | 1-1 | 0 | 26/10/68 |
| Dundee | Parkhead | 3-1 | 0 | 02/11/68 |
| Arbroath | Gayfield | 5-0 | 0 | 09/11/68 |
| Raith Rvrs | Parkhead | 2-0 | 2 | 16/11/68 |
| Partick Th. | Firhill | 4-0 | 0 | 23/11/68 |
| Hibernian | Easter Road | 5-2 | 0 | 30/11/68 |
| St.Mirren | Parkhead | 5-0 | 0 | 07/12/68 |
| Falkirk | Brockville | 0-0 | 0 | 14/12/68 |
| Kilmarnock | Parkhead | 1-1 | 0 | 21/12/68 |
| Airdrie | Broomfield | 0-0 | 0 | 28/12/68 |
| Clyde | Parkhead | 5-0 | 0 | 01/01/69 |
| Rangers | Ibrox | 0-1 | 0 | 02/01/69 |
| Dunfermline | Parkhead | 3-1 | 0 | 04/01/69 |
| Aberdeen | Pittodrie | 3-1 | 0 | 11/01/69 |
| Dundee Utd | Tannadice | 3-1 | 0 | 18/01/69 |
| Hearts | Parkhead | 5-0 | 1 | 01/02/69 |
| Arbroath | Parkhead | 7-1 | 0 | 05/03/69 |
| Raith Rvrs | Stark's Park | 3-1 | 0 | 08/03/69 |
| Partick Th. | Parkhead | 1-0 | 0 | 15/03/69 |
| Hibernian | Parkhead | 1-1 | 0 | 24/03/69 |
| St.Mirren | Love Street | 3-0 | 0 | 29/03/69 |
| St.Johnst'ne | Muirton | 3-2 | 0 | 01/04/69 |
| Falkirk | Parkhead | 5-2 | 0 | 09/04/69 |
| Airdrie | Parkhead | 2-2 | 0 | 19/04/69 |
| Kilmarnock | Rugby Park | 2-2 | 0 | 21/04/69 |
| Morton | Parkhead | 2-4 | 0 | 28/04/69 |
| Dundee | Dens Park | 2-1 | 0 | 30/04/69 |

**Scottish Cup**

| | | | | |
|---|---|---|---|---|
| Ptk Thistle | Firhill | 3-3 | 1 | 25/01/69 |
| Ptk Thistle | Parkhead | 8-1 | 0 | 29/01/69 |
| Clyde | Shawfield | 0-0 | 0 | 12/02/69 |

| | | | | |
|---|---|---|---|---|
| Clyde | Parkhead | 3-0 | 1 | 24/02/69 |
| St.Johnst'ne | Parkhead | 3-2 | 0 | 01/03/69 |
| Morton | Hampden | 4-1 | 0 | 22/03/69 |
| Rangers | Hampden | 4-0 | 0 | 26/04/69 |

**European Cup**

| | | | | |
|---|---|---|---|---|
| St.Etienne | Parkhead | 4-0 | 0 | 02/10/68 |
| Red Star | Parkhead | 5-1 | 1 | 13/11/68 |
| Red Star | Belgrade | 1-1 | 0 | 27/11/68 |
| A.C.Milan | Milan | 0-0 | 0 | 19/02/69 |
| A.C.Milan | Parkhead | 0-1 | 0 | 12/03/69 |

**played 50 goals 8**

# 1969-70

**League Cup**

| | | | | |
|---|---|---|---|---|
| Airdrie | Parkhead | 6-1 | 0 | 09/08/69 |
| Rangers | Ibrox | 1-2 | 0 | 13/08/69 |
| Rangers | Parkhead | 1-0 | 0 | 20/08/69 |
| Airdrie | Broomfield | 3-0 | 0 | 23/08/69 |
| Aberdeen | Pittodrie | 0-0 | 0 | 10/09/69 |
| St.Johnst'ne | Hampden | 1-0 | 0 | 25/10/69 |

**League**

| | | | | |
|---|---|---|---|---|
| Kilmarnock | Rugby Park | 4-2 | 0 | 03/09/69 |
| Dunfermline | East End | 1-2 | 0 | 06/09/69 |
| Hibernian | Parkhead | 1-2 | 0 | 13/09/69 |
| Aberdeen | Pittodrie | 3-2 | 1 | 29/10/69 |
| Ayr United | Somerset | 4-2 | 2 | 01/11/69 |
| Hearts | Parkhead | 0-2 | 0 | 08/11/69 |
| Motherwell | Fir Park | 2-1 | 0 | 15/11/69 |
| Morton | Cappielow | 3-0 | 0 | 29/11/69 |
| St.Mirren | Parkhead | 2-0 | 0 | 01/12/69 |
| Dundee | Parkhead | 1-0 | 0 | 06/12/69 |
| St.Johnst'ne | Muirton | 4-1 | 0 | 13/12/69 |
| Dundee Utd | Parkhead | 7-2 | 1 | 17/12/69 |

| | | | | |
|---|---|---|---|---|
| Kilmarnock | Parkhead | 3-1 | 0 | 20/12/69 |
| Partick Th. | Parkhead | 8-1 | 0 | 27/12/69 |
| Clyde | Shawfield | 2-0 | 0 | 01/01/70 |
| Rangers | Parkhead | 0-0 | 0 | 03/01/70 |
| Hibernian | Easter Road | 2-1 | 0 | 17/01/70 |
| Dunfermline | Parkhead | 3-1 | 0 | 31/01/70 |
| Dundee Utd | Tannadice | 2-0 | 0 | 07/03/70 |
| Morton | Parkhead | 4-0 | 0* | 10/03/70 |
| Ayr United | Parkhead | 3-0 | 0* | 21/03/70 |
| Aberdeen | Parkhead | 1-2 | 0 | 25/03/70 |
| Hearts | Tynecastle | 0-0 | 0 | 28/03/70 |
| Motherwell | Parkhead | 6-1 | 1 | 04/04/70 |
| Dundee | Dens Park | 2-1 | 0 | 06/04/70 |
| St.Mirren | Love Street | 3-2 | 0 | 18/04/70 |

**Scottish Cup**

| | | | | |
|---|---|---|---|---|
| Dunfermline | Parkhead | 2-1 | 0 | 24/01/70 |
| Dundee Utd | Parkhead | 4-0 | 0 | 07/02/70 |
| Rangers | Parkhead | 3-1 | 0 | 21/02/70 |
| Dundee | Hampden | 2-1 | 0 | 14/03/70 |
| Aberdeen | Hampden | 1-3 | 0 | 11/04/70 |

**European Cup**

| | | | | |
|---|---|---|---|---|
| Benfica | Parkhead | 3-0 | 0 | 12/11/69 |
| Benfica | Lisbon | 0-3 | 0 | 26/11/69 |
| Fiorentina | Parkhead | 3-0 | 0 | 04/03/70 |
| Fiorentina | Florence | 0-1 | 0 | 18/03/70 |
| Leeds | Elland Road | 1-0 | 0 | 01/04/70 |
| Leeds | Hampden | 2-1 | 1 | 15/04/70 |
| Feyenoord | Milan | 1-2 | 0 | 06/05/70 |

**Glasgow Cup**

| | | | | |
|---|---|---|---|---|
| Clyde | Parkhead | 4-1 | 0 | 15/10/69 |
| Rangers | Hampden | 3-1 | 0 | 10/08/70 |

**played 46 goals 6**

# 1970-71

### League Cup

| | | | | |
|---|---|---|---|---|
| Clyde | Shawfield | 2-0 | 0 | 19/08/70 |
| Hearts | Parkhead | 4-2 | 0 | 22/08/70 |
| Dundee Utd | Tannadice | 2-2 | 0 | 26/08/70 |
| Dundee | Dens Park | 2-2 | 0 | 09/09/70 |
| Dundee | Parkhead | 5-1 | 0 | 23/09/70 |
| Dumbarton | Hampden | 0-0 | 0 | 07/10/70 |
| Dumbarton | Hampden | 4-3 | 0 | 12/10/70 |
| Rangers | Hampden | 0-1 | 0 | 24/10/70 |

### League

| | | | | |
|---|---|---|---|---|
| Morton | Parkhead | 2-0 | 0 | 29/08/70 |
| Clyde | Shawfield | 5-0 | 0 | 05/09/70 |
| Rangers | Parkhead | 2-0 | 1 | 12/09/70 |
| Hibernian | Easter Road | 0-2 | 0 | 19/09/70 |
| Dundee | Parkhead | 3-0 | 0 | 26/09/70 |
| Dunfermline | East End | 2-0 | 0 | 03/10/70 |
| Airdrie | Broomfield | 3-1 | 0 | 17/10/70 |
| Hearts | Parkhead | 3-2 | 0 | 28/10/70 |
| Motherwell | Fir Park | 5-0 | 0 | 31/10/70 |
| Cowdenb'th | Parkhead | 3-0 | 0 | 07/11/70 |
| Kilmarnock | Parkhead | 3-0 | 1 | 14/11/70 |
| Falkirk | Brockville | 0-0 | 0 | 21/11/70 |
| St.Mirren | Parkhead | 3-0 | 0 | 28/11/70 |
| Dundee Utd | Tannadice | 2-1 | 0 | 05/12/70 |
| Aberdeen | Parkhead | 0-1 | 0 | 12/12/70 |
| Ayr United | Somerset | 2-1 | 0 | 19/12/70 |
| Morton | Cappielow | 3-0 | 0 | 26/12/70 |
| Hibernian | Parkhead | 2-1 | 0 | 09/01/71 |
| Dundee | Dens Park | 8-1 | 0 | 16/01/71 |
| Dunfermline | Parkhead | 1-0 | 0 | 30/01/71 |
| Falkirk | Parkhead | 4-0 | 0* | 27/03/71 |
| Motherwell | Parkhead | 3-0 | 0* | 12/04/71 |
| Clyde | Parkhead | 6-1 | 0 | 01/05/71 |

### Scottish Cup

| | | | | |
|---|---|---|---|---|
| Qu.South | Parkhead | 5-1 | 0 | 23/01/71 |

### European Cup

| | | | | |
|---|---|---|---|---|
| Kokkola | Parkhead | 9-0 | 0 | 16/09/70 |
| Kokkola | Finland | 5-0 | 0 | 30/09/70 |
| Waterford | Dublin | 7-0 | 2 | 21/10/70 |
| Waterford | Parkhead | 3-2 | 0 | 04/11/70 |

### Glasgow Cup

| | | | | |
|---|---|---|---|---|
| Ptk Thistle | Firhill | 4-3 | 1 | 30/03/71 |
| Clyde | Shawfield | 1-2 | 0 | 06/05/71 |

**played 38 goals 5**

## 1971-72

### League Cup

| | | | | |
|---|---|---|---|---|
| Rangers | Ibrox | 2-0 | 0 | 14/08/71 |
| Morton | Cappielow | 1-0 | 0 | 18/08/71 |
| Ayr United | Somerset | 3-0 | 0 | 21/08/71 |
| Morton | Parkhead | 0-1 | 0 | 25/08/71 |
| Rangers | Ibrox | 3-0 | 0 | 28/08/71 |
| Ptk Thistle | Hampden | 1-4 | 0 | 23/10/71 |

### League

| | | | | |
|---|---|---|---|---|
| Clyde | Parkhead | 9-1 | 1 | 04/09/71 |
| Rangers | Ibrox | 3-2 | 0 | 11/09/71 |
| Morton | Parkhead | 3-1 | 0 | 18/09/71 |
| Hibernian | Easter Road | 1-0 | 0 | 09/10/71 |
| Dundee | Parkhead | 3-1 | 0 | 16/10/71 |
| Dunfermline | East End | 2-1 | 0 | 27/10/71 |
| Dunfermline | Parkhead | 1-0 | 0 | 19/02/72 |
| Ayr United | Parkhead | 2-0 | 0 | 04/03/72 |
| Aberdeen | Pittodrie | 1-1 | 0 | 11/03/72 |
| Ptk Thistle | Parkhead | 3-1 | 0 | 01/04/72 |
| Kilmarnock | Rugby Park | 3-1 | 0 | 08/04/72 |
| East Fife | Bayview | 3-0 | 0 | 15/04/72 |

| | | | | |
|---|---|---|---|---|
| Motherwell | Parkhead | 5-2 | 2 | 22/04/72 |
| Dundee Utd | Parkhead | 3-0 | 0 | 25/04/72 |
| Hearts | Tynecastle | 1-4 | 1 | 29/04/72 |

**Scottish Cup**

| | | | | |
|---|---|---|---|---|
| Albion Rvrs | Parkhead | 5-0 | 1 | 05/02/72 |
| Dundee | Parkhead | 4-0 | 0 | 26/02/72 |
| Hearts | Parkhead | 1-1 | 0 | 18/03/72 |
| Hearts | Tynecastle | 1-0 | 0 | 27/03/72 |
| Kilmarnock | Hampden | 3-1 | 0 | 12/04/72 |
| Hibernian | Hampden | 6-1 | 0 | 06/05/72 |

**European Cup**

| | | | | |
|---|---|---|---|---|
| BK Copenhagen | Copenhagen | 1-2 | 0 | 15/09/71 |
| Sliema Wanderers | Parkhead | 5-0 | 0 | 20/10/71 |
| Ujpest Dosza | Hungary | 2-1 | 0 | 08/03/72 |
| Ujpest Dosza | Parkhead | 1-1 | 0 | 22/03/72 |
| Inter Milan | San Siro | 0-0 | 0 | 05/04/72 |
| Inter Milan | Parkhead | 0-0 | 0 | 19/04/72 |

**played 33** **goals 5**

# 1972-73

**League Cup**

| | | | | |
|---|---|---|---|---|
| Stirling Alb | Annfield | 3-0 | 0 | 12/08/72 |
| East Fife | Parkhead | 1-1 | 0 | 16/08/72 |
| Arbroath | Gayfield | 5-0 | 1 | 19/08/72 |
| Stirling Alb | Parkhead | 3-0 | 1 | 26/08/72 |
| Stranraer | Stair Park | 2-1 | 0 | 20/09/72 |
| Stranraer | Parkhead | 5-2 | 1 | 04/10/72 |
| Dundee | Dens Park | 0-1 | 0 | 11/10/72 |

**League**

| | | | | |
|---|---|---|---|---|
| Kilmarnock | Hampden | 6-2 | 1 | 02/09/72 |
| Morton | Cappielow | 2-0 | 2 | 09/09/72 |
| Rangers | Hampden | 3-1 | 0 | 16/09/72 |
| Dundee | Dens Park | 0-2 | 0 | 23/09/72 |
| Ayr United | Parkhead | 1-0 | 0 | 30/09/72 |

| | | | | |
|---|---|---|---|---|
| Airdrie | Parkhead | 1-1 | 0 | 07/10/72 |
| Partick Thistle | Firhill | 4-0 | 0 | 14/10/72 |
| East Fife | Parkhead | 3-0 | 0 | 21/10/72 |
| Dumbarton | Boghead | 6-1 | 0 | 02/12/72 |
| Arbroath | Gayfield | 2-0 | 0 | 16/12/72 |
| Dundee | Parkhead | 2-1 | 0 | 13/01/73 |
| Ayr United | Somerset | 3-1 | 0 | 20/01/73 |
| Airdrie | Broomfield | 1-2 | 0 | 27/01/73 |
| Kilmarnock | Rugby Park | 4-0 | 0 | 07/02/73 |
| Ptk Thistle | Parkhead | 1-1 | 1 | 10/02/73 |
| East Fife | Bayview | 2-2 | 0 | 17/02/73 |
| St.Johnst'ne | Parkhead | 4-0 | 0 | 28/02/73 |
| Aberdeen | Parkhead | 2-0 | 0 | 03/03/73 |
| Hearts | Tynecastle | 2-0 | 0 | 24/03/73 |
| Falkirk | Parkhead | 4-0 | 0 | 31/03/73 |
| St.Johnst'ne | Muirton | 3-1 | 0 | 14/04/73 |
| Dumbarton | Parkhead | 5-0 | 0 | 18/04/73 |
| Arbroath | Parkhead | 4-0 | 0 | 21/04/73 |
| Hibernian | Easter Road | 3-0 | 0 | 28/04/73 |

**Scottish Cup**

| | | | | |
|---|---|---|---|---|
| East Fife | Parkhead | 4-1 | 0 | 03/02/73 |
| Motherwell | Fir Park | 4-0 | 0 | 24/02/73 |
| Aberdeen | Parkhead | 0-0 | 0 | 17/03/73 |
| Aberdeen | Pittodrie | 1-0 | 0 | 21/03/73 |
| Dundee | Hampden | 0-0 | 0 | 07/04/73 |
| Dundee | Hampden | 3-0 | 0 | 11/04/73 |
| Rangers | Hampden | 2-3 | 0 | 05/05/73 |

**European Cup**

| | | | | |
|---|---|---|---|---|
| Rosenburg | Hampden | 2-1 | 0 | 13/09/72 |
| Rosenburg | Norway | 3-1 | 0 | 27/09/72 |

**played 40 goals 7**

# 1973-74

**League Cup**

| | | | |
|---|---|---|---|
| Arbroath | Gayfield | 3-1 | 0 |
| 29/08/73 | **played 1** | **goals 0** | |

**Total appearances 504** (including Glasgow Cup)
**Total goals 110**

# Middlesbrough

# 1973-74

**League**

| | | | | |
|---|---|---|---|---|
| Blackpool | Bloomfield | 0-0 | 0 | 22/09/73 |
| Bristol C | Ayresome | 2-0 | 1 | 29/09/73 |
| Orient | Ayresome | 3-2 | 0 | 02/10/73 |
| Swindon Tn | County Gd | 1-0 | 1 | 06/10/73 |
| Hull City | Ayresome | 1-0 | 0 | 13/10/73 |
| W.B.A | Ayresome | 0-0 | 0 | 20/10/73 |
| Carlisle U | Brunton Pk | 1-1 | 0 | 23/10/73 |
| Millwall | The Den | 1-0 | 0 | 27/10/73 |
| Luton Town | Ayresome | 2-1 | 0 | 03/11/73 |
| Oxford Utd | Manor Gd | 2-0 | 1 | 10/11/73 |
| Notts Co | County Gd | 2-2 | 0 | 24/11/73 |
| Sheff Wed | Hillsboro | 2-2 | 0 | 08/12/73 |
| Preston N.E | Ayresome | 3-0 | 1 | 11/12/73 |
| Nott'm F | Ayresome | 1-0 | 0 | 15/12/73 |
| Bristol City | Ashton Gate | 1-1 | 0 | 22/12/73 |
| Sunderland | Ayresome | 2-1 | 0 | 26/12/73 |
| Crystal Pal. | Ayresome | 2-0 | 0 | 29/12/73 |
| Aston Villa | Villa Park | 1-1 | 0 | 12/01/74 |
| Portsmouth | Ayresome | 3-0 | 0 | 19/01/74 |

| | | | | |
|---|---|---|---|---|
| Nott'm F | City Ground | 1-5 | 0 | 02/02/74 |
| Blackpool | Ayresome | 0-0 | 0 | 09/02/74 |
| Swindon Tn | Ayresome | 3-1 | 0 | 23/02/74 |
| Sunderland | Roker Park | 2-0 | 0 | 02/03/74 |
| Millwall | Ayresome | 2-1 | 0 | 09/03/74 |
| W.B.A | Hawthorns | 4-0 | 0 | 16/03/74 |
| Fulham | Craven Cott. | 4-0 | 0 | 19/03/74 |
| Oxford Utd | Ayresome | 1-0 | 0 | 23/03/74 |
| Luton Town | Kenlw'th Rd | 1-0 | 0 | 30/03/74 |
| Notts Co. | Ayresome | 4-0 | 0 | 06/04/74 |
| Bolton W | Ayresome | 0-0 | 0 | 09/04/74 |
| Cardiff City | Ninian Park | 2-3 | 0* | 13/04/74 |
| Bolton W | Burnden Pk. | 1-2 | 0 | 15/04/74 |
| Sheffield W | Ayresome | 8-0 | 1 | 20/04/74 |
| Preston N.E | Deepdale | 4-2 | 0 | 27/04/74 |

**League Cup**

| | | | | |
|---|---|---|---|---|
| Man Utd | Old Trafford | 1-0 | 0 | 08/10/73 |
| Stoke City | Victoria Gd. | 1-1 | 0 | 31/10/73 |
| Stoke City | Ayresome | 1-2 | 0 | 06/11/73 |

**F.A.Cup**

| | | | | |
|---|---|---|---|---|
| Grantham | Grantham | 2-0 | 0 | 05/01/74 |
| Wrexham | R'crse Gd. | 0-1 | 0 | 26/01/74 |

**played 39 goals 5**

# 1974-75

**League**

| | | | | |
|---|---|---|---|---|
| Birmingh'm | St.Andrews | 2-0 | 0 | 17/08/74 |
| Carlisle Utd | Ayresome | 0-2 | 0 | 20/08/74 |
| Luton Town | Ayresome | 1-1 | 0 | 24/08/74 |
| Carlisle Utd | Brunton Pk. | 1-0 | 0 | 27/08/74 |
| Stoke City | Victoria Gd. | 1-1 | 0 | 31/08/74 |
| Chelsea | Ayresome | 1-1 | 0 | 07/09/74 |
| Sheffield U | Bramall Ln | 0-1 | 0 | 14/09/74 |
| Man City | Ayresome | 3-0 | 0 | 21/09/74 |
| Tottenham | W H Lane | 2-1 | 0 | 28/09/74 |

| | | | | |
|---|---|---|---|---|
| Wolves | Ayresome | 2-1 | 0 | 05/10/74 |
| Liverpool | Anfield | 0-2 | 0 | 12/10/74 |
| Luton Town | Kenilworth | 1-0 | 0 | 16/10/74 |
| Coventry | Ayresome | 4-4 | 0 | 19/10/74 |
| Derby Co | Baseball Gd | 3-2 | 0 | 26/10/74 |
| West Ham | Upton Park | 0-3 | 0 | 02/11/74 |
| Newcastle | Ayresome | 0-0 | 0 | 09/11/74 |
| Leeds | Elland Rd | 2-2 | 0 | 16/11/74 |
| Q.P.R | Ayresome | 1-3 | 0 | 23/11/74 |
| Birmingham | Ayresome | 3-0 | 0 | 14/12/74 |
| Burnley | Turf Moor | 1-1 | 0 | 21/12/74 |
| Sheffield U | Ayresome | 1-0 | 0 | 26/12/74 |
| Everton | Goodison | 1-1 | 0 | 28/12/74 |
| Ipswich | Portman Rd | 0-2 | 0 | 11/01/75 |
| Arsenal | Ayresome | 0-0 | 0 | 18/01/75 |
| Newcastle | St.James' Pk | 1-2 | 0 | 01/02/75 |
| West Ham | Ayresome | 0-0 | 0 | 08/02/75 |
| Leeds | Ayresome | 0-1 | 0 | 22/02/75 |
| Q.P.R | Loftus Rd | 0-0 | 0 | 25/02/75 |
| Stoke City | Ayresome | 2-0 | 0 | 01/03/75 |
| Tottenham | Ayresome | 3-0 | 0 | 15/03/75 |
| Everton | Ayresome | 2-0 | 0 | 18/03/75 |
| Chelsea | Stamford Bg | 2-1 | 0 | 22/03/75 |
| Man City | Maine Road | 1-2 | 0 | 28/03/75 |
| Burnley | Ayresome | 2-0 | 1 | 29/03/75 |
| Derby Co | Ayresome | 1-1 | 0 | 05/04/75 |
| Leicester | Filbert St | 0-1 | 0 | 09/04/75 |
| Wolves | Molineux | 0-2 | 0 | 12/04/75 |
| Liverpool | Ayresome | 1-0 | 0 | 19/04/75 |
| Coventry | Highfield Rd | 2-0 | 0 | 26/04/75 |

**League Cup**

| | | | | |
|---|---|---|---|---|
| Tottenham | W H Lane | 4-0 | 0 | 11/09/74 |
| Leicester | Ayresome | 1-0 | 0 | 08/10/74 |
| Liverpool | Anfield | 1-0 | 0 | 12/11/74 |
| Man United | Old Trafford | 0-3 | 0 | 18/12/74 |

**F.A. Cup**

| | | | | |
|---|---|---|---|---|
| Sunderland | Ayresome | 3-1 | 1 | 25/01/75 |
| Peterboro' | London Rd | 1-1 | 0 | 15/02/75 |
| Peterboro' | Ayresome | 2-0 | 0 | 18/02/75 |
| Birmingham | St.Andrews | 0-1 | 0 | 08/03/75 |

**Texaco Cup**

| | | | | |
|---|---|---|---|---|
| Carlisle | Ayresome | 0-1 | 0 | 03/08/74 |
| Newcastle | St.James Pk | 0-4 | 0 | 10/08/74 |

**played 88 goals 7**

# 1975-76

**League**

| | | | | |
|---|---|---|---|---|
| Tottenham | W H Lane | 0-1 | 0 | 16/08/75 |
| Newcastle | St.James' Pk | 1-1 | 0 | 20/08/75 |
| Wolves | Ayresome | 1-0 | 0 | 23/08/75 |
| Birmingham City | Ayresome | 2-0 | 0 | 26/08/75 |
| Burnley | Turf Moor | 1-4 | 0 | 30/08/75 |
| Stoke City | Ayresome | 3-0 | 0 | 06/09/75 |
| Man City | Maine Road | 0-4 | 0 | 13/09/75 |
| Aston Villa | Ayresome | 0-0 | 0* | 04/10/75 |
| West Ham | Ayresome | 3-0 | 0 | 18/10/75 |
| Liverpool | Ayresome | 0-1 | 0 | 01/11/75 |
| Leeds Utd | Ayresome | 0-0 | 0 | 15/11/75 |
| West Ham | Upton Park | 1-2 | 0 | 22/11/75 |
| Derby Co | Baseball Gd | 2-3 | 0 | 29/11/75 |
| Man Utd | Ayresome | 0-0 | 0 | 06/12/75 |
| Wolves | Molineux | 2-1 | 0 | 13/12/75 |
| Tottenham | Ayresome | 1-0 | 0 | 20/12/75 |
| Sheffield U | Bramall Ln | 1-1 | 0 | 26/12/75 |
| Everton | Ayresome | 1-1 | 0 | 27/12/75 |
| Man City | Ayresome | 1-0 | 0 | 10/01/76 |
| Newcastle | Ayresome | 3-3 | 0 | 31/01/76 |
| Birm'hm C | St.Andrews | 1-2 | 0 | 07/02/76 |
| Sheffield U | Ayresome | 3-0 | 0 | 17/04/76 |

**League Cup**

| | | | | |
|---|---|---|---|---|
| Bury | Gigg Lane | 2-1 | 0 | 09/09/75 |
| Derby Co. | Ayresome | 1-0 | 0 | 07/10/75 |
| Peterboro' | Ayresome | 3-0 | 0 | 11/11/75 |
| Burnley | Turf Moor | 2-0 | 0 | 03/12/75 |
| Man City | Ayresome | 1-0 | 0 | 13/01/76 |
| Man City | Maine Road | 0-4 | 0 | 21/01/76 |

**F.A.Cup**

| | | | | |
|---|---|---|---|---|
| Bury | Gigg Lane | 2-3 | 0 | 03/01/76 |

**Anglo-Scottish Cup**

| | | | | |
|---|---|---|---|---|
| Aberdeen | Ayresome | 2-0 | 0 | 15/09/75 |
| Aberdeen | Pittodrie | 5-2 | 0* | 30/09/75 |
| Mansfield | Ayresome | 3-0 | 0 | 21/10/75 |
| Mansfield | Quarry Lane | 2-0 | 1 | 03/11/75 |
| Fulham | Ayresome Pk | 1-0 | 0 | 26/11/75 |
| Fulham | Craven Cott | 0-0 | 0 | 09/12/75 |

**played 28 goals 0**

**Anglo Scottish Cup not included**

## International Record

| | | | | | |
|---|---|---|---|---|---|
| Italy | Hampden | 1-0 | WCQ | 0 | 09/11/65 |
| Wales | Hampden | 4-1 | Home | 2 | 24/11/65 |
| Italy | Naples | 0-3 | WCQ | 0 | 07/12/65 |
| England | Hampden | 3-4 | Home | 0 | 02/04/66 |
| N.Ireland | Hampden | 2-1 | Home | 1 | 16/11/66 |
| N.Ireland | Belfast | 0-1 | Home | 0 | 21/10/67 |
| Cyprus | Nicosia | 5-0 | WCQ | 1 | 11/12/68 |
| W.Germany | Hampden | 1-1 | WCQ | 1 | 16/04/69 |
| Wales | Wrexham | 5-3 | Home | 0 | 03/05/69 |
| N.Ireland | Hampden | 1-1 | Home | 0 | 06/05/69 |
| England | Wembley | 1-4 | Home | 0 | 10/05/69 |
| Austria | Vienna | 0-2 | WCQ | 0 | 05/11/69 |

**12 Caps 4 goals**

Printed in Great Britain
by Amazon

73530618R10180